LESSONS FROM THE FRONT LINE

Other Books in the Wiley Investment Series

Angel Financing: How to Find and Invest in Private Equity
Gerald A. Benjamin & Joel Margulis

Cyber-Investing: Cracking Wall Street with Your PC, Second Edition
David L. Brown & Kassandra Bently

The Investor's Anthology: Original Ideas from the Industry's Greatest Minds
Charles Ellis with James R. Vertin

Mutual Funds on the Net: Making Money Online
Paul B. Farrell

It Was a Very Good Year: Great Investment Moments of the 20th Century
Martin S. Fridson

The Conservative Investor's Guide to Trading Options
LeRoy Gross

Stock Investing for Everyone: Tools for Investing Like the Pros
Arshad Khan & Vaqar Zubei

The Psychology of Investing
Lawrence E. Lifson & Richard Geist

Merton Miller on Derivatives
Merton Miller

REITS: Building Your Profits with Real Estate Investment Trusts
John Mullaney

The Inner Game of Investing: Access the Power of Your Investment Personality
Derrick Niederman

Patterns in the Dark: Understanding Risk and Financial Crisis with Complexity Theory
Edgar E. Peters

The Art of Short Selling
Kathryn F. Staley

The Stock Market, Seventh Edition
Richard J. Teweles & Edward S. Bradley

Market Magic: Riding the Greatest Bull Market of the Century
Louise Yamada

LESSONS FROM THE FRONT LINE

MARKET TOOLS AND INVESTING TACTICS FROM THE PROS

Michael Brush

John Wiley & Sons, Inc.

New York • Chichester • Weinheim • Brisbane • Singapore • Toronto

To Emilia, Eliza, Laura, and Alison

This book is printed on acid-free paper. ∞

Copyright © 2000 by Michael Brush. All rights reserved.

Published by John Wiley & Sons, Inc.

Published simultaneously in Canada.

This publication is designed to provide accurate and authoritative information in regard to the subject matter covered. It is sold with the understanding that the publisher is not engaged in rendering professional services. If professional advice or other expert assistance is required, the services of a competent professional person should be sought.

Library of Congress Cataloging-in-Publication Data:

Brush, Michael, 1957–
     Lessons from the front line : market tools and investing tactics
from the pros   Michael Brush.
          p.   cm.–(Wiley investment series)
     Includes index.
     ISBN 0-471-35017-6 (cloth : alk. paper)
     1. Investment. I. Title. II. Series.
HG4521.B763   1999
332.6–dc21   9932876

Printed in the United States of America

10   9   8   7   6   5   4   3   2   1

CONTENTS

Acknowledgments   ix

Introduction   xi

PART 1 INVESTOR INTELLIGENCE

CHAPTER 1   THE WALL STREET ANALYST'S REPORT   3
Yes, they are self-serving. But if you know how to use these reports, they can be a big help. The pros explain what you really need to know when reading a Wall Street analyst's report.

CHAPTER 2   HOW TO PARTICIPATE IN YOUR COMPANY'S
CONFERENCE CALL   27
Meant to link top management with money managers and analysts, these calls are usually open to individual investors as well. How to get the most out of them while avoiding the pitfalls.

CHAPTER 3   READING THE INSIDER TEA LEAVES   37
Corporate insiders have an excellent record for calling the ups and downs of stocks. But interpreting their moves is not as straightforward as you might think. Here's the best way to do it.

CHAPTER 4   THE SEC TREASURE TROVE   50
A guide to where the good stuff is in the documents companies must file with the Securities and Exchange Commission.

CHAPTER 5   THE TORPEDO RATIOS   60
Financial analysis is complex. But two quick ratios used all the time by the pros can tell you when trouble is looming, so you can get out of a stock before the real damage occurs. How to do the math yourself, using SEC documents available on the Internet.

CHAPTER 6   THE PRICE TO SALES RATIO   70
Although the price to sales ratio is less popular than valuation measures like the price earnings or price to book ratios, it can be a much better tool. Here's why.

CHAPTER 7   CASH ON THE BALANCE SHEET   80
If too much debt is bad, does that mean a lot of cash is good? Not necessarily. The pros explain how to know when that cash hoard is a sign of trouble.

CHAPTER 8   WHAT THE ECONOMIC INDICATORS
             REALLY MEAN   90
A quick guide to the major economic indicators. Which ones really matter and why.

PART 2 PROFITABLE STOCK MARKET PATTERNS

CHAPTER 9   THE EARNINGS "CONFESSION" SEASON   109
When it comes to the earnings season, the markets follow a predictable pattern that can be profitable if you understand how to use it.

CHAPTER 10   THE LOCKUP RELEASE   117
How to profit from the stock market's version of the clearance sale.

CHAPTER 11   THE RUSSELL RESHUFFE   124
Each year at the same time, the Frank Russell Company rebalances its indexes. This creates a good buying opportunity, but making it work for you is not as simple as you might think.

PART 3 ADVANCED INVESTMENT TACTICS

CHAPTER 12   INVESTING IN ROLL-UPS   135
The consolidation of mom-and-pop shops can be a great investment play, as long as you know how to judge whether management is using the "roll-up" strategy for the right reasons.

CHAPTER 13   INVESTING IN IPOs   143
How to invest in initial public offerings.

CHAPTER 14   REVERSION TO THE MEAN   157
Because investing is driven by psychology, stock prices bounce
around maddeningly. Here is the best way to take advantage of the
investment opportunities this creates.

CHAPTER 15   THE BASICS OF BIOTECH INVESTING   163
How to invest safely in biotech stocks.

CHAPTER 16   SHAREHOLDER ACTIVISM
Improving your returns with shareholder activism.

PART 4 WHEN TROUBLE STRIKES

CHAPTER 17   WHAT TO DO WHEN YOUR
              STOCK BLOWS UP   187
How to decide whether to hold or get out when a stock sinks. The
pros explain how they handle the most common scenarios.

CHAPTER 18   WHEN GOOD STOCKS GO BAD   203
High-flying momentum stocks that tank because of one weak quarter
may seem like bargains. Most often, they are not. Why "trolling the
momentum trash" is a loser's game.

CHAPTER 19   AFTER-HOURS MARKETS   208
The pitfalls of night trading.

CHAPTER 20   AVOIDING THE CON ARTISTS   212
Holding on to your money. How to spot and avoid the most common investment frauds.

PART 5 EPILOGUE

CHAPTER 21   TRICKS OF THE PROS   227
Learn from the basic investing rules of thumb followed by professional money managers.

CHAPTER 22   SOME BASIC POINTERS   250

The often neglected but simple advice that will save you money
and peace of mind.

Index   253

Acknowledgments

Above all, I would like to thank my sources, without whom none of this would have been possible. I would also like to thank the Knight Bagehot Fellowship program at Columbia University, Columbia Business School, Columbia Law School, and the Johns Hopkins School of Advanced International Studies, all of which allowed me to learn more about business, economics, law, and the markets than I could have ever imagined. Finally, special thanks to Carl La Vo of the *Bucks County Courier Times,* Bob Lyle of *Radio Free Europe/Radio Liberty,* Frank Flaherty of the *New York Times,* Doug Dundas who was my editor at *Money New Media,* and Martin Giles of *The Economist,* editors and colleagues who managed to teach me how to do my best work, though it might not always have been good enough.

INTRODUCTION

Some people like to compare the stock market to a battlefield. While this shows disrespect for people who have risked their lives serving in the military, the analogy is apt. Every trading day, investors battle it out over the prices of securities, and the losers can suffer some serious damage.

If the market is like a battlefield, then the key strategists behind the action on the front lines are the professional money managers. And if you want to refine your investing skills, who could possibly be better teachers than these pros who make tough judgments every day on what to buy and sell?

That is the idea behind this book.

For several years as a financial writer covering the markets for the *New York Times* and *Money* magazine, I had the privilege of interviewing money managers about their battles–taking in their war stories and observing the way they make decisions. Later, I went back and gathered more information in follow-up conversations.

Much of what I learned about their tactics and strategies is in this book. It is full of valuable market insights and useful lessons drawn from the experience of some of the best professional investors around. In short, it contains the condensed wisdom of professional investors who go in to work every day and deal with the markets for a living. *Lessons from the Front Line* offers an insiders' look at how Wall Street thinks.

Used well, the lessons here should improve your investment results noticeably. But even if the book merely saves you the time it would otherwise take you to understand how to do more advanced research, spot trouble in financial statements, or figure out some important market patterns, it will be worth your while. For the price of just a trade or two, you get a collection of essential insights and lessons that would take you years to learn through your own experience and study.

This book is for all individual investors, from the neophyte to the expert. Although it assumes some basic knowledge of investing, even beginners can understand many of the concepts right at the start—and they can grow into the book and go back to it to learn more as they advance.

Lessons From the Front Line will be particularly useful for people who have been investing in stocks for at least a little while and want to take their knowledge of the markets to the next level without having to plow through a dense book that is written like an MBA text. The market is full of introductory investing books that do a great job. But few books move you ahead without presenting information in a hard-to-follow academic style.

Even if you have been in the stock market for years, this book will be helpful. Many of the insights here will be new to even the most experienced individual investor. Remember that while the chapters are organized around themes, they do not build on each other and you don't have to read them in any particular order.

On one level, this book gives you several of the tools you need to uncover winning stocks on your own. Even if you don't initiate investing ideas yourself, you will want to be able to check out the ones that come from your broker or one of the multitude of news sources churning out tips on a regular basis. On another level, this book demystifies many of the market's natural twists and turns that present profitable buying opportunities. Whether it's the discounting of good stocks caused by the "earnings confession season" or lock-up releases—or dips caused by the herd behavior of investors—many market anomalies give you the chance to buy stocks at the right price. Once you understand what is happening in the market, you can more fully take advantage of it to buy stocks at a discount.

On this subject, I would like to point out that generally speaking, it can be a real challenge to make any money as an active trader. If you *do* trade, the techniques in this book will serve you well by helping you get into a stock at the right time. However, it's probably better for most people—especially those who don't have the time or resources to trade—to be long-term investors. If that's what you are, you will be able to use the ideas in this book to find superior stocks. Next, you can use the market concepts to get good entry points which will boost your returns. All this becomes a lot easier to do, once you have learned the lessons from the front line.

PART ONE

INVESTOR INTELLIGENCE

CHAPTER 1

THE WALL STREET ANALYST'S REPORT

Picking stocks that actually earn you money is not easy. So it's a good thing you can get detailed brokerage reports from Wall Street analysts. These well-trained graduates of prestigious business schools conveniently boil down weeks of hard-nosed research on a company into one crisp word like "buy," "accumulate," or "hold." With their reports in hand, you can cut through the nonsense and get down to making some serious money by simply following their advice. Right?

Well, not quite. The truth is, the world of the Wall Street analyst report ranks high on the list of places where things are not always quite what they seem.

Consider a simple word like "hold," for example. To the uninitiated, this may seem like a clear indication that a stock is worth hanging on to because it is going to move up soon. Wrong. In the confounding world of the Wall Street analyst's report, "hold" actually means "sell." Well, if that's true, what could "sell" possibly mean? "Sell is often an indicator that the company is going to go down the toilet," explains Jeff Ricker, an investment strategist based in San Francisco. To confuse matters even more, "sell" is not the only word used to describe the worst stocks. In an apparent effort to dissuade you from converting shares to cash, some brokerages use the word "swap" in place of "sell." Investors who "swap" one security for another buy more shares than if they had simply sold–meaning they spend more on commissions.

Why do analysts use such Alice in Wonderland language in their reports? Critics say it's because these people don't always have your interests as an investor in mind when they write reports—for a number of reasons.

One of the biggest reasons has to do with how brokerage houses make a good chunk of their money. The brokerage where your analyst works most likely has an investment banking side that helps companies issue new shares or advises them on financing and mergers. It is supposedly separated from the brokerage business by a "Chinese wall." But the fee income from the investment banking side of the business is usually far greater than what the analysts generate through commissions. Because of this imbalance, activities in the investment banking side get through the Chinese wall and have an impact on what the analysts do and say.

Indeed, one way or another, some of that lucrative investment banking income makes its way to the analyst who helps land a banking deal. The analyst might help by writing reports that please management at a company that will soon be shopping around for an investment banker. In short, when it comes to covering publicly traded companies—which are potential clients for the investment banking side of the brokerage house—the analysts may have more than just you, the investor, in mind.

"Research coverage is a way of getting the ear of the company's financial people and pitching them investment banking business," says Ricker. "The analysts are often the ones making the pitch." Many insiders would disagree, but Ricker claims the practice is endemic. "In some firms there are no Chinese walls. You have the analyst putting deals together. But they don't like to say that."

Indeed, many "buy-side" analysts—the ones who work for portfolio managers buying stocks— gripe about what they say is the poor quality of Wall Street research. They claim the low quality is due to the fact that picking good stocks has little to do with the pay packages of "sell-side" analysts—those who work for brokerage houses pitching stocks. The result, according to these buy-side analysts, is that the sell siders don't dig around or aggressively question companies or their competitors, customers, and suppliers. Instead, they perform more of a reporting function than real research, the portfolio managers say.

People who defend the sell-side analysts say the portfolio managers are just looking for someone to blame. For what? The fact that their performance usually trails the market averages, even though these fund managers collect high fees from investors for their supposed expertise at stock picking. Whoever is right, many mutual fund firms like Fidelity Investments or Alliance Capital Management rely more and more on in-house research departments—a sign of what they think of the brokerage house analysts. Obviously, no one wants you to believe that all sell-side analysts are lazy or crooked. Just be aware of the potential conflict of interest when you read their reports. Studies show that analysts whose firms have investment banking ties with the companies they cover tend to put out higher earnings forecasts and more buy ratings on those companies.

The conflict of interest was not always there. Back before deregulation in 1975 made commissions come down, brokerage houses built up big research staffs to attract clients. Once commissions fell, the securities industry began focusing more on fee-based income that comes from things like stock underwriting, mergers, and acquisitions. That's when the job of the analyst began changing from simply commenting on investment banking deals to helping make them happen.

Aside from the tendency of these analysts to get involved with pitches for the investment banking deals, there are other reasons to be suspicious of their reports. For one thing, the investment banking side of the brokerage house may have stock in a company left over from an offering it carried out–stock it still needs to place in the market. Positive reports by analysts can help in that effort.

The brokerage house probably also has a trading desk that acts as a market maker in the stocks covered by the analyst. If so, "buy" recommendations and lots of exciting company updates can be profitable because these reports generate lots of turnover.

Turnover is good for the trading desk–which earns money by trading the spread on the stock. The spread is the difference between the price at which individual investors like you can sell a stock to a market maker (the bid) and what you can buy it for (the ask). (The bid, of course, will be lower than the ask.) Spreads often get wider when a stock is moving fast–say because a positive analyst's report has come out or there is other news. This is especially true for smaller stocks with lower average volume. When spreads widen, the market maker earns even more when he buys a stock from you at the bid and sells it to someone else at the ask price. True, trading income at brokerage houses declined after federal regulators forced market makers to narrow their spreads in the late 1990s. But it is still a good source of revenue.

Another problem with analysts is that they may simply be reluctant to write reports that are too harsh on management for fear of being cut off from the valuable flow of information. "If they issue a bad report, maybe the company won't talk to that analyst in the future," says Tom Baker, a portfolio manager for Bingham Osborn & Scarborough, a San Francisco investment advisory.

Many analysts tread lightly when discussing problems at a company because of this concern about offending managers. This can lead to the use of subtle language, euphemisms, or double-speak, at best. At worst, analysts may write overly positive prose, or gloss over problems, because they are thinking about that potential investment banking business.

Does all this mean you should just throw analysts' reports in the trash? Yes, say some buy-side analysts. "Don't bother with these reports," says William Fleckenstein of Fleckenstein Capital in Seattle. "They are 100% useless claptrap. These guys don't have an interest in analyzing stocks. They just want to sell stocks."

Although there is a lot of truth to what Fleckenstein says, his view is probably too extreme. For one thing, few industry observers believe that analysts actually fib very often, when it comes to writing reports. "It is not in their best interest to drum up interest in a stock when they know in their heart of hearts that their recommendation is the opposite of what will happen in the real world," says Richard Pucci, the director of research for IBES International, a firm that analyzes and tracks earnings estimates. After all, the brokerage houses and their sales staff need repeat business, especially for their big institutional clients.

Second, even if they are subject to some potential conflicts of interest, the reports can be useful because they contain important information from management which is not available elsewhere. Some parts of the analyst's report, like the broad overview section written about the sector, can save you a lot of leg work, and they tend to be less biased anyway. So it would be a mistake to reject them out of hand. In short, the research is by no means completely tainted or useless.

Just keep in mind at all times what these reports are really about. First and foremost, they are marketing tools used by brokerage houses to sell stock to investors, notes Carl Wiese, a portfolio manager with Hokanson Capital Management in Solana Beach, California. As in any business, there are lots of good deals and some real clunkers. "Among the stocks that are worth buying, there are also companies that are not well positioned, stocks that the analysts have to push as well," says Wiese.

Knowing how to tell the difference between the two is crucial. You will do a lot better at this if you understand the subtleties of the art of interpreting the various parts of the analyst's report. Educated investors, who know how to read between the lines because they have a sound knowledge of the ways of Wall Street analysts, can put the research reports to good use. Here are some of the key things you need to know about how to use analysts' reports, according to professional money managers who read them every day.

TIPS ON HOW TO USE ANALYSTS' REPORTS

Look for the investment banking connection and other potential sources of bias. The first thing to do when you pick up an analyst's report is to check the footnotes and the fine print for what is probably the most important piece of information you will find in it. You want to see whether the investment banking side of the analyst's brokerage house has a relationship with the company being covered. In other words, look for whether the bankers have helped issue shares of the company or raise cash in the past.

If so, should you just discard the report? Again, some money managers think so. "If the analyst comes from a firm whose investment banking side is part of the syndicate that has floated shares, I would throw the report in the trash," says Ken Winans, a financial advisor at Winans International in Mill Valley, California. "Many of the analysts would rather go out and find deals than write reports. It is like the college professor who teaches but really likes the job of getting research grants."

It is probably better, however, to just be aware of the potential source of bias but use the reports anyway. Otherwise you may miss out on some useful information. The reports contain management guidance on earnings and internal sales forecasts that you probably can't find elsewhere. Or they might have information on upcoming events that will affect the company. And they probably even have some sensible analysis. "They are all biased," notes Sil Marquardt, the director of research at John Hancock Funds. "But that does not mean that one of them is not right."

Besides, the banking link is not necessarily always a bad thing. "It may actually be positive, because the analyst might have better contacts and insights," says Marc Klee, who co-manages John Hancock's Global Technology Fund. "You just have to be aware that there is a business relationship that can color the viewpoint of the writer. It is a critical component of the report, because there is a tendency for the reports to be somewhat more optimistic when the firm has a banking relationship."

As a rule of thumb, you should be most suspicious of analysts who work for a brokerage whose investment banking side was a lead underwriter in a share issue, as opposed to a lower ranking member of the underwriting team. And you can pretty much take it as a given that after the quiet period for an initial public offering (IPO) ends, all the analysts involved in the deal will come out with solid buy recommendations. Those are fairly meaningless. On the other hand, consider it a red flag if you *don't* see a glowing report from the analyst whose bankers handled the deal.

Even when the investment banking side of the analyst's brokerage has not been active in deals, you still have to be on guard. Their reports may be influenced by the fact that they are trying to pick up investment banking business. But for really big companies, this argument is probably overblown. For the most part, bigger firms have more or less cemented their banking relationships. So analysts know they are not going to be able to help their bankers muscle in at the larger firms. Still, the analyst might be worried about speaking too harshly about a company, for fear of getting cut out of the loop by management.

And keep in mind that brokerage houses have an interest in beating the drum about stocks because of earnings from commissions and trading the spread. A brokerage house, for example, might play up short-term news about a stock to generate interest, even though the development is really not that important. In sum, do not let analysts' reports serve as a form of investment pornography that arouses the urge inside of you to trade more than is good for you.

Finally, you should be aware of another bias you will find in the Wall Street reports. In general, analysts are often overly optimistic about the industries and companies they follow. They think they are the best sectors and firms around, or else they would be covering something else, points out Chuck Hill, a former analyst who is the director of research at First Call. They also tend to be overly optimistic about their earnings estimates.

SOME SOURCES OF INDEPENDENT RESEARCH

Research services like Value Line and Standard & Poor's, as well as the brokerage Sanford Bernstein, have no investment banking divisions. This means their research won't be tainted by the desire to land banking deals. And the St. Louis-based A. G. Edwards gets good marks among investors for its research—in part because it is not a major investment bank. Many boutique research services like Lipton Financial Services or DuPasquier & Co. are independent too, though their work is mainly available to institutional clients only. When it comes to the analysts who work for brokerage houses with investment banking divisions, be sure to consult the *Institutional Investor* annual ranking by professional money managers who use their reports. It is called the All America Research Team, and you can find it at Institutional Investor's Web site.

Be familiar with how the company deals with analysts. Is it heavyhanded with them? Some companies browbeat analysts by threatening to cut them off from information. With other firms, analysts are free to "call 'em as they see 'em." Know the difference. Typically, the bigger, well-run companies don't push analysts around that much, but this is not always the case. Roberto Goizueta, CEO of Coca-Cola, was notorious for giving firm and explicit instructions on how analysts should come up with earnings estimates. How do you know whether a company might be leaning on analysts to kowtow? Unfortunately, if you are not in the inner circle, it is hard to find out about the relationship between companies and their analysts. You can get some clues by reading press accounts or listening in on conference calls.

Consider the source. Each industry has its best and most influential analysts. Know who they are, and give their reports more weight when you make decisions. Tom Kurlak, for example, was "the axe" for semiconductor stocks when he worked at Merrill Lynch. His calls were not always right, but his reasoning was often very insightful. And he could move markets. You have to be aware of an analyst with that kind of power.

Analysts, like most people, tend to have their strengths and weaknesses. It is best to know what they are and follow the advice of the analysts accordingly, points out Ryan Crane, an equity analyst with AIM Aggressive Growth Fund. Some analysts may be good with the earnings and revenue estimates. Some excel at understanding and telling the story behind a company. Others may simply be outstanding at choosing stocks, even though they get the numbers wrong. "If someone is a good stock picker but weak on the numbers, I may not pay attention to their numbers," says Crane. "Their estimates may be way out of line, but an upgrade in their rating on a stock is still a good sign."

"There are some analysts who know everything about an industry, but they can't translate it into a rating," agrees Marquardt. "Since they know how tight every nut is on every bolt in the industry, however, it is useful to read their stuff. That is where you go when you want to know the details." Understanding the nuances of the analyst's community comes with experience. Talk with other investors. Listen to how the analysts are introduced on television. Look at the *Institutional Investor* ratings. Read the predictions of an analyst and watch what happens.

When checking out an analyst, be sure to consider these questions. Does he or she have a growth or value slant? How experienced is the person? Does the analyst have a reputation for being a mouthpiece for management? Has the analyst been feuding with any companies in the sector? Is the analyst successful because he has been good at bringing in investment banking business or selling stocks? Is the analyst a raw business school graduate, or someone who has been covering the industry for 10 years?

Know what to take from the various parts of the reports. Analysts' reports come in various shapes and sizes. Inside, they have distinct components. Generally, an analyst will do one big report on the company and its sector when she initiates coverage. These are followed by regular updates. Inside the reports and updates, the key parts include the section on new developments; the "buy," "hold," or "sell" rating; the earnings estimates; and the price target. Knowing how to interpret each section of the reports you get from your broker is important.

The Background Report. Typically, the big background reports—which tend to come out when coverage is initiated—will be the least biased. These are very useful for getting yourself up to speed on trends in a sector. And they often do a good job of outlining the story behind the stock. A good background report will give you much of the information you need to start forming an opinion about a company.

The Update. These may be driven by events, or a brokerage may simply put them out on a regular basis. Either way, this is where you turn to get the analyst's spin on developments—on why inventories are building up or who put in a recent big order.

It may seem like an obvious point, but you might want to start reading an update by trying to figure out why the analyst wrote it and what is really behind it. Ask yourself, "What is different from the last report?" Is there a significant change, real news, or some original research—like a survey by the brokerage of buyers in the field? Or is the analyst just reacting to a well-published event like an industry conference or an earnings release? If you have a "me too" update, or an analyst simply following a trend and jumping on the bandwagon, the report is less useful.

Sometimes, a report might come out because the stock has been shellacked, and the company asked the analyst to support the share price. This is more likely to be the case if the analyst works for the same firm that handles the investment banking for the company. Or a report might get issued because the analyst is looking to make a statement to the company, notes Howard Schachter, of Schachter Capital Management. When shopping for investment bankers, companies look for decent research (and a strong market maker) because they want a firm that will support a stock when trouble comes.

Earnings Estimates. Next to background reports, and updates that are written for the right reasons, the earnings estimates may be the most useful part of a report. Often, earnings revisions are the key thing to focus on. "A change in estimates for the right reason speaks more loudly than enthusiastic language," says Wiese, of Hokanson Capital Management. "When it comes down to it, companies are valued on their earnings."

Typically, what an analyst does with the earnings number is more important than changes to a rating. "The ratings are based more on their opinion," says Ben Zacks, of Zacks Investment Research. "This is where the analysts have a tendency to be more favorable. I pay a lot more attention to the changes in estimates. There is more information in the fact that they changed their estimates than that the rating went to an outperform from a neutral."

When the estimates and the rating diverge, trust the estimates. An analyst may say something like: "We are lowering our earnings estimates but maintaining our buy rating on the stock because we still think the company is a good value." Or the analyst might write, "We are lowering our estimates but reiterating our buy rating because we feel the market has discounted the news." Don't believe it. If the estimates are coming down, that says a lot more than the positive commentary or the fact that the rating has not changed. In short, base your decision more on what analysts do with the numbers than what they say with their ratings. They have a tendency to use the rating to put a positive spin on things. But they are less likely to mess with the estimates for spin control.

Similarly, if estimates have been going up, and suddenly there is a downgrade in a rating—but no change in the earnings numbers—the sell-off that follows can be a buying opportunity. This is especially true if the downgrade was "for valuation," meaning the analyst thinks the stock is getting ahead of itself. Once the effect of the downgrade wears off in two or three days, investor enthusiasm for the stock is likely to return, and it may begin its march upward again. Even downgrades in ratings for what seem like legitimate concerns can create a buying opportunity—as long as the analysts are not bringing the numbers down as well. You have to give it a day or two to see if they adjust their earnings estimates. They don't always do it immediately after news develops.

It is a good idea to put an earnings estimate or ratings change in context by using a service like IBES International, First Call, or Zacks Investment Research. These firms compile estimates and ratings from most of the analysts covering a stock—giving you the big picture. Consulting one of these services will help you understand whether the revision you heard about was just a laggard catching up with the group or someone on the leading edge of a trend. Look at whether the estimate ratings change goes above or below consensus. If an estimate that gets cut goes below consensus, that is worse than if it was just too high to start with. One note of caution. Each of these services polls a slightly different subset of analysts, since not all analysts cooperate with each firm. So don't be surprised if you see small contradictions in consensus estimates. Each of the three services has a retail product available on the Internet.

Be sure to look closely at what is behind changes in the earnings estimates. Although earnings revisions can say a lot about where a stock is headed, you have to be careful when you interpret them. It is important to verify that the earnings numbers are going up because of changes that will have a lasting impact. Your goal will be to distinguish between one-off increase in earnings and sustainable growth.

A "numbers bump," as it is called among money managers, that happens because of a one-time change in tax payments or a share buyback is not that interesting. Financial restructuring that brings lower interest expenses can only increase profits for a year or two. The same thing goes for other kinds of cost cutting. After all, there is a limit to how much a company can trim expenses. Likewise, a decline in capital spending won't produce long-term earnings growth. At some point, the company will have to increase capital spending again to stay competitive.

Generally speaking, you want to look for reliable top-line (sales or revenue) growth that will sustain increases in earnings over the long term. But be critical of the assumptions an analyst makes. Some just assume incremental growth. You have to look at what is driving the increases. Leadership in a rapidly growing sector is a reassuring source of revenue growth. Dell has been a good example. A company that is taking over market share or consolidating a sector is also likely to deliver sustained top-line growth. Wal-Mart and any of the other "category killers" are good examples of this. When analyzing the top line, remember that professional investors like to see sources of recurring revenue, either because a product gets replaced frequently or upgrades occur at regular intervals. Microsoft and other software producers fit into this category. Investors also like to see earnings gains that come from a shift in the product mix toward higher-margin goods or services. The least desirable revenue comes from one-off sales.

Keep in mind that while you shouldn't get too excited about gains from cost cutting because they are not repeatable, don't dismiss cost savings out of hand. For one thing, they can give a stock a nice bump up over the course of a year or two. Moreover, when they are part of a turnaround of a poorly run company, you might see improvements at the company that boost the rate of sales growth for a longer time. What looks like a one-time cost-cutting measure may actually be part of a bigger, successful plan. Wal-Mart drove costs down in part by developing its hub and spoke delivery system and getting better deals from suppliers. Then it cut prices and proceeded to use lower prices to romp the competition and take over market share. One of the reasons Dell was so successful was that it contained costs by virtually eliminating inventory. This price advantage was one of the tactics that helped it beat competitors. Not all financial restructurings have short-lived effects on earnings either. If a company spins off slower growing divisions to concentrate on its most rapidly expanding business lines, the new focus may contribute to sustained growth.

When it comes to upward earnings revisions caused by a merger, be especially careful. In judging the impact of the merger on earnings, the analysts may not really have done all the work. Instead, they could have simply borrowed assumptions from management. But there is a bigger reason to be suspicious: Making a merger work is hard. Fewer than half of them add any value in the medium term—except for shareholders in the firm getting bought out. It is not easy to put together two different business cultures. The transition can distract management. The much-ballyhooed synergies might not really come about. As a general rule, mergers are more likely to succeed when companies buy businesses they know something about than when managers are building empires by piecing together disparate businesses.

The Rating. The biases from the investment banking side of a brokerage are more likely to seep through the Chinese walls and into a stock rating than earnings estimates. "Sometimes a broker starts coverage of a stock with a strong buy rating, and two months later they do a secondary issue of more stock," says Crane. "What a coincidence!" Analysts are also more likely to bump their ratings up to support a stock that is sagging or cut them when they sense trouble but don't have enough certainty to cut their estimates. In contrast, earnings are usually more concrete, even if they do actually contain a lot of assumptions about growth.

All this means that when you are looking at stock ratings, be wary of an upgrade that is not accompanied by a change in the earnings numbers. Likewise, if earnings estimates go down and the rating does not, be suspicious. "That is a sign the analyst does not want to go into a negative mode," says Marquardt. "You see that all the time. They say, This quarter is bad but we are keeping our long-term buy rating." But bad quarters, notes Marquardt, tend to come in fours. Of course, it may just be a sign of uncertainty when the rating changes but the earnings numbers do not. Whenever this happens, remember to pay more attention to the earnings numbers.

Despite the fact that analysts may use stock ratings to send mixed signals, they are still useful to you as an investor. You just have to know how to interpret them. How you do this will depend on your investment style and your philosophy of human behavior. You have to develop a system that is right for you. Here are some of the common ways experienced investors read stock ratings. None of them is right all the time.

Many investors believe a preponderance of positive recommendations may really be a contrary indicator. After all, these investors reason, if most of the brokerage houses have moved their clients into a stock, who is left to buy it? Good news may continue to drive it higher, of course. But the big pools of uncommitted money are no longer out there.

"I wouldn't buy a stock if there is a consensus that it is a good buy, because it is probably overbought," says Daniel Weaver, an associate professor in the Zickland School of Business at Baruch College in New York. "Think about prospecting for gold. Where will you have the best chances of making a big strike? In a stream where you are the only one there, or where you are in one square foot toe-to-toe with thousands of people?"

A lot of investors like to look among stocks that have an abundance of negative recommendations. They reason that these issues are beaten down and forgotten but may come back. If you are looking for these kinds of stocks, don't forget that "hold" is a code word for sell.

Along these lines, some investors like to look closely at stocks that have neutral ratings by big firms like Merrill Lynch or Goldman Sachs. They believe that these brokerage houses still hold out hope for the stock, or else they would drop coverage altogether. Sooner or later, the brokerage is likely to put the stock back on the buy list and drive the price up, the thinking goes.

Other investors believe that you have to watch for trends and catch a stock when a few analysts have spotted a change in business and upgraded their ratings. That way, when the rest of the analysts jump on board, they will drive the stock even higher, and you can enjoy the ride.

Chuck Hill, at First Call, says it is important to consider the relative strength of the rating. To do so, compare the rating on the stock you are thinking about buying to the consensus recommendation for stocks in the S&P 500. To do this, rank the ratings used by your broker on a scale of 1 to 5, with 1 being a strong buy. (All the brokers used different words for their rankings, so you have to convert them to a numbered scale.) Then see how that compares to the consensus recommendation for the

S&P 500 stocks, which is usually between 2.1 and 2.3. In this way, you get a sense of the relative strength of the rating.

Be sure to understand the rating system used by the brokerage. Unless you are familiar with the scale used by Goldman Sachs, for example, it may not be obvious that a "market outperform" is actually not such a hot rating, since it is the third best ranking the firm issues (behind "recommend list" and "trading buy").

Many brokerages use long-term and short-term ratings. The short-term rating tends to change more often. But it is not always clear what the difference is. "What does it mean when the short term is hold and the long term is buy?" asks Crane. "Frankly, I don't know, either."

Despite all the potential confusion about what stock ratings may really mean, one thing is sure: they do affect stock prices. So when the rating changes for one of the stocks you follow, you will be faced with the task of trying to figure out what to do. Unfortunately, unless you are a premier client, chances are a lot of people have heard the news before you. So the price will have already moved by the time you find out. But if there is a change in the long-term outlook, you will still need to do some thinking even if you missed the initial price reaction. What you do will depend on the specifics of the situation. But when considering your options, keep in mind this useful basic rule of thumb. The effect of a downgrade to a "sell" tends to last longer than the impact of an upgrade to a "buy." In practice, this means it often pays to wait a few days after an upgrade for a stock to cool off before buying it. But when they say sell, sell. The negative effects of a change in a rating to a "sell" tend to linger a lot longer. The chances are good that the stock will continue to lose value and then tread water for a long time.

Keep in mind another reason a stock may not actually be worth buying even though it is rated a "buy." Analysts are only human, and they make many of the same mistakes individual investors do. They get "married" to a stock, and they refuse to downgrade it as it declines after the fundamentals have changed. Or they may be afraid to upgrade it when it moves up because they fear the stock will reverse once they change their rating.

The Price Target. In theory, the price target captures all the factors affecting a stock's potential and sums them up in one neat number. People who have been trained at business school like to boil all things down to one number when they can, and this is a useful habit. In practice, though, few professional investors really think that a stock will be trading at the price target within 12 months, the usual time frame for the target. Instead, it is just a guideline.

The analyst comes up with the price target by projecting what earnings will be a year from now and then assuming a price-to-earnings ratio. Combine the two, and you have an expected price. Embedded in the price target reached through these two calculations are all the assumptions about things like revenue growth, the company's ability to control costs, earnings growth, and a fair value for the company. When evaluating a price target, you have to question all these assumptions. If the analyst says the company deserves a valuation (price to earnings or price to book value) that is higher than the industry average, ask why. Does the reasoning make sense? In general, don't let the price target have a big impact on the opinion you form about a stock. The target may be too optimistic, or the stock may hit the price target in just a few months. Don't think of it as a projection that has a decent chance of actually being accurate. Again, it is just a tool used to sum up all the analyst's assumptions about stock. Instead of simply looking at a price target and thinking "gee, that sounds like a nice return" as many investors do, it is much more important to analyze the trends for the stock and the sector that are behind the target.

The trend is your friend. One report in and of itself does not tell you what you need to know. Instead, the incremental change in the analyst's opinion over several reports is what counts. Look at many reports by the same analyst and get a feel for how his opinion has been changing over the months or years. Even though the stock may still be rated a buy, a decline in enthusiasm by the analyst can be a red flag.

"For me, the directional change is more important than the absolute value of an opinion," advises Klee. "So you have to get some understanding of the perspective they have had on the stock and how it has changed. They may be enthusiastic now, but they might have been more enthusiastic in the past. And are they saying anything inconsistent? If so, why is that?"

Likewise, rather than simply looking at the sheer number of positive ratings, the smart investor tries to get a handle on the trends in the changes in ratings by all the analysts covering a stock. Is there a steady stream of conversions to stronger recommendations? If so, that is when you want to buy the stock, not after all the analysts have completed their upgrades and the stock has run up in price. It may still have further to run. But the easy earnings have probably already been made. Again, services like IBES International, First Call, and Zacks Investment Research do a good job of tracking trends in analysts' ratings.

Get reports from several different analysts. Professional investors have access to reports written by most of the analysts covering a stock.

This is important because the quality of the analyst can vary from brokerage to brokerage or from sector to sector within one brokerage house.

Although the pros have access to many brokerage reports through their news services, you may be able to afford accounts with only one or two brokers. This is not a problem. "Call the investor relations department at the company and say you are an investor," says Winans. "Ask them for copies of other brokerage reports." (In general, you should develop a relationship with the investor relations department of companies you invest in.)

If you take this route, be careful about getting fooled by "reports" that look like they come from analysts, even though they were prepared by the company. Many of them prepare their own overviews of the company, and they often use the format of Wall Street analysts because it is convenient and easy to read. The company is not deliberately trying to mislead you.

Get a sense of the company's approach to accounting. Most experienced investors agree that when you analyze companies, it is very important to focus on earnings from continuing operations. This is *not* the same as the line item on the income statement known as operating income. Operating income is net income (or the bottom line) with depreciation, amortization, taxes, and interest added back in.

Earnings from continuing operations, in contrast, is net income with extraordinary or one-time costs added back in. This is the number you hear about when a company reports its profits for the quarter. Investors like to add nonrecurring costs back in to net income because this gives an earnings number that better reflects the strength of a company's ongoing business. Charges defined as "extraordinary items" on the income statement which get added back in to net income are things like: the effects of an accounting change, most early retirement of debt, and the cost of discontinuing operations. One-time charges (typically cited in the footnotes of financial statements) which also get added back in are things like restructuring charges, acquisition charges, and gains or losses from the sale of assets.

But there is still a lot of wiggle room. Accountants at the company have to make judgments about matters like revenue recognition, how much to reserve for things like restructuring charges, and the useful lives of assets—which has an impact on depreciation and amortization. The bottom line is that different accountants will reach different conclusions about these kinds of things, and their decisions can have a big impact on earnings from continuing operations. Knowing that investors tend to ignore big one-time charges and look instead at the future, for example, some companies load more operating expenses into restructuring charges than they should.

In short, there can be dramatic differences in reporting practices among companies in the same industry. If accountants are too liberal when making choices about financial reporting, the result can be bad earnings surprises in the future–bringing down a stock's price. So you want to try to get a feel for the accounting practices, as well as the general reputation, style, and credibility of management at the company. In general, it is important to develop a sense of the difference between conservative and liberal accounting policies. If a company is conservative, you are less likely to get nasty earnings surprises in the future.

In some sectors, professional investors don't focus on earnings from continuing operations. The insurance industry is an example. Here, the pros look at earnings from what is called the "core business," which excludes gains or losses from securities operations. Bank analysts focus on earnings from the "core business," too. But banks include proceeds from securities holdings in the number. This explains why they often have fewer negative earnings surprises. If they need to make up a small shortfall, they can simply realize some gains by selling some securities and add that to earnings.

Small company reports require special handling. Analyst coverage of small-cap stocks can be a two-edged sword. On the bright side, you can profit from the greater "information inefficiencies" surrounding these less covered companies. On the other hand, coverage of smaller companies is more likely to be a thinly disguised attempt to generate business for the investment banking side of the analyst's brokerage house.

First the downside. "With small-cap companies, whatever coverage exists is filled with pitches for deal flow," says Ricker. The reason is simple. Many analysts will follow a big company like Microsoft–even if their firm's banking side has no chance of getting a deal–simply because it is such an important, high-profile company. With smaller companies, this kind of motivation does not exist. Therefore, any analyst covering a smaller firm is more likely to be fishing for investment banking business. Among the analysts following a major company, in contrast, there are many who know their investment banking side has little hope of ever getting a deal from the company.

Now for the good news. The flow of information about smaller firms is so much more inefficient that if you do your homework, you are much more likely to find companies whose bright prospects have not been discovered by the market and factored into the stock price. There are several reasons for this.

First, if 30 analysts cover a big company that has a well-paid investor relations team, there is bound to be a pretty efficient distribution of information in the market. "It is not likely that one analyst is going to make a superior call," says Crane. "And incrementally, I don't know if I can do a better job of analyzing Microsoft than the thousands of people who do that."

In contrast, only four or five analysts may be covering a smaller company. They are likely to have different levels of access to various people in management at the company. And their skills at predicting how well the company will do are bound to vary. In this kind of environment, one analyst is much more likely to break out of the pack and do a better job. Unfortunately, figuring out which analyst is making that better call is not easy. Indeed, your own analytical skills come into play, and you should take advantage of this opportunity. "With a smaller company," says Crane, "there are so few people following it, then incrementally I can probably do a better job."

At the extreme is the small company that takes care of its own financing out of cash flow and has little need for investment bankers. Because there is no potential investment banking business, this company will probably be covered by very few analysts. It pays to look for these kinds of firms, because you can find excellent investments in this group of overlooked companies.

Here is another advantage to following small-cap companies that are not extensively covered. News in this part of the world travels more slowly. When a major brokerage house like Merrill Lynch upgrades a big stock, it usually moves right away. When a smaller brokerage increases the rating or earnings estimates of a smaller company, the market does not react as fast. "So you can get in on the stock before it goes up, hopefully ahead of the pack," notes Crane. "At least with these companies you have a chance to be early."

A better chance than you may think, according to some research. Studies[1] have confirmed that information about smaller, less covered companies tends to spread through the market much more slowly. To demonstrate this, researchers looked at two groups of recent winners in the stock market, defined as shares that were in the top 30% by performance. One group consisted of very small stocks with a market cap

---

[1] Jeremy Stein, Harrison Hong, and Terence Lim, "Bad News Travels Slowly: Size, Analyst Coverage, and the Profitability of Momentum Strategies," *Journal of Finance* (in press).

of around $100 million to $500 million. These stocks had limited coverage by analysts. The other group was made up of big companies with a market cap of around $5 billion. They had lots of coverage. Over the course of time, the smaller, less covered companies outperform the bigger ones by a wide margin, implying that the positive information that initially made them top performers took a while to get to other investors.

The study makes another interesting point. Thinly covered losers tend to keep on declining more than thinly covered winners continue to go up. The authors of the study conclude that this happens because companies are less eager to let out bad news than good news. And a lack of analyst coverage probably helps them keep the bad news from becoming public. This is more evidence, in other words, that the markets are less efficient when it comes to smaller companies. The definition of "small cap" varies, but generally, it means anything under $1 billion in market capitalization.

THE SWEET SPOT OF NEW ANALYST COVERAGE

New analyst coverage normally boosts a stock. Studies show that the effect is the biggest when a company is already being covered by three to six analysts. Any more, and the effect starts to weaken. Any less, and the company still does not have enough exposure—or investors still don't have enough confidence in a stock—for new coverage to have as big an impact. There is one exception: Previously uncovered stocks make a decent move up when an analyst initiates positive coverage.

Once you start poking around in the world of small-cap stock analyst reports, you will find yourself dealing with some of the smaller, regional brokerage firms. They may have strange names you have never heard of before, which may make you doubt their abilities. After all, the big money and prestige are at the larger, well-known brokerage houses in New York City. If these local analysts were really any good, they would be at Merrill Lynch or Goldman Sachs, you may think. Are the regional analysts really inferior?

Absolutely not. In many cases, they have an edge over the analysts from the bigger brokerage houses. For one thing, the analyst at a regional brokerage lives in the same community as the company, which could make him more familiar with the firm. "He may know the company like the back of his hand because he lives in the same town and his kids play little league ball with kids of the managers," says Crane.

Certainly, you should put more credence in a regional analyst's coverage of a local firm as opposed to its research of a large-cap multinational. "But an analyst at a major wire house may not have the contacts or guidance that the local brokerage firm has with the smaller companies," says Zacks. "You should stick with the specialty of the local wire house."

"Don't think that regional ones are less capable," agrees First Call's Chuck Hill. "The regional analysts may be more on top of things that are in their back yard. Sometimes, they get a hold of information sooner than the bigger brokerage firms."

Furthermore, many talented analysts prefer to work for the smaller firms where they have more flexibility and more freedom to pick up new companies to cover. And many of the very same high-profile analysts at the big firms recently worked at the smaller brokerages, which are often the proving grounds for the bigger brokerage houses. When dealing with the smaller brokerage house, just keep in mind that a higher percentage of the regional analysts are making pitches for deal flow.

A few more words of caution. When looking for deals among the less covered companies, the same information inefficiencies you are trying to exploit can also work against you. An outstanding, but unnoticed, company may continue to go unnoticed for a long time. So you have to have patience and confidence in your conclusions to get you through the waiting spell without giving in to the temptation to close out your position right before the market catches on to what you already know.

Second, managers at smaller companies tend to be less seasoned. This means that if there are problems with a quarter and the company looks like it will miss earnings expectations, management may not tell anyone until the last minute, in the hopes that it will be able to make the number. "Smaller companies are more prone to coming out with a big surprise at the last minute," says Klee.

Be sure you understand the brokerage's rating system. Each brokerage will have its own names for the various levels of ratings. Some will be as simple as "strong buy," "neutral," "underperform," or "sell." Others will use expressions like "priority list," "recommend list," or "accumulate." If you are new to the game, it may not be clear to you that phrases like "market outperform," "accumulate," and "trading buy" are actually second- or third-best ratings that indicate less than 100% enthusiasm for a stock. "Trading buy" may sound great for at least a

short-term flip, until you realize it is the fourth best ranking at one brokerage house (Goldman Sachs), three notches below the most enthusiastic rating of "recommend list." You would not know this unless you
read the fine print explaining the rating system. Translate the words into
a five-point scale (there are usually five levels), so that you can compare
rankings among brokerage houses.

Use common sense. Don't sell yourself short when it comes to analyzing the assumptions and reasoning built into the analyst's report. The
report may exude confidence and use intimidating language. Ignore all
that. Just make sure you understand the rationale behind the conclusions. Then decide whether or not it all makes sense.

The report should explain the business model and how it adds value.
Does it do this in a believable way? If the analyst assigns the company
a valuation or rate of earnings growth that is higher than its industry's
average, does this seem sound? How long can it last? What is the company's competitive advantage? Is it gaining market share? Does it really
have a distribution system that cannot be replicated? Do the assumptions about sales growth, pricing, and product mix make sense? Are the
investment risk factors more serious than they are made out to be?
Don't accept all the built-in assumptions. Examine the reasoning behind
them, then decide. Think about where things can go awry.

"Typically, analysts just take the last year or two and extrapolate it,"
says Marquardt of John Hancock. "They don't look at enough time in
the past. They make the mistake of confusing the current environment
for the stock as being the case for the stock. You have to weed out envi-
ronmental characteristics like economic or currency trends. The envi-
ronmental factors are often only temporary."

"Consider the analyst's report in the context of all the information
you have and ask yourself if it fits in with the big picture," advises Wiese,
of Hokanson Capital Management. "Are they overly optimistic or pes-
simistic? Ask yourself what you think. There is a bit of common sense
in all of this."

Make sure the outlook for the stock is based on an economic scenario
that you think is correct. Don't deviate from your own outlook for a sector or the economy, just because the story sounds good. An analyst may
be writing positive reports about changes at an oil company. "But it does
not matter if the oil sector is not the right place to be," says Wiese.

And don't be fooled into thinking that any recent news described in
an analyst's report is not already priced into the stock unless it is a small
company. The long-term trends described will continue to have an
effect as time goes by. But unless you are a high roller or a buy-side ana-

lyst with a big portfolio, you are probably near the bottom of the list when it comes to getting the news in the reports. Unfortunately, that means the news is probably already priced into the market by the time you see it. "The more you pay for your investment advice, the quicker you get it," says Weaver. "If you have the money, then you go to the front of the line. Money comes to money."

BROKERS ON BROKERS: WHO YOU GONNA CALL?

Once you are wise to the ways of Wall Street analysts, their reports can be a good source of investment guidance. But who do you turn to when you want the lowdown on the brokerage houses themselves?

After all, analysts face some especially thorny issues when they cover their own industry. For one thing, there is a much greater risk to potential deal flow on the investment banking side. Trashing the management of a single company may close out the possibility of future investment banking deals with that firm. Trashing another brokerage can multiply the effect. Why? Because loan syndications or stock offerings are typically originated by one or two "lead" banks which then divide the deal up among several other investment banks, in part to spread out risks.

"Analysts may be reluctant to be harshly critical of another securities firm because that firm may soon be the lead underwriter in a deal," says John Eade, a research analyst with Argus. "And the lead underwriter might not want to bring in the analyst's firm if the analyst wrote a report that was too harsh." On the other hand, who wants to praise the competition too much?

Here is another problem. Analysts often base their reports on the facts they gather in meetings with managers. When those managers happen to work for a competing brokerage house, they are not likely to be very forthcoming with the details of in-house strategy. What's more, an analyst may be reluctant to say bad things about potential future bosses.

Because of obstacles like these, say many buy-side analysts, reports on fellow brokerage houses are likely to be so watered down that they are far less useful than the typical Wall Street report. "We have found that the coverage of their own industry is more cautious than warranted," notes Ron Muhlenkamp, the portfolio manager of the Muhlenkamp Fund. "And the greatest bias against brokerage houses is to not cover them." Some brokerage houses don't even bother to follow their industry at all.

So where can you turn for information about brokerages? Old stand-bys, like Value Line and Standard & Poor's, come to mind. But in the end, the best approach might be to roll up your sleeves and do the job yourself. Ironically, one good place to start your research is with the brokerage reports themselves—as long as you know how to use them.

"I do not listen to the opinions of analysts in the reports," said Robert Male, a securities analyst who follows the financial services industry for the USAA mutual funds. "But I use them for information on industry trends and things like financial numbers for the companies—information that would otherwise take me a little longer to obtain." The rest of the details you need can be found in annual reports and other Securities and Exchange Commission filings. With these documents in hand, follow these rules used by seasoned independent brokerage analysts.

Check out how well the brokerage house manages costs. "Whether a brokerage makes money or not depends on cost control," explains Muhlenkamp. "When Wall Street has a good year or two, they lose sight of expenses, and costs get out of whack." To judge the ability to control costs, Tom Finucane, an assistant portfolio manager for the John Hancock Financial Industries fund, likes to monitor compensation as a percentage of revenue. "Once it gets higher than 50%, you have to start asking questions."

The late Perrin Long, who was an independent brokerage analyst after a stint with Brown Brothers Harriman, liked to examine trends in profit margins before taxes. To do so, you have to figure out pretax income as a percentage of total revenue for the same period. (Divide pretax income by total revenue and multiply by 100.) Calculate this at several points in time and look for the trend.

"This tells you how well the brokerage manages all of its costs in relation to revenues," according to Long. Consider it a good sign if pretax margins hold fairly steady over the years—especially if there has been a lot of growth at the brokerage. Usually, companies have trouble controlling costs as they grow. You should also check to see how pretax margins fared in difficult years for the industry—like 1988–90 and 1994. Was the brokerage successful in keeping pretax margins high by cutting costs in those years? If not, it may have the same problem the next time a bout of trouble hits the sector.

Check how well the brokerage uses its assets. Another useful measure of efficiency is the pretax return on assets, according to Long. "You want to see how many dollars of assets it takes to generate a dollar of revenue." To do so, divide total revenue before taxes by the value of assets for the same period. "If this is declining, watch out, because it means it is taking more assets to produce a dollar of revenue." An upward trend is preferable, but no change is acceptable.

Look for adequate growth. Long believed revenue growth per share is one of the key yardsticks to use when analyzing brokerage houses. To calculate this, divide the revenue earned in a year by the number of shares outstanding during that year. Then compare the change over several years. "If a company's revenue per share does not increase over time, it is highly likely that earnings and book value will not increase either," said Long.

Bargain hunt. Analysts also apply some basic value measures. As a value investor, Male looks for price to book of at least 1 or below. Anything with a price to book value of more than 2 is probably overvalued. Analysts also look for a price to forward earnings ratio of around 10 or below, depending on the asset mix of the brokerage. Keep in mind that it can be important to look for relative value (rather than blindly follow rules using absolute numbers) if growth trends for the sector look like they will stay in place. Analysts measure industry trends by monitoring things like trading volume in the market, the flow of money into mutual funds, and the number of initial public offerings, mergers, and acquisitions. They also look at longer term demographic trends that affect the rate of personal savings and investment.

To measure the value of a brokerage stock against internal growth, Muhlenkamp likes to look for a price earnings ratio below the return on equity and the revenue growth rate. This is similar to the "peg" ratio investors use to evaluate stocks. Many investors consider a stock to be potentially undervalued if the ratio of its price earnings ratio to its long-term (three- to five-year) growth rate—the peg ratio—is less than one.

Consider reducing volatility. Be warned that brokerage stocks can be notoriously volatile. Since much of their business is linked to the level of activity in the markets, the stocks of brokerage houses tend to move in tandem with the markets. Often, however, they will move down a lot more than the broader market indexes, because a depressed market can dramatically cut both trading and underwriting revenues. Likewise, the stocks tend to move up a lot in bull markets—often more than the overall market.

If stock price volatility makes you nervous, Michael Gasparac, an investment analyst with Zurich Kemper Investments, advises buying brokers with more predictable revenue streams. Brokerage houses earn steadier revenue from activities like asset management, fund distribution fees, and recordkeeping services. Trading and underwriting are more volatile sources of revenue.

Even if you choose stocks that are supposed to be less volatile, you should be well prepared for anything–like an increase in interest rates–that could make the markets and brokerage stocks decline, according to Long. "Anybody who buys brokerage stocks must be willing to see the value of their investment go down 30% or 40%, because these stocks are highly cyclical."

CHAPTER 2

How to Participate in Your Company's Conference Call

When it comes to investing in stocks, you need every advantage you can get. So you will probably want to listen in on the conference calls companies have with the professional stock analysts. Companies use these calls every quarter to explain earnings. They also schedule them as needed to discuss extraordinary news events. Although conference calls are meant to link top management with analysts and money managers, individual investors are usually welcome as well.

You can get the conference call phone number and access codes by simply calling the firm's investor relations department. Even if you only own a hundred shares of a stock, the company should let you listen in. Because, in theory, all investors are supposed to have equal access to important information that comes from management. You can also get the access numbers by asking your broker or checking in the investment "chat areas" on the Internet. Don't worry if you don't have time when the original call is held. Replays usually run for about a week. Many companies broadcast their conference calls over their websites.

Conference calls can be very helpful, but you should use them carefully. Remember that old saying about how a little knowledge can be a dangerous thing. Interpreting what management says in a conference call is no easy task. Not only do you need to know the jargon used in discussing business and financial statements. It also pays to know how to read between the lines and interpret the subtle signals. Understanding the calls can be a challenge for amateur investors, and a false interpretation of what was said can lead to trouble. If you reach a different conclusion than the analysts and the markets, you might end up making a big mistake.

Indeed, former Hambrecht & Quist analyst Joe Noel thinks that amateurs shouldn't even listen in because of the risks involved. "Conference calls have developed into an art form. It takes quite a while to understand the nuances of these calls and what management is saying. Unless you know what is going on, it is almost impossible to compete with the institutional investor. It is like playing basketball with Michael Jordan." Another risk, says Noel, is that management itself may be new to the game and make the mistake of sending off a false signal. "An inexperienced management team might not understand that every little word between the lines is analyzed, and they might say the wrong thing. Investors will think the CEO is sending a signal. But instead, he is just saying something stupid."

Despite these risks involved in using conference calls, with time, study, and experience you can probably get the hang of them. To help get you started, several money managers who have used conference calls for years explain in this chapter how to interpret them, what to take from them, and what to watch out for.

The first thing to know is that there are several kinds of conference calls. Some are sponsored by brokers to help management discuss an initial public offering. Others go over a big news event. More commonly, they are used to explain a quarterly earnings release and how things went during that quarter. Generally, this third type is the kind of call you will find yourself listening to most often, simply because they are more common.

The second thing you should keep in mind is that it is a bad idea simply to listen to one call and then make a snap decision about an investment. Instead, do your homework thoroughly. Read annual reports, news stories, and analysts' reports. Even if you already understand a company and its sector, be careful about drawing conclusions from the first conference call you hear. It takes several calls and a lot of practice to really understand what is going on in them and how management communicates. Mastering the conference call takes a lot of experience. To get you started, here is some advice from the pros.

TIPS ON MASTERING CONFERENCE CALLS

Be prepared. Obviously, you need to be familiar with the quarterly financial statements or press release behind the call. Just as importantly, you have to have a solid understanding of the company—based on a thorough knowledge of its quarterly and annual reports, and any other material you can get your hands on. If not, listening to the call will not bring as many insights. "Since investment analysis is a business of incremental knowledge, it is critical to have a decent background before listening to a call," says Marc Klee, a portfolio manager at John Hancock's Global Technology Fund. "They may never talk about the Far East, and all of a sudden they are talking about the Far East. Why? Do they have plans to expand there?" In short, you have to know the company and what to expect. "Otherwise how do you know if something is new or different?" asks Howard Schachter, of Schachter Capital Management. "Often people overact because they don't know the context."

Be familiar with the company's style. Each management team has its own style in dealing with analysts in a conference call. Some companies, like Intel and Microsoft, are extremely conservative when commenting on the future. Others are overly optimistic. If you don't know which style a company follows, you can easily misread the signals during the call. A "no comment" may not be a negative sign if management is always tight-lipped. At another company that is typically more open, those words could spell trouble. You won't know the difference unless you have heard several calls and understand management's style.

"You have to know the history of the company and whether what it says can be taken at face value," says Chuck Hill, a former analyst who works for First Call. "Does it usually try to play things conservatively, or gild the lily? Management might always say, 'We are going to have a hard time showing growth,' and then always announce decent growth. You have to know they have a habit of low-balling it." Being familiar with management's style can be helpful in another way. Many professional managers prefer to invest in firms that err on the side of being too conservative in their conference calls. "The more successful companies tend to be the more conservative ones," notes Hieko Thieme, the manager of the American Heritage Fund. "The less successful ones want to tout their stocks. We prefer the company that does not need to push itself, like Intel, Microsoft, or Applied Materials."

When trying to get a feel for management's style, don't rush to judgment. "It takes more than one conference call to get a feel for the management team," says Carl Wiese, a portfolio manager at Hokanson Capital Management, Solana Beach, California. "In successive calls, look to see if they are saying the same thing and delivering. You want to look for credibility, and they have to establish that over a period of time."

Pay attention to the "body language" during the call. Most buy-side analysts prefer one-on-one meetings to conference calls. Personal encounters allow you to read facial expressions and body language. To some degree, however, you can gather the same intelligence during conference calls.

"You can find out where the potential problems are through the body language," says Sil Marquardt, the director of research at John Hancock Funds. "If they handle a question badly, pass it off, or fumble it, you know they are evading it because it may touch on a problem." It can pay to focus on the emotional aspects of the call, even though you might not think that would be the case in the hard, cold world of business and investment management. "Investors are not only looking for information about things like earnings reports, but for the tone of the call," says Noel. "Stocks will trade up or down on the tone of the call." But be on guard for fake-outs. "Managers can be optimistic, just not too aggressive," says Louis Navellier, of Navellier & Associates. "If they are too aggressive, something smells. You should be skeptical."

Know the structure of the conference call and what to take from each part. Typically, the chief financial officer (CFO) will start by walking the analysts through the numbers for the quarter. Then the chief executive officer (CEO) will have comments on the quarter and some broader issues. Finally, there will be a question and answer session. Generally, the part presented by the CFO will be a look back. The CEO comments and the question period will give a look forward, in addition to covering the past.

Which section is most important? It varies. The meat of a call about quarterly results will be the CFO's presentation of the numbers. Some analysts prefer to focus on this part. "I like CFOs and treasurers better than presidents, because Wall Street is obsessed with numbers," says Navellier. But if the call is about a news event or merger, you will probably want to focus on the CEO, to hear how strategy issues are addressed. There is another reason to zero in on the CEO—in any type of conference call. In most companies, the CEO has subordinate managers boxed in with instructions on what they are allowed to talk about in public. "But the CEO can divulge whatever he wants," says Marquardt. "He knows exactly where the line is so he can come right up to it. Whereas, if you are one of the minions, you have to stay several yards away from it."

What you focus on in the call can be a matter of your investing style. Thieme likes to assign an analyst at his firm to listen to the CFO's presentation—to get the details. He listens to the CEO for the big picture. "I invest in companies for their long-term potential, so I like the vision. I am more of a conceptualizer."

When listening to CEOs, pay attention to their attitude toward the analysts. "A lot of CEOs do not get Wall Street," says Navellier. "A good CEO sucks up to Wall Street, and you want to see that. The ones that are more aloof are more likely to have disappointments."

You can learn as much from the questions as the answers. "The information brought up by other investors is useful," says Eric Efron, the co-portfolio manager of the USAA Aggressive Growth Fund. "It helps you get a feel for the sentiment toward a stock and how the thoughts of other investors are changing. The market is psychological as much as it is fundamental."

The questions can tell you what issues are bothering other people and can make you consider things you might not have thought about before—like that increase in inventories or days sales outstanding. If you hear three analysts ask different versions of the same question and none of them gets a decent answer, then you know the market is going to be worried about this issue. Be aware of who is asking the questions. Questioners usually have to identify themselves. Generally, they will be the sell-side analysts (those who work for brokerage houses) and the bigger money managers—or the people who move the stock every day. They know the company and often ask a lot of good questions. Some of the sell-side analysts are just currying favor, and you need to be able to separate them from the rest in your thinking.

Listen to the tone of the questions. Are they argumentative? Or more along the lines of "I just wanted to get a better feel for how the numbers are changing". If a lot of the questions from the sell-side analysts start with "Great job, congratulations on a great quarter!" that is a good sign that they are pleased with how things went, and they are likely to raise their numbers. In other words, that kind of banter is usually more than just glad-handing.

Listen closely to the questions from the lead analyst for the sector. On a more sophisticated level, tune in to whether an analyst with a neutral rating (like market perform or accumulate) is asking a lot of positive questions. That might signal an upgrade is coming. Likewise, you can get a read on whether analysts who have been hot on the stock might be cutting their ratings.

Then there is the matter of short sellers. Some professional investors believe they deliberately lob in terrorizing questions during a conference call to shake up the markets. More likely, the tone of their questions is just a by-product of their job, and their questions are no more biased than those coming from the long side. Shorts, of course, want stocks to go down. But more to the point, they tend to be a touchier group than investors who go long, because their potential losses are higher. If you go long a stock at $20, the most you can lose is $20. But if you short that stock at the same price, your potential losses are much bigger. It could go to $100. So you would expect shorts to sound a bit more nervous.

If you are long a stock, you should ignore the fact that the short sellers sound extremely nervous. But don't tune them out. Instead, welcome questions from the short side, because you always want to know the bear story for a stock you own. A conference call can be a great place to get that.

But not always. Companies often exclude short sellers from the calls because they don't want to face the hard questions. Bill Fleckenstein, of Fleckenstein Management, is a short seller who is regularly banned from conference calls. Fleckenstein is more frustrated about what he sees as the reasons for his being kept out rather than the fact that he is excluded. "Things are so warped now," he says. "Managers used to pride themselves on integrity. Now it is OK to mislead people. What is the penalty? If they get caught cooking the books, they just rewrite their options. There is this whole cheerleading aspect of management and the analyst community now."

You may notice other weaknesses to the question and answer period. Many money managers, like Martin Whitman of the Third Avenue Value fund, finds this part of the call to be shallow, because analysts tend to focus on the short term. If your goal is to understand the long-term prospects for a company, he says, you won't find much useful information in the question and answer section, let alone the rest of the conference call.

"Many managers are geared toward what the analysts want. And analysts just want to know what the next quarter will be or whether dividends will be raised. Their objective is speculation, or predicting what a securities price will be in the next month, or year," says Whitman. "So the questions are directed in that way. The questions don't have to do with understanding the business but predicting a stock price. Good investors figure out what a business is worth and what the dynamic will be. They do not carry all that excess analytic baggage that says you have to make stock market predictions." There are other reasons why analysts don't cover all the issues during the question and answer session. First, time is limited. Second, many of the analysts have questions they don't want to ask in public. They wait until they get the CFO on the phone, so they don't tip their hand.

Take advantage of the opportunity to see how management responds to challenges. Just about every Wall Street analyst and investment banker has to endure a "stress test" as part of the job interview. Some analysts like to put managers through the same kind of trial. This gives you a chance to see how they do under pressure. "The most interesting part is not so much the canned presentation by management, but the interaction between investors and management, which can get adversarial at times," says John Cabell, the co-portfolio of the USAA Aggressive Growth Fund.

Whether or not questioners are playing the stress test game, you should expect sharp, credible answers that come out quickly. If not, be careful. "I like to look for a manager who can answer the question immediately, off the top of his head, demonstrating he knows the business inside and out," says Wiese. "I give negative points for broader, nonspecific answers that demonstrate a lack of knowledge of the overall business. And you should be careful about managers who talk too much. That might mean they have something to prove. You don't want a sales pitch. Look out for signs that they are trying too hard."

Access may be limited. Don't always expect to get in on the live version. For one thing, companies are often charged for the number of ports used to patch everyone together. So they may have an incentive to limit access. And as an individual investor, you won't be able to ask any questions if you do get into the live version. Questions are reserved for the professional investor.

If this makes you feel left out, you are not alone. In addition to the short sellers, some buy-side analysts (the ones who work for fund managers) are excluded because they have the nasty habit of asking more penetrating questions than sell-side analysts. Buy-siders, after all, are actually putting money on the line. In addition, some companies will exclude sell-side analysts who have published negative reports or asked too many negative questions in the past.

You should be aware that management can also manipulate the lineup for questions. The result is that the sell-side analysts who are more prone to using kid gloves may be first in line. One trick is "priority cueing," which allows managers to decide who gets to the top of the question cue, regardless of which analyst was there first. Managers who do this, of course, want to favor the friendly analysts who ask softball questions.

You won't hear any major news during a conference call. As useful as they are, conference calls are rarely going to give you any really important news. To ensure that the little investor has equal access to big news—like mergers, the loss of a major contract, or earnings results—regulators expect firms to announce major events with a press release. Conference calls are then held to fill in the details. They usually occur after the close of the market, to dampen big market swings and give investors time to digest the contents.

But the rules on this are far from airtight. Big news may slip through in a conference call from time to time—or more likely in a private call with a small group of analysts, a call you can't listen in on. The Securities and Exchange Commission (SEC) does not like this practice, known as "selective disclosure." For one thing, it is unfair. Second, the SEC knows that if investors think the capital markets are rigged, eventually they will stay away, and it will be harder for companies to use them to raise money. At the same time, the SEC is well aware that selective disclosure goes on. It sees the tell-tale spikes in volume between the time companies give analysts price-sensitive information and the time it is put out in a press release.

"My preference is that calls to analysts should not come before a press release, and that even then, these discussions should not divulge new material information not contained in that press release," says SEC Chairman Arthur Levitt. "Our law has no tolerance for favoritism. Everyone deserves a fair shot at success in our nation's securities markets."

Unfortunately, not everyone has a fair shot, and it isn't easy for the SEC to do anything about it. The reason is that selective disclosure does not fit neatly under the rules against insider trading. Those rules, developed by courts over several years, were clarified in a Supreme Court holding in a case known as *Dirks vs. SEC*. Simply put, the ruling says that the person who gets the information has to know that the tipper violated his "fiduciary duty" to the corporation, or the obligation to put the interests of the company above his own. And the tipper has to benefit in some way. Typically, the benefits to the tipper have been things like money, gifts, or a better reputation. This is the part that trips up regulators.

"It is complicated to reach selective disclosure under the *Dirks* case, because it requires that the tipper gets some kind of benefit," says a lawyer in the SEC's enforcement division. It is not always clear what benefit the company receives when it discloses information selectively to analysts. In some cases, the company may be trying to do the analyst a favor so the analyst will put a more positive spin on the story in conversations with the press. Or else the company is exchanging advance access to information for favorable coverage by the analyst. These cases probably violate the *Dirks* rules. "And if the CFO is selectively giving out information to enhance his reputation, then maybe we can get him," says the SEC lawyer. "But there are no clean rules out there. So we are working on how to write them." Indeed, by the time you read this, they may have been written.

Here is another reason why you should not expect to hear much big news in a conference call. Contrary to popular belief, companies are under no obligation to disclose material information. Yes, there are a few exceptions. One is when a mandatory reporting period (the quarter, for instance) comes to a close and the company has to file a document with the SEC, like a quarterly or annual report. Another exception is when a company finds out a public statement it has made is wrong. Once the company knows this, it has to correct the statement. Other than that, companies don't have to disclose bad news, even if asked directly about a big problem it knows it has. Managers are not allowed to lie, but dodging the question is perfectly legal. So, don't be lulled into a false sense of security when managers are asked about a problem and they respond with some form of "no comment," a phrase like "The company never comments on unusual movements in its stock price."

Be aware of the code words and what they mean. Take some time to get a feel for the nuances and special language found in conference calls, before you rush to judgment. Like politicians, managers often use code words to talk about touchy subjects.

Don't think "transitional quarter" means a change for the better, for example. It means just the opposite. A "lengthening sales cycle" may sound positive. Longer, after all, is often better. And who wouldn't want a sales cycle for a product to keep going? Actually, the phrase means it is taking the company more time to generate the same amount of sales. A quarter that is "back end loaded" may seem innocent enough. But it really means lots of the orders came in at the last minute. In fact, they may have been crammed in there to build up an otherwise weak three months. "Our eyes get big when we hear phrases like these," says Efron.

Try to figure out what the pack is going to think. The economist John Maynard Keynes once noted that if you want to predict who will win a beauty contest, the first thing you have to do is forget about which contestant appeals to you the most. Instead, your job is to guess which competitor the judges like best. His point was that it is the same way with stocks. This is a good concept to remember, especially if you are a trader making decisions based on what you hear in a conference call. Like it or not, in the short term, at least, it doesn't matter what you think. It's more important to understand what the crowd took from the call and where the crowd is headed. You might be absolutely right in your interpretation of what managers said. But that won't matter if the markets reach a different conclusion and investors run for the exits. Of course, if you have it right and the herd was wrong, sooner or later the markets will come around. In the short term, however, you will have made the wrong decision, at least if you are a trader.

Don't get cocky. Remember that even though you may think you know what was said during the conference call, understanding them is really tricky business. Be careful about making decisions based on what you hear in a call, at least until you have a lot of experience with them.

CHAPTER 3

READING THE INSIDER TEA LEAVES

Who could possibly know more about a company's future than the top managers who run it? After all, they have the front row seats. Unfortunately, they don't always tell you, the investor, everything they know about trends in profits or about that new hit product that is about to be launched.

But there is still a way you can figure out what is on their minds. Simply watch whether they are buying or selling their own company's stock. Actions, after all, often do speak louder than words. This approach can be so effective that it has spawned a whole cottage industry of analysts who pour over the stock trading activities of these "insiders" on behalf of professional fund managers and retail investors. "There are no better experts," believes David Coleman, of Watershed Asset Management in Washington, D.C. "Insiders are the source of all the information used by the Wall Street analysts. And what they give the analysts is just the tip of the iceberg." By tracking the trading patterns of the insiders, analysts like Coleman try to fathom the rest of their knowledge.

They can do this because, by law, top managers–known as "insiders" in the securities industry–must tell stock regulators at the Securities and Exchange Commission (SEC) whenever they buy or sell shares in their companies. Insiders include board members, senior managers, and anyone who owns more than 5% of a company's stock. The papers they file divulging their trades are public documents. This is how the insider analysts know what the senior managers are doing. (By the way, the term *insider trading* here is a reference to the legal kind. Insiders can and do trade illegally on confidential information, but that is another matter.

"Insider" in that case has a different and more complicated legal definition, which loosely means anyone who has a duty to put shareholder interests first, but profits from trading on insider information nonetheless.)

You can get the same information on the insider trades as the experts. But knowing what to do with it is not as simple. Understanding insider trading requires some sophisticated analysis. Although it is not a science, the reasoning goes a lot deeper than merely thinking, "The CEO just bought 50,000 shares in his own company. I am buying some too!" As you will see, the problem with this simplistic approach is that there are many reasons why insiders will buy or sell shares in their own company that have little or nothing to do with where they think the stock is headed. However, there are ways to weed out these false signals and cull useful investing intelligence from the moves of insiders.

Professional insider trading analysts use their techniques for more than just predicting the movements in individual stocks. They also make sector and market calls. The approach can even be used to forecast interest rates. Insider analysts, for example, will watch buying and selling patterns at utilities—reasoning that the top managers have an uncanny knack for predicting where interest rates are headed. "They have access to commercial power usage, which tells them a lot about how strong the economy is," says Bob Gabele, the editor of *Insiders' Chronicle,* one of the newsletters that tracks insider activity.

To make any of these kinds of forecasts, you have to know the tricks. You will by the end of this chapter. Often, insider analysts build computer models that adjust for the important factors we will go over here—such as how high the insiders are on the company ladder or what their past trading patterns were. Most of us don't have fancy computer models. But don't let that worry you. They are not essential for interpreting the moves of insiders. What you need to know are the main points the pros keep in mind when interpreting insiders' moves.

TIPS ON READING THE INSIDER TEA LEAVES

Insider buying is more significant than insider selling. There are many reasons executives sell the shares of their company that have nothing to do with how business is going. They might want to buy a new house, pay college tuition, or diversify their assets after a good run in their company's stock. Top bosses at tech companies regularly sell because much of their pay comes in the form of stock. Selling for these reasons is not negative. Indeed, it is pretty common to see a lot of selling in a high-flying stock and then watch that stock keep moving up. "An increase in selling can be warranted by a run-up in prices," notes Coleman. Insider selling, in other words, is not always a bad thing. Insider purchasing is another matter. Managers are more likely to be buying for one simple reason: They think good things are about to happen.

There are other reasons why interpreting insider sales is a challenge. For one thing, high-profile chief executives, like Bill Gates of Microsoft or Michael Dell of Dell Computer, know very well they are being watched. So they carefully sell shares in their own companies on a regular basis in relatively equal blocks (though they might sell a bit less if the stock slips because they think they are not getting good value). Given these attempts by the most visible managers to disguise their thinking, insider analysts try to gather insights by looking for a departure from normal patterns when considering sales by the high-profile corporate titans.

When looking at sales, keep in mind that a burst of activity can occur for purely innocent reasons. At the end of 1998, for example, executives at a company called Network Appliance dumped lots of shares. Was this a sign that insiders saw trouble ahead for the company which makes servers that store data? Maybe not. Executives had been barred from buying or selling stock for two quarters before the flood of sales because the company was negotiating a deal with Dell Computer. Once the restrictions were lifted, there was a rush to unload the stock because sales had been blocked for so long, the company explained.

That makes sense. But you should always be cautious about justifications by companies about insider selling. They know that investors are watching what insiders do, so many companies will try as hard as they can to put a good spin on insider sales. Not only that, but sometimes they play with the numbers. Suppose a senior manager holds 4 million options, exercises them all, and then sells 3.2 million of those shares. Devious public relations reps at his company might then put out a press release stating he has picked up 800,000 shares. While this is technically true, he has also reduced his holding by 80%, if you consider options as holdings, which is the way you should look at them, says Gabele. "Beware of companies that work the math in their favor. I am very wary whenever companies announce their insiders are buying because that smells of promotion."

Although it is a basic tenet of insider analysis that sales are less significant than buys, you shouldn't simply ignore sales because you think they don't matter. "We get plenty of information out of them," says Gabele. "The categorical assumption that sales do not count is wrong." A good way to tease clues out of the sales numbers is to look at the insider's pattern of behavior over time and determine whether the current activities are an anomaly, notes Gabele. Just keep price in mind. Anomalistic selling when a stock has quadrupled might not matter. But if exceptional selling occurs while a stock is moving sideways, that is a warning signal.

A fundamental rule when it comes to insider selling is that you should always look at it in relation to buying. If selling picks up but buying holds steady, it may not be a bad sign. The steady buying means that insiders are still positive about the market. And keep in mind that insider selling (and buying) always has to be analyzed in the context of the seller's past habits. "If someone has been a seller all along and the company has always done well, then it obviously doesn't matter," said Coleman. Reversals, say from a general buying trend to a lot of selling, are significant.

AN INSIDER'S STEALTH BOMBER: THE ZERO-COST COLLAR

Insiders have an easy way to cover up their tracks when they want to cut exposure to their company's shares because they know trouble is coming. They simply use put and call options to hedge their exposure to their own shares. A put option allows you to sell a stock at a prearranged price. It protects you against downside. A call option allows you to buy a stock at a price agreed on beforehand. When insiders know bad news is on the way, they can hedge away exposure to their own stocks by buying put options, financing the cost by selling call options on their stock.

Since the rules governing the disclosure of these activities are unclear, the transactions don't always get reported. And when they do get reported, they are not always well-monitored by firms tracking insider trades. A recent study shows that investors should be paying more attention. The study found that on average, stocks fall by 7% relative to a benchmark 20 days after an insider puts on this kind of hedge. And stocks fall by almost 30% 120 days later. By comparison, when managers sell shares outright, the average price decline after 100 days is only around 5%. The study, by Carr Bettis, John Bizjak, and Michael Lemmon of Arizona State University, is called "Can Insiders Hide Trades in Their Own Equity? An empirical examination of the use of zero-cost collars and equity swaps by corporate insiders."

Even insider buying can be relatively meaningless. Let's face it. If you were in upper management and you knew the markets were closely watching every insider for signs of how well the company is going to perform, what would you do? Find ways to encourage senior management and insiders to buy more shares, of course. And that is exactly what many companies do. Because of this, you can't always assume an insider's big buy is a vote of confidence.

One trick companies use to get executives to buy is to set up a loan program to help them purchase shares. Often, the company won't make the loan program public until months after the purchases were made. This doesn't seem fair, because it deceives investors who follow insider moves closely. So the SEC requires that loans to executives above $60,000 be reported in financial statements. Sometimes, however, the loans don't show up in the documents until months later. Or if they do, the company will neglect to point out that part of the loan agreement is that the executives never really have to pay it back. This kind of behavior frustrates insider trading analysts like Gabele. He estimates that while only about 5% of companies have loan programs, they can account for a much bigger percentage of insider buying overall. As much as 20% of buying might be motivated by some form of incentive program, he says. "Be careful about companies that issue press releases heralding the wonderful event of insider buying. Some companies have massive loan programs, and you see more buying than at most other companies. But then the stock goes down by 50%."

Here is another false signal you have to watch for. Insiders may be buying because their company has a stock ownership rule stating that executives must own a multiple of their salary in stock. This is often the case in the banking sector. Typically, the executives are given several years to meet the ownership guidelines. In some industries, like the oil sector, insiders tend to buy a lot simply because it is part of the business culture. While all these kinds of buys may be some form of public relations stunt, the forced purchases still benefit investors because to some degree, these purchases align the interests of corporate managers with shareholders. And tracking purchases made because of these kinds of rules can at least tell you what the insiders think about valuation.

Insiders closest to day-to-day operations are the most important to watch. In descending order of importance, insider analysts typically like to watch the moves of the chairman, the president, the chief financial officer, vice presidents, and directors. For example, purchases by a CEO are more important than transactions made by the vice president for transportation. But since the chairman and president are so keenly aware that all eyes are on them, and they behave accordingly, many insider analysts like to fly below the radar and focus on the CFO and heads of strategic divisions.

When you are following the paper trail of inside transactions, be aware that what certain types of insiders do is fairly meaningless. You don't want to get faked out by their selling or buying. These are the "beneficial owners" and shareholders who are legally considered insiders simply because they own a big chunk of the company's stock.

These shareholders have to notify the SEC of their transactions simply because they own more than 5% or 10% of the stock in a company—two cutoff levels that trigger certain reporting requirements. Anyone who goes over 5% has to tell the SEC about the position (with a form 13-D or 13-G) and notify the SEC afterward whenever there is a change in that position. They do so with an amended version of the 13-D or 13-G or a Form 4. Shareholders who own more than 10% of a stock are considered insiders under securities law. They also have to report their sales or purchases. But since these kinds of insiders aren't necessarily that close to day-to-day goings on at the company, they are not really the same as the true insiders who work at the firm. So you should ignore the Form 4s of these kinds of insider, even though these beneficial owners may be behind some of the bigger insider trades. You can spot their Form 4s because they will have the name of an institutional investor on them, as well as the symbol B.O., for beneficial owner.

Selling from these kinds of insiders—and it is more often selling—might be simple profit taking by a venture capitalist who helped the company get started. Trusts, hedge funds, or the occasional value investor who takes large positions to help force a change at the firm are often the shareholders who are filing amended 13-Ds or 13-Gs because they have over 5% and are changing their positions.

Yes, they probably know the company well, if they own a large stake. But they are not as close to the business as the true insiders, so you have to play down the importance of their sales.

It usually means a lot more when many insiders trade around the same time. The experts look for a "cluster" of buying or selling by insiders. This gives a sense of unanimity about the company's prospects. You have to figure out, however, whether the cluster occurred for the wrong reasons. If so, the cluster is meaningless. What are the wrong reasons? Some firms will only let their managers buy or sell during a defined time frame, creating windows in which the trading can occur. Compaq, for example, has permitted insider buying and selling only

THE MOST IMPORTANT SEC FORMS YOU NEED TO TRACK INSIDERS, AT A GLANCE

Form 4   Insiders use this form to report buying or selling.

Form 144   Insiders use this form to report the intention to sell restricted securities, meaning shares that have not yet traded in the market.

Form 13-G and 13-D   Anyone who buys more than 5% of the shares of a company has to tell the SEC. They do so with these forms. Changes in the position are reported on amended versions of these forms.

Form 14a   This is a proxy statement. It can tell you the total number of options that insiders hold.

after earnings come out. Clusters of activity caused by these kinds of rules don't mean much.

Options-related trades and other special transactions mean less than open-market transactions.   Many insiders have lots of options priced well below the market—often at pennies on the dollar. They can raise some quick money by cashing in these options and selling the stock in the open market. Likewise, insiders might have stock they received as a gift or an award. The sale of stock that insiders own for any of these reasons is usually less indicative of what an insider really thinks about her company. Insider analysts heavily discount these kinds of sales.

But you can't altogether ignore options-related sales by insiders. If the options-related selling occurs at prices that are well off recent highs, this can be a warning of trouble ahead. And in many cases, insiders will "hold" just about their whole position in the company in the form of options, so *all* of their trades are options related. One of these insiders could cut his position in the company in half by exercising options and selling the stock. That would be a meaningful move. But you would have missed it if you were ignoring options-related trades. Form 4s indicate whether the insider got the stock by exercising an option, and the price paid. To get the total position of that insider in options, you have to consult the 14a proxy statement, which is produced once a year for a vote at annual meetings.

On the buy side, many fast-growing companies in areas like high tech pay their managers with options. This has weakened the signals insider analysts used to get from straightforward open-market transactions. "These guys are getting so many shares through options programs that it is hard to imagine when they would ever want to go buy on the open market," says Richard Cuneo, an analyst with Argus Research, which publishes *Vickers Weekly Insider Report*. "You don't see many obvious buy signals at companies like IBM or Microsoft."

To compensate for the effect of options on insider buy signals, Cuneo has lowered the bar. "Whereas I used to want to see five insiders buying stock in the open market, now when I see two or three I seriously consider that company, because I know they probably did not have to go into the open market to buy stock."

The larger the transaction, the more significant it is. This may be obvious, but remember that you have to compare the number of shares in the transaction to the number the insider already owns. Buying by an insider who already has a lot of the stock is more meaningful than purchases by someone who does not have a big position. The dollar amount is important, too. For example, Argus Research, which analyzes insider activity for retail investors, gives added weight to transactions of $250,000 or more. Some insider analysts also like to see heavy buying in one stock confirmed by a lot of purchases in the same industry. The same goes for using insider activity to call the overall market. "When insiders move in unison across a broad spectrum of industries, it has always proven worthwhile to take notice of what they are saying," notes Coleman.

Insider analysts are sometimes not overly impressed by big insider purchases by the chairman and president because they are so aware of the fact that they are being closely watched. Analysts also know that even the people at the top can misjudge the future of the company because the leader with the big vision might be missing the forest for the trees. "A single big buyer can be wrong," says Gabele. "So it is nice to see a supporting cast around that big buy or sell. Lots of little buys by the guys in the middle can be very meaningful. We look for the more subtle stuff rather than what hits us between the eyes."

One trick is to compare the size of the purchase to the insider's salary. A purchase of $10,000 worth of stock by someone who makes $60,000 a year can be a more meaningful vote of confidence than five much more highly paid vice presidents buying $2,000 worth of stock each. You can find the salaries of insiders on the 14a proxy statement which is voted on at annual shareholder meetings.

Insiders tend to be early with their transactions. You should not expect a stock to shoot up right after insiders buy it. They are good at spotting value in their own shares, but they are lousy market timers because they don't follow the markets that closely. They buy early, and it is not unusual for a stock to decline even after heavy insider buying. The chances are good, however, that when there has been heavy insider buying, the company is either about to see some good news or at least it will be free of nasty surprises. Likewise, insiders tend to bail out early when trouble is on the way. In short, don't count on them to call bottoms or tops in their stock.

You have to interpret insider buying or selling in the context of the overall market trends. Suppose you see a selling frenzy during a market rebound after several months of an overall weakness. Is it time for the market to tank again? Not necessarily. Much of the selling might be due to the fact that insiders who wanted to lighten up positions during the market slump were holding off for a rebound. Even when there was no recent bear market, you can expect to see more selling during a rally. "It's logical that in a high market some insiders will be taking some of their money off the table," says Russell Brooks, the president of Market Profile Theorems Inc. in Seattle, a firm that analyzes insider activity for money managers.

Similarly, a big increase in purchasing in the absence of a market pullback can be an extra positive sign. The same thing goes for when insiders continue purchasing into higher prices on the way up. But if you see a lot of insiders in a sector or a stock move quickly to capitalize on sharp increases in their stock by selling, this is a sign that valuations are getting too rich. It does not mean that a correction is imminent, but it is a clear warning sign that prices have moved up too fast.

Remember, however, to consider the historical context for the company. "If there is always a lot of selling, what is the significance of another sale?" asks Michael Painchaud of Market Profile Theorems. Finally, keep in mind that insider activity does not immunize you from the overall market trends. In a correction, even stocks with strong insider buying are likely to go down with the market in the short run.

You get news of insider transactions with a slight time lag, but it does not matter. Insider trades can be over five weeks old by the time they are filed with the SEC. Don't worry about this. It is the overall trend that matters, and insiders tend to act too soon anyway. Besides, you should never base an investing decision on just one or two insider moves. They are just pieces in the puzzle. The important thing to consider is the insider trend that has been developing over the most recent quarter or two, tempered with additional research on the company.

Insiders can be wrong. Because insiders have such a good track record and following their moves makes so much sense intuitively, it is easy to become too confident in this investing tool. Remember, as good as insiders are at calling turns in their stock or the market, they can be wrong. Even after you have adjusted for all the factors above, you can still get a false signal from insider activity.

Now that you have the theory, let's take a look at how some of the pros put these ideas into practice. You may not be able to replicate their systems fully. But seeing how they work can teach you more about how to interpret insider trading and help you understand what some of the insider tracking services have to offer investors.

HOW THE PROS DO IT

Argus Research (800 645–5043) publishes an insider newsletter for retail investors called *Vickers Weekly Insider Report.* It uses several tools to measure insider sentiment. Its main weapon for making broad market calls is what Argus calls the "eight-week sell/buy ratio." This simply presents a ratio of total sales to buys over the preceding eight weeks. Since insiders normally sell 2 to 2.5 times more than they buy, any eight-week sell/buy ratio in that range is considered neutral. A ratio below that is bullish because it means insiders are buying more than normal, and a ratio above 2.5 is bearish. Historically, whenever the ratio has gone below 1, there has been at least a 23% increase in the market within one year. The eight-week sell/buy ratio is one of the more useful tools because it smooths out short-term blips that may turn out to be anomalies.

Vickers also uses an indicator that measures the short-term blips–the one-week sell/buy ratio. As with the eight-week version, a ratio between 2 and 2.5 is neutral. Although this ratio tends to be more volatile, and therefore less reliable, it serves as a useful leading indicator.

Another leading indicator is the volume of the forms that insiders use to let the SEC know they plan to sell restricted securities, meaning shares that have not yet been traded in the market. Insider analysts call these Form 144 filings, named after the paperwork involved. In theory, insiders have to file a Form 144 before or at the time of the sale of restricted stock. (Form 4s, used to report the sale of nonrestricted stock, can be filed after the sale.) This is why the volume of Form 144 filings, compared to the long-term average, can be a leading indicator. "The fluctuation in rate of Form 144 filings can be a proxy for next month's insider sell/buy ratio," says Richard Cuneo, of *Vickers Weekly Insider Report*. In practice, though, insiders often file the Form 144 at the same time that they make the sale, which weakens the usefulness of this measure. When tracking Form 144 filings, Argus draws the line at sales valued under $100,000, ignoring filings for sales of less than that amount.

Form 4, used by insiders to indicate that a transaction has occurred, is supposed to be filed by the tenth of the month after the month of sale. Usually, there is a flurry of filings leading up to the tenth of the month, and then the volume lightens up. This often reduces the significance of changes in insider tracking indicators around the middle of the month. As in technical analysis of stocks and stock indexes, any changes that happen on lighter-than-normal volume are less significant. The lower volume means there is less conviction behind these kinds of changes. And when volume is light, it takes a smaller amount of sales to shift the indicators.

Argus also tracks transactions that result in a 10% or more change in aggregate holdings–since this is considered a more meaningful sale. You can get the size of the overall holding because insiders have to report how much they own after the transaction, on the Form 4.

Vickers also puts together a reading for individual stocks. Aside from the level of buying compared to selling, it weighs several other factors. These include things like the rank of the insider, whether or not several insiders are making the same move at the same time, and the size of the transaction. "If someone sells 50% of their holding, we give that a more negative weighting than if they sell 1%," says Cuneo. The index also considers the overal market conditions at the time of the sale. If someone buys when the market–or the stock–is going down, that is more significant. Selling on a decline in the stock's price is extra negative. Selling into a rising market is less significant.

Insiders' Chronicle, published by First Call-Investnet, (800-243-2324), uses many of the same tools that Argus applies. The newsletter, edited by Bob Gabele, tracks a sell/buy ratio that filters out beneficial owners, since they are not true insiders. A ratio of 2 to 2.1 is considered neutral. Anything above is negative, and ratings below that are bullish. The newsletter also presents a moving average of the ratio, which helps give an understanding of the trend by smoothing out short-term volatility. The newsletter also offers sector analysis, industry rankings, and stock picks, along with comments explaining why certain groups look good or bad. Computers screen for telling insider moves, but when making calls on sectors or stocks, Gabele looks for anomalies in trading patterns.

The Insider Bulletin (www.insider.net), written by David Coleman, offers market comment, highlights sectors and stocks with unusual insider activity, and presents a model portfolio. The newsletter lists individual trades to back points about a stock or sector.

Market Profile Theorems Inc., uses insider activity along with other forms of analysis to develop advice for institutional money managers. It has culled the academic research to figure out the most important things to consider. In addition to obvious factors such as the size of the transaction or whether it was options related, analysts look at whether a purchase or sale was a first-time transaction. If so, it gets less merit because it was probably a "political" decision. Newcomers to a company, for example, are likely to buy shares as a show of faith. Market Profile Theorems also considers the historical bias of insider activity at the firm, how much time has passed since the transaction, and the level of the insider at the company.

When making overall market calls, Market Profile Theorems comes up with a broad insider indicator by dividing sales by total transactions. A ratio of .60 to .45 is neutral. The firm also uses a market stability rating that not only considers the absolute value of selling versus buying, but also captures the rate of change in insider activity. Analysts only use insider transactions in New York Stock Exchange stocks. This gets rid of the volatility caused by insider activity at microcap and tech stocks. Market Profile Theorems does not offer a product for retail investors.

RESEARCHING INSIDER TRANSACTIONS

What is the best way to get a look at the insider buying and selling records filed with the SEC? You might think the SEC's own Edgar database would be the first stop. Although the site is a great service to investors because it presents a vast array of corporate documents for free, it does not contain all of the forms insiders file to reveal their trading. The problem is that the forms insiders use don't have to be filed electronically, says the SEC. So the SEC can't post them on its Web site easily. Until this changes, you have to go elsewhere. (A lot of insiders do file the forms electronically, so you will see some of them at the SEC site.)

Many financial Web sites like Quote.com have what you need as part of their package of investor tools. Insider trading records are also available at Yahoo! and other financial sites. One useful service can help you get a jump on the competition. Edgar Online (www.edgar-online.com)

pays to get SEC filings from Lexis Nexis, a huge legal and news data-base used by law firms. It then e-mails you alerts when SEC forms regarding your companies are filed, including the forms on insider activ-ity. Another advantage of the Edgar Online site, a pay service, is that it posts all the SEC documents a day before they appear at the SEC's own site. Edgar Online also offers software that permits you to do more com-plex searches of the lengthy SEC documents than you can carry out by using the "find" function in the Web browser.

CHAPTER 4

THE SEC
TREASURE TROVE

One of your best resources as an investor is the information in filings that publicly traded companies have to turn over to the Securities and Exchange Commission (SEC) on a regular basis. These documents are a real treasure trove. Indeed, that was the purpose of the federal securities laws passed in the early 1930s—the laws which make companies submit these reports. The SEC filings contain everything from company financials and sector analysis to the latest on insider buying or selling news, and how much your bosses' options are worth.

All good stuff. So don't let the coarse packaging and formal language scare you away. Once you learn the format and the code words, mining these documents gets a lot easier. You will learn to recognize boilerplate language, which sections to skip over, and what to focus on. Take advantage of Web sites that offer advanced, or Boolean, search techniques. Or at least use the search function on your Web browser. The private sites also offer e-mail alerts which are useful because they let you know when your companies have filed papers.

You might have doubts about how valuable the SEC filings really are, given that the companies themselves prepare them. This means the documents are not about to include any damaging information or useful tidbits that were not previously known, right? Not really. Sure, the filings are drawn up by the companies. But they have to follow a strict set of rules that force managers to disclose information they might not otherwise want to divulge. And they are supposed to do so in a manner that is understandable to investors.

"Every corporate lawyer knows the documents that are filed with the SEC will get substantial scrutiny and make the company legally vulnerable," says Harvey J. Goldschmid, a securities law professor at Columbia Law School, who went on leave to become general counsel for the SEC in the late 1990s. "So they are taken very seriously. The companies are required to prepare disclosure documents under a set of instructions meant to force out material that the investing public ought to have."

Nevertheless, managers can be pretty cautious about making predictions or the kinds of comments they think might land them a lawsuit from disgruntled investors down the line if things go bad. Therefore, corporations often hold back on what would otherwise be a useful discussion of what the future might bring. Despite this, the filings contain a lot of great analysis and information.

Useful things can pop up anywhere (especially the footnotes), but some sections stand out as the most interesting. Here are three of the more important ones. First, be sure to read the segment that is blandly labeled "The Company." This section is found in most quarterly and annual reports, and in the prospectus. It provides an excellent survey of how the company's game plan and products fit in to the business landscape. Another good part is the "Management Discussion and Analysis." It can be a frank review of how trends are affecting the company. And don't miss the section that discusses the most recent quarterly results. You will find it right below the table that contains those results. Aside from the numbers themselves, these three segments are the ones that are consistently the most useful.

Remember to look at filings by competitors, customers, and suppliers of the company you are thinking of investing in. And one final word of advice: Read the footnotes! Lots of interesting things are lurking there. Here are some of the most common ways investors use SEC filings.

WHAT YOU CAN LEARN FROM THE SEC FILINGS

Find out why your stock might be tanking. If one of your stocks is slipping in value on no news, check the 13G and 13D filings, which identify the big shareholders who have owned the stock recently. Some hedge fund managers, like Geoffrey Vinik, have a reputation for getting out of stocks in an aggressive manner, regardless of what it does to the price. Many of the momentum players will do the same thing. Even if nothing has changed at the company, one of these "mad bombers" may be taking your stock down simply because they want out for reasons that have nothing to do with business conditions. Also check the 424s and

S-1, S-2, or S-3 forms for a lockup release (see chapter 10). If a big insider or one of the venture capital firms that funded your company just got the green light to sell, they may be doing just that. This can have a big impact on mid-cap and small-cap stocks.

Find out how much the bosses' options are worth. This is public information that has to be reported to the SEC, if the person is high enough up in the company. Typically, the DEF14A annual proxy statements contain information on executive compensation, including stock options and salary. If a company recently came on the market in an initial public offering, the information will be in the S1 filing.

General research on a company. Most of the documents can be useful for this purpose, but the 10Ks and 10Qs and the prospectus offer some of the best surveys of the company and business conditions in its sector. A good place to look which you might not think of checking is the contracts that the company makes with other firms. These may contain some revealing details which tell you a lot more than what the company said in its press release on the business deal.

Track new developments. The 8-Ks announce new developments that could have an impact on business. These forms also may contain many more details than the press release on the same matter.

Find out whether insiders are buying or selling. What the insiders are up to can tell you a lot about a company's prospects, even if interpreting their moves requires some care (see Chapter 3). Check the 144 forms, or Forms 3, 4, and 5.

Look for options repricing. When out-of-the-money options get priced lower, you should be on guard. This is not a good sign. Not only does this dilute earnings per share, but it could also be a signal the company is having trouble keeping its top managers. Options repricing is a "material event" which has to be reported in an 8Ks, or it may turn up in a 10Qs.

Find out what the shareholder activists are up to, if anything. Proxy statements submitted by other shareholders can be found in the DEF 14A filings.

WHERE TO FIND THE SEC FILINGS

One of the biggest favors the SEC has ever done for investors was to put the SEC filings from public companies on the Internet. They are available for free (with a time lag of about 24 hours after they have been filed) at the SEC's Edgar database at www.sec.gov. ("Edgar" stands for

Electronic Data Gathering and Retrieval.) If you are a buy and hold investor, the 24-hour delay should not be a problem.

As useful as the SEC's database is, it has a few shortcomings. These problems stem from the fact that there are still some forms that companies are not required to file electronically through the SEC's Edgar system. Because that's the case, these forms don't go on the SEC Web site. Primarily, this means the documents that have to be filed by company insiders when they intend to sell shares in their own firm (Forms 3, 4, 5, and 144). Not having access to these electronically is a big drawback for the individual investor because watching what insiders are doing is often a good way to divine the fortunes of a company. Another interesting form you won't necessarily find on Edgar is the one that investment managers–like mutual fund portfolio managers–use to report their equity holdings (Form 13F), although this will probably change soon. In addition, foreign company filings do not have to be filed electronically through Edgar.

From time to time, any of these forms may show up in the SEC's database because companies or individuals voluntarily file them electronically. But if you really want to be sure you know whether any of these forms are filed, you will have to turn to an Edgar database run by a private company, like Edgar Online at www.edgar-online.com. These private Web sites get all the documents by buying a feed from a service like Lexis Nexis, which scans in all the SEC forms that are filed on paper. This arrangement also allows Edgar Online and some of the other private sites to get you the documents without the 24-hour delay. They also offer e-mail alerts and provide more sophisticated search services. For example, you can search all SEC filings for the past couple of years for names, ticker symbols, or types of service or products.

WHERE TO FIND SEC FILINGS ON THE INTERNET

SEC (www.sec.gov)

Edgar Online (www.edgar-online.com)

EdgarScan(edgarscan.tc.pw.com)

Disclosure (www.disclosure-investor.com)

Livedgar (www.livedgar.com)

Keep in mind that if you are researching very small publicly traded companies, you won't find any documents on them in Edgar. Many firms are too tiny to file the reports or even register their securities for that matter. Companies raising less than $5 million in a 12-month period, for example, may be exempt from registering the transaction, under a rule known as Regulation A. Instead, these firms must file a hard copy of the "offering circular" with the SEC. It contains financial statements and other information.

In addition, small companies raising less than $1 million don't have to register with the SEC. But they do have to file a Form D. This is a brief document that includes the names and addresses of the owners and stock promoters, but little other information. If you can't find a company on Edgar, you can call the SEC at (202) 942-8090 to find out if the company filed an offering circular under Regulation A or a Form D. You should check with state securities regulators as well.

THE FORMS

THE REGULAR UPDATES

After companies register their securities with the SEC, they have to keep the registration current by filing Forms 10-Q, 10-K, and 8-K on a regular basis.

10-K   This is basically the same as the **annual report** which gets sent to shareholders. It gives a broad overview of the company's business, complete with the financials and a discussion of new products, research and development, and business trends. This is the main document companies use to disclose things to shareholders. It is a rich source of information. The report has to be filed within 90 days after the end of the fiscal year. **The 10-KSB** is the annual report filed by small companies.

10-Q   The **quarterly report** includes unaudited financial statements and an update of business conditions. It is filed for each of the first three quarters of the company's fiscal year. The fourth quarter is covered by the annual report. The quarterly is due within 45 days of the close of the quarter. The small company version is the **10-QSB.**

8-K   This report has to be filed when there are **unexpected events** or changes which are important for shareholders or the SEC to know about. This can include things like the resignation of a director, a change in the accounting firm (which might occur because the previous one found problems in the financials), a change in control of the company, and the catchall "other materially important events." The 8-Ks provide more current information on specific events than any other SEC filing. Don't get alarmed every time you see one from one of your companies, however. They can report fairly mundane events, too.

INSIDER TRADING

Forms 3, 4, and 5   Under the 1934 Securities Act, every director, officer, or owner of more than 10% of the stock in a company must file a statement of ownership with the SEC. The initial filing is on **Form 3.** Changes are reported on **Form 4.** The annual statement of ownership by these people is done on **Form 5.** The forms explain the relationship of the person to the company and provide details on purchases and sales of the stock. These forms don't have to be filed electronically with the SEC, so they won't necessarily show up in the SEC's Edgar database. You have to turn to a private service to find them.

Form 144   Insiders use this form to let the SEC know they plan to sell "restricted" or unregistered shares. By filing this form, insiders are automatically exempted from having to register the shares, which means they can then sell the stock.

Although these "intention to sell" papers are supposed to be filed prior to the actual trade, the majority of them come in on the day of the sale or even afterward. By waiting, the sellers may be trying to cover up their tracks because they think it is better to unload their shares before other investors find out that insiders are selling. Some filers go so far as to mail the Form 144s from a distant post office, so that their sales can take place before the forms arrive at the SEC and the trades are made public. Insiders are not *required* to sell shares once they have filed Form 144. The filing remains active for three months.

The 144 sales often come in clusters sparked by a lockup release or a price that makes a lot of insiders want to cash out options. Insider trading analysts use 144 filings as a leading indicator, since early 144s are often followed by others. People who sell big-ticket items for a living have been known to track 144s to figure out who just came into a lot of money. Insiders have to file Form 144 when they want to sell more than 500 shares or $10,000 worth in any three-month period. Since these forms do not have to be filed electronically, they do not necessarily show up in the SEC's database. Instead, you need to consult a private Edgar service.

STATEMENTS OF OWNERSHIP

13D   A "schedule" 13D must be filed by anyone who buys more than 5% of the shares in a company. Many investors like to keep an eye on these forms because a 5% or greater position can indicate someone may be thinking of taking over the company. Or maybe someone is planning to begin playing a bigger role in the company as an "activist" shareholder. Value investors, for instance, often like to take big stakes so they can have a say in what goes on, because they think they can help turn a company around. The form requires owners to state the reason for their purchase. However, they don't always tell the whole truth. The 13D must be filed within 10 days of the acquisition of the shares. The name of the "beneficial owner" has to be on the form. A beneficial owner is anyone who directly or indirectly has voting power through the shares or the power to sell the security.

Additional purchases, or sales, have to be reported in an amended 13D (which will be called a **13D/A**). Anyone who makes a tender offer that would put them over 5% ownership has to file a **schedule 14D-1** with the SEC. It also has to be sent to the company and competing bidders.

13F   This is the form money managers use to disclose their entire portfolio each quarter. Any manager with $100 million or more in assets has to file a 13F within 45 days of the end of the quarter. This includes mutual funds, pension funds, insurance companies, banks, and foundations. Investors use this filing to see what the hot fund managers are up to or to see who else was recently in a stock they are thinking of owning. Mutual fund analysts use the form to see what stocks a manager recently held and to get a sense of the manager's thinking. Unfortunately, the manager may have sold the stock or trimmed the position by the time this form is filed. The private Edgar Web sites offer a more convenient summary of who has filed ownership statements than the SEC Web site.

13G   Schedule 13G is an abbreviated version of 13D that can be used by some banks, broker dealers, and insurance companies. They use this form when the securities were bought in the course of ordinary business, and not with the intention of influencing the control of the issuer.

REGISTRATION STATEMENTS

Under the 1933 securities act, companies that want to issue stock have to register them first with the SEC. This process includes the disclosure of "material" business and financial information to help investors decide whether they want to buy the stock. The registration statement contains the prospectus, which gets distributed to potential investors. In its draft form, a prospectus is called a "red herring." Once the company finishes registering the shares, it can distribute the prospectus and start selling the stock. The most widely used registration forms are the following. All of these can go through several amendments, so make sure you have the latest one.

S-1   This is the registration form submitted when a company decides to go public in an initial public offering. The company discloses three years of financials and gives a detailed description of its business. This filing contains the red herring, which will become the prospectus if everything goes well and the registration is approved. The S-1 is also used for secondary offerings. A secondary is when stocks are sold by company insiders and other existing shareholders (like venture capital firms) of a company that has already gone public.

S-2   This is a simplified registration form for stocks to be offered in a secondary issue. It can be used by companies that have been reporting to the SEC for at least three years. This form can "incorporate by reference" the necessary documents like the 10-K or the 10-Q.

S-3   This is the simplest registration form that can be used by companies that have been reporting to the SEC for three years. This form is used for secondary offerings.

S-4   This form is used to register stock used in a merger or other type of business combination.

S-8   This form is used to register shares to be offered to the company's employees in stock option plans.

SB-1 and SB-2   The SB-1 is used by small companies to register securities when the amount being raised is less than $10 million. A small business can also use an SB-2 to register shares, in which case there is no limit on the amount being raised. An SB-1 contains balance sheets for the previous year and income statements for two years. The SB-2 requires two years of balance sheets and three years of income statements.

Form 10   This is the disclosure document for a spinoff. It is like a prospectus but usually shorter.

424B Filings   Once an initial public offering gets the green light, companies use these forms to report the final prospectus and make amendments to it.

Aside from the prospectus itself, these filings contain useful information like the timing of a lockup release, which is likely to drive the stock price down and create a temporary buying opportunity. You can also find out who the underwriters were, how much stock each one got to distribute, and what the "green shoe" or overallotment provisions are. The **424B1-5** forms are either variations of the 424B or forms that are used to add changes. A **424A** is used to file the red herring.

PROXY SOLICITATION MATERIALS

Shareholders use proxies to delegate someone else to vote for them at company meetings. All sorts of documents related to proxies have to be filed with the SEC, most of which are public. Usually, the most important is the **DEF 14A,** or the proxy statement. It provides notification of matters to be brought to a vote at a shareholders' meeting. It is also supposed to give shareholders the information they need to vote on matters raised at shareholders' meetings. Copies of the final proxy statements and proxy cards are filed with the SEC when they are sent to security holders.

Most often, proxies are used to vote on directors or adopt employee compensation and share option plans. But many other interesting issues are raised in proxy statements. If shareholder activists are trying to use the corporate voting machinery to make changes in the company, you will see it here. You can also use these documents to learn more about directors, like what other boards they might serve on and how much they get paid. The initial proxy filings that relate to mergers, consolidations, acquisitions, and similar matters are not made public when they are first filed with the SEC. All other proxy filings are publicly available.

Filings related to proxies basically fall into two camps: preliminary documents (which start with the letters PRE) and "definitive," or final documents (which start with the letters DEF). Here is a quick overview of what each of the filings does. **PRE 14A** is a preliminary proxy statement meant to notify shareholders of matters that will be brought to a vote at a shareholders' meeting. **PREC14A** and **PREC14C** deal with contested proxy solicitations. **PREN14A** contains proxy statements that do not come from management. **PREM14A** and **PREM14C** will have information on proxy statements relating to a merger or acquisition. **PRES14A** and **PRES14C** contain information about a special meeting. **PRE 14C** is a preliminary proxy statement containing all other information. **PRER14A** and **PRER14C** provide revised, preliminary proxy soliciting materials. **PRE13E3** contains an initial statement on a proposal to take the company private. **PRRN14A** contains revised, preliminary proxy soliciting materials from nonmanagement for contested solicitations and other situations. **PX14A6G** provides notice of exemptions.

The "definitive," or final filings include the following. **DEFM14A** provides notification of matters relating to a merger or acquisition. **DEFM14C** contains information about a merger or an acquisition. **DEFS14A** provides notice regarding a special meeting. **DEFS14C** will have information about a special meeting. **DEFC14A** contains a proxy statement related to contested solicitations. **DEFC14C** provides information about contested solicitations. **DEFA14A** contains proxy soliciting materials. **DEFN14A** contains a final proxy statement filed by nonmanagement for matters not related to contested solicitations. **DFRN14A** contains a revised, final proxy statement filed by nonmanagement. **DFAN14A** contains additional proxy soliciting materials filed by nonmanagement. **DEF13E3** contains a final statement on a proposal to take the company private. **DEFA14C** adds new information, and **DEFR14C** revises information already filed.

When the names of any SEC documents are followed by "/A," it means it is an amendment to a form that was already filed but is still pending. If a form is followed by "POS," it means it is an amendment to a filing that is in effect.

CHAPTER 5

THE TORPEDO RATIOS

Have you ever found yourself wondering why your stock is tanking even though it just announced earnings that beat expectations?

It could be that while you were feeling good about that earnings surprise, the professional investors were busy calculating the "torpedo ratios." These are the tools that measure underlying financial trends which can spell trouble for a stock—even while earnings look good. Whenever a company releases quarterly results, you have to dig beneath the bottom line. It is important to pick apart the rest of the numbers to see exactly how the company got to the earnings. The Devil may or may not be in those details, but the fate of your investment surely is.

There is a lot to look at. People study financial analysis and accounting for years before they fully understand it. That said, the pros often turn first to a few simple "torpedo ratios," effective financial statement tools that are fairly easy to understand. They are useful because they quickly capture disquieting trends on the balance sheet. These torpedo ratios measure the extent to which inventories and accounts receivable are building up compared to sales growth.

On a company balance sheet, inventories include anything from raw materials and unfinished products to goods ready to be shipped. Accounts receivable basically measures the amount of outstanding bills the company has to collect from customers. Both are considered assets on a balance sheet—so you might think it is nice to have a lot of them. This is true, but you don't want to see too much. And certainly not more than you did last year, compared to sales revenue. Professional investors know that when these two accounts are building up relative to sales, it may be a sign of trouble.

Investors have good reason to think this way, according to a study by Claudia Mott, of Prudential Securities.[1] Mott's research shows that these ratios send off reliable sell signals for stocks of all sizes. "An increase in either of these is a sign that something is getting out of balance in the company's business that is going to impact earnings down the road," says Mott. A buildup in accounts receivable signals that companies are not able to collect on what they sell, or that they are booking revenue more aggressively to meet their earnings numbers. A buildup in inventory might mean they can't sell their goods as quickly as planned.

Mott's study of mid-cap companies (defined as those with a market cap of $600 million to $6 billion) between 1987 and 1998 shows how effective the torpedo ratios are. She found that the stocks flashing the strongest sell signal because of an accounts receivable buildup (the worst 5% of the group) underperformed mid-cap stocks as a group by around 5.2% a year during the 10 years covered in the study. The bottom 10% of the universe underperformed by an average of 3.3% a year. These big differences in performance show how powerful an investing tool the torpedo ratios can be. But before you go to work on the balance sheets, keep a few things in mind.

WHERE THE TORPEDO RATIOS WORK BEST

First, the two torpedo ratios are not equally effective. A buildup in inventories tends to be a less accurate forecaster of problems (see Table 5.1). Stocks sending off the strongest sell signal on the inventory front (again, the worst 5%) underperformed by only 1.5%, compared to 5.2% for accounts receivable offenders. Mott says sophisticated modern inventory systems may be making the inventory to sales ratio less effective.

Second, you should also know that the torpedo ratios work better for growth stocks than for value stocks. Growth stocks with the worst accounts receivable buildup lagged by 5.7% on average each year. Growth companies with the biggest inventory buildup trailed by 3.4%. When it comes to value stocks, an accounts receivable is a pretty good predictor of problems. But inventory buildup is not. Undervalued stocks with the biggest accounts receivable increases trailed by 3.4% a year. Value stocks with the worst inventory buildup problems did not lag at all.

---

[1] Eddie Cheung and Claudia Mott, *Focus on the Balance Sheet to Avoid Mid-Cap Torpedoes* published by Prudential Securities in Small Cap *Quantitative Perspectives,* June 19, 1998.

Table 5.1

Relative Return: How Well the Torpedo Ratios Work for Growth and Value Stocks[a]

	Accounts Receivable/Sales			Inventory/Sales		
	All Stocks	Growth	Value	All Stocks	Growth	Value
Top 20%	2.1%	3.0	0.7	2.2	2.5	1.7
Second 20%	0.7	0.1	0.6	0.9	1.4	-0.4
Third 20%	1.8	0.9	0.1	0	-0.6	-1.5
Fourth 20%	-0.3	-0.4	-0.3	-1.4	-2.8	-2.0
Bottom 20%	-2.1	-3.4	-1.4	-1.3	-3.6	0.6
Bottom 10%	-3.3	-6.7	-2.0	0.3	-3.1	0.3
Bottom 5%	-5.2	-5.7	-3.4	-1.5	-3.4	-0.9

[a] This table shows you how well the torpedo ratios predicted performance for different types of stocks. The column on the left ranks the stocks based on their accounts receivable and inventory to sales ratios. The top 20% had the biggest declines in those ratios, which is a good sign. The bottom 5% had the biggest increases, an ominous trend. The percentages inside the table show the average annual performance differences for each group, compared to all mid-cap stocks ($600 million to $6 billion in market capitalization) from 1987 to 1998.
Source: Prudential Securities.

Table 5.2

Trouble Ahead: How Well the Torpedo Ratios Predicted Problems by Sector[a]

Accounts Receivable/Sales		
Excellent	*Mixed*	*Poor*
Business services -4.9%	Consumer staples -2.7	Energy 0
Health care -4.3	Basic industry -1.7	Financial services 1.6
Technology -4.2	Utilities -1.2	
Capital spending -2.9		
Consumer services -2.9		
Consumer cyclical -2.7		

Inventory/Sales		
Excellent	*Mixed*	*Poor*
Business services -7.2	Energy -1.1	Consumer staples 1.2
Capital spending -6.8		Financial services -0.6
Health care -4.6		Utilities -1.3
Basic industry -4.5		
Consumer services -4.3		
Consumer cyclical -4.1		
Technology -2.5		

[a] The table gives the relative performance of the 20% of companies with the biggest increases in accounts receivable or inventory to sales ratio, a negative sign. Their performance is compared to the overall group of mid-cap stocks ($600 million to $6 billion in market capitalization) between 1987 and 1998.
Source: Prudential Securities.

The accuracy of the torpedo ratios also depends on the sector (see Table 5.2). Both ratios do a pretty good job of sending sell signals in business services. Stocks in this group with the strongest warning signs trailed by up to 7% on average each year. In health care and technology, both ratios did a good job of helping investors spot potential trouble. They also work well in the capital spending, consumer services, and basic industries groups. The torpedo ratios do not work well in the energy and financial services sectors.

You can use these tools to find winners, too. Declines in inventories and accounts receivable–relative to sales–suggest that a stock is about to do well. Overall, stocks with the best improvements in these two ratios outperformed by over 2% a year.

Once again, these ratios work better as buy signals for growth stocks than for value stocks. Value stocks with solid gains in the inventory to sales ratio did not outperform at all. (Indeed, if you just zero in on 1993 to 1998 in the study, you find that the accounts receivable to sales ratio was a much better indicator for value stocks on both the upside and the downside.) The torpedo ratios are good for predicting upward stock moves in consumer services, technology, and capital spending sectors, but they weren't so effective in other groups (see Table 5.3).

Table 5.3

Buy Now! How Well the Ratios Did at Predicting Winners[a]

Accounts Receivable/Sales		
Excellent	*Mixed*	*Poor*
Consumer services 5.0%	Business services 1.8	Basic industries –1.2
Technology 4.5	Capital spending 1.1	Consumer staples –1.8
	Consumer cyclical 1.3	Energy –0.5
	Utilities 1.4	Financial services –3.9
		Health care –0.2

Inventory/Sales		
Excellent	*Mixed*	*Poor*
Business services 2.8	Basic industry 0.7	Consumer cyclical –3.7
Capital spending 8.6	Financial services 0.2	Consumer staples –2.8
Consumer services 3.0	Utilities 1.0	Energy –0.5
Technology 2.1		Health care –2.2

[a] The table gives the relative performance of the 20% of companies with the biggest decreases in accounts receivable or inventory to sales ratio–a good sign. Their performance is compared to the overall group of mid-cap stocks ($600 million to $6 billion in market capitalization) between 1987 and 1998.
Source: Prudential Securities.

HOW TO MEASURE THE
TORPEDO RATIOS

As an individual investor, you can measure a change in these ratios as well as the pros. Just go to a site like the Securities and Exchange Commission's Edgar database and collect the numbers from the 10-Q or 10-K forms (the quarterly and annual company statements). When analyzing the accounts receivable and inventory numbers, be sure to compare the most recent quarter to the same quarter last year—as opposed to the quarter just before. This way you account for any seasonality in the company's numbers.

And it is better to compare the most recent quarter's worth of accounts receivable and inventory to a full trailing 12 quarters of sales. That way you capture a better measure of the sales growth. Use the search function in your browser to quickly get to the key words—like accounts receivable—in the lengthy documents. Try searching on "revenue," if nothing comes up under "sales."

Once you have the numbers, calculate the torpedo ratio by dividing the amount of inventories (or accounts receivable) for the most recent quarter, by the trailing 12 months worth of sales. Then take the amount of inventories or accounts receivable from the quarter a year before, and divide by its trailing 12 months' worth of revenue. The two ratios should be about equal. If the most recent one is bigger, look out. Problems may be developing.

Remember that if you see either of these accounts grow, you should not necessarily jump to conclusions. (Likewise, not all declines are buy signals.) First you have to understand what is behind the buildup because it may be happening for legitimate reasons. A change in a company's billing software, for example, can cause a temporary increase in accounts receivable, which is not necessarily a sign of trouble. Or else a firm might be increasing inventories because it is anticipating greater sales. Although there are some acceptable reasons for these two accounts to grow, they usually expand for one simple reason: because the company is running into trouble. Listen to management's explanations. But put more faith in the torpedo ratios than any stories that sound far fetched. On the other hand, if the market sells off the stock but management's explanation makes sense, you may have a good buying opportunity. It is not uncommon for the pros to sell part of their positions just to be on the safe side, even though managers present a plausible reason for the buildup in either of these accounts.

YOU ARE ON YOUR OWN

Indeed, one area of investment research where it can really pay to do your own work is this kind of financial statement detective work to turn up signs of either impending problems or outright accounting trickery. Why? Because no one else is doing it for you. You might think that stock analysts and auditors are supposed to be on your side. But studies[2] show they regularly fail to warn investors about obvious changes in the books which clearly point to difficulties ahead.

Analysts probably pick up the warning signals from the torpedo ratios as well as anyone else. But they normally won't cut their earnings estimates until the underlying problems actually start having an impact on reported earnings, notes Richard Sloan of the University of Michigan School of Business Administration. The news usually has to come out in the form of an earnings preannouncement, or an actual earnings shortfall, before analysts will change their estimates. By then, of course, it is too late for investors because the stock has already started to tumble.

As for the outside auditors, they are not really there to offer you investment advice. You might think that you can get advance warning of serious trouble or fraud anyway by keeping a lookout for a "qualified opinion"—one in which the auditor approves the books with some reservations. But like the analysts, auditors usually go along with the company's accounting methods even when there are obvious signs of trouble, says Sloan. Qualified opinions are actually pretty rare. Auditors typically resign, or they are fired, before they get to issue a qualified opinion. Once it comes to this, it may be too late to get out of a stock.

Why do the analysts and auditors stay mum when problems are growing? In the case of analysts, they might be trying to support the price of the shares through an upcoming secondary issue of stock. Or maybe they are wary of offending management and risking the loss of business by their investment banking side. The auditors are probably afraid of losing business, too, says Sloan. So they keep quiet until they have no choice but to either speak up or leave. More and more, auditing firms get a lot of their revenue from technology and business consulting, or merger advisory work. Often they provide these services to the very same companies whose books they are auditing, creating a potential conflict of interest. Nonauditing services make up more than 50% of the revenue at the Big Five accounting firms. And many auditors

---

[2] Mark T. Bradshaw, Scott A. Richardson, and Richard G. Sloan, *Earnings Quality and Financial Reporting Credibility: An Empirical Investigation.*

switch over to the corporate finance departments of their clients for more pay. When they do, their books are being audited by their former partners, creating another potential conflict.

Keep in mind that the auditors are not really there to hunt for fraud anyway. They are only obligated to ensure that financial statements follow "generally accepted accounting principles." They report fraud only if they find it while checking to see whether a company follows those standards. When managers conspire to commit fraud, it is difficult for auditors to detect it.

Once problems surface or outright accounting tricks are exposed, a company typically misses earnings, and its stock tanks. At this point it may seem like all the bad news is out. But don't assume that the worst is all behind and it is a good time to buy a beaten-down stock. On average, earnings continue to decline for two years after the SEC sanctions a firm for manipulating earnings, according to Sloan's work.

Since you can't necessarily rely on the analysts and auditors before all of this actually comes to pass, you are pretty much on your own when it comes to spotting dodgy accounting that will hurt earnings and tank a stock. Fortunately, there is often plenty of time to pick up on the trouble before disaster strikes. Often, several months go by in which problems are clearly developing on the balance sheet but the analysts and auditors are not warning anyone, and the stock price is not reacting. This gives you time to trim your position or get out of a stock completely—as long as you are doing the work that uncovers the trouble.

THE CATCHALL QUALITY OF EARNINGS RATIO

One of the best ways is to use the catchall "quality of earnings" ratio, in addition to the two torpedo ratios described above. This tool is very useful because it measures the extent to which "accruals" are building up anywhere on the balance sheet. In accounting, accruals are used to recognize income or expenses as they are earned or incurred, even though they may not have been *received* or *paid* in cash at the same time. Accountants use accruals all the time and rightly so. One of the main points of accounting is to smooth out earnings by matching expenses with the income generated by those expenses.

Unfortunately, accruals can be used to disguise problems. Here is just one example. Say a company uses cash to buy inventory. Instead of charging that cash expense against earnings right away, accountants accrue (postpone) the expense until the inventory is sold. When it is sold, the company gets money for the product, and at that point it recognizes both the income and the expense, meaning the cost of the inventory. Everything is hunky dory.

But what if the inventory is not moving and the chances are becoming slim that it will ever sell? The recognition of the cost of that inventory continues to be postponed, even though it is starting to look worthless. At some point, the company has to acknowledge the inventory won't sell and write if off—reducing earnings. Meantime, it can ignore the problem, even though some day it will hurt earnings. "In retailing, for example, if you overstock, it costs you nothing in the short run," says Sloan. "And if you are selling a lot of high-margin stuff at the same time, your profits will look good. But at some point you will have to write down the overstock, which will hit earnings."

Accruals can build up all over the place on the balance sheet—in accounts for inventories, receivable, taxes, and elsewhere. Again, in theory, there is nothing wrong with them. When they start piling up too much, though, it is usually a sign of trouble. Firms with extremely high accruals typically take a hit on earnings at some point over the following three years, according to Sloan's research. Meanwhile, he notes, you won't get much warning from the analysts or the accountants about the looming problems.

But you can spot the buildup in accruals yourself, using the quality of earnings ratio. When working through the math, keep in mind that accruals are simply the difference between earnings and cash flow, which are called *net income* and *cash from operations* on the income statement. The basic concept is that if net income is growing faster than cash flow, the company is using something other than hard cash to produce the earnings growth. If that something else is accounting hocus pocus, then problems may be around the corner.

To compute the quality of earnings ratio, subtract cash from operations from net income. You can find both items on the income statement. Then divide the result by average total assets. You compute this by taking the average of the amount of assets on the balance sheet at the beginning and at the end of the year. If the answer is less than negative .14, according to Sloan, the company has high-quality earnings. Its earnings are backed by a lot of cash. If the answer is greater than .06, the company has poor quality earnings. The earnings are not backed by enough cash. Look into why this is the case and consider selling the stock if you do not get a plausible explanation.

"It means the accountants have invented some noncash assets and stuck them on the balance sheet, and that is what is supporting earnings," says Sloan. "In the long run, however, earnings have to be supported by cash flow, or there will be trouble." In Sloan's study covering 10 years, the best 10% of stocks measured by the quality of earnings ratio outperformed the worst 10% by 12% over the subsequent 12 months.

THE CATCHALL QUALITY OF EARNINGS RATIO

$$\text{Quality of earnings} = \frac{\text{Net income–Cash from operations}}{\text{Average total assets}}$$

A value $> .06$ = low-quality earnings

A value $< -.14$ = high-quality earnings

Not every company that gets a poor rating by this measure will run into trouble, of course. Sometimes accruals can build up for legitimate reasons. Indeed, if you get a warning sign from the quality of earnings ratio, your next step is to find out what is causing it. On average, though, companies with lousy ratings eventually run into problems with earnings, and the stock tumbles.

OTHER DIVINING RODS INVESTORS USE TO FIND PROBLEMS BENEATH THE SURFACE IN COMPANY FINANCIAL STATEMENTS

Gross vs. Net Profit Margins

There are two types of profit margins. Whenever the two don't follow the same trend, it is a sign there may be some funny business going on. Gross profit is calculated by taking sales and subtracting the cost of goods sold, which is the cost of making the goods. Net profit equals sales minus the cost of goods sold, minus general and administrative costs (overhead), interest, and taxes. If gross profits fall but net profits don't go down by the same amount, it is time to take a closer look at the books for trouble. True, there may be innocent explanations. Often, however, this divergence is a sign of hanky panky. The reason is that compared to gross profits, net profits take into account many more items–like taxes and research and

(continues)

development. This means there is a lot more room to fiddle with the books and make net income look better than it is.

How a Company Accounts for Expenses

Companies have the choice of expensing a cost (charging it against this year's profits) or capitalizing it (charging it against future profits). Generally, a company can't capitalize a cost unless it can demonstrate that whatever it bought with the money will be generating income in future years. If you notice a company is capitalizing costs that look like they should be expensed, like outlays for marketing, be careful. It might be bending the accounting rules to boost current earnings.

The Footnotes

As boring as they seem, the footnotes in company financial statements often contain some of the best hints that a company is playing accounting tricks. Read them.

FURTHER RESOURCES

Analysts' Accounting Observer, a Baltimore investment advisory service owned by Jack Ciesielski

The Center for Financial Research & Analysis in Rockville, Md.

The Quality of Earnings Report, a newsletter

The Olstein Financial Alert Fund (800-799-2113) run by Robert Olstein, who puts an emphasis on financial sleuthing when picking stocks

CHAPTER 6

THE PRICE TO SALES RATIO

Earnings are squishy. Sales are sales. Both of those statements are exaggerations, but together they summarize a useful investing concept. When you are valuing companies to see whether they are too expensive, it helps to look beyond the popular price to earnings (p/e) and price to book ratios. You should also make use of a lesser-known but in many ways more effective instrument: the price to sales ratio (PSR). This tool compares a company's stock price to its sales per share, telling you how much investors pay for each dollar the company gets in revenue.

The PSR often gives you a much better X ray of a company's value. Indeed, James O'Shaughnessy, author of *What Works on Wall Street* and the president of O'Shaughnessy Capital Management, calls it "the king of all value indicators." What makes it so effective? For one thing, companies use accounting tricks to manipulate the p/e or price to book ratio. But it is harder to distort revenue. Sales don't lie. Or at least not as much. "Revenue is one of the things that is least fiddled with," said Ken Fisher, of Fisher Investments in California. "So with sales you get something that does not have a whole lot of phony baloney in it. In contrast, there is a fair amount of phony baloney in earnings, and some in book value."

Do companies really use accounting tricks to add a dash of "earnings helper" to the books? Not all of them, of course. Many practice commendable, conservative accounting, but a lot of them do resort to tricks. You can blame crooked accounting on the increased obsession among fund managers with quarterly results, in part. Because of this trend, accountants at many companies have the temptation now more than ever to bend the rules a little here and there to squeeze that extra penny or two out of a weaker-than-expected quarter. Companies may also feel pressure to manipulate earnings to comply with tight loan covenants.

True, sales can be manipulated, too. But sales in general tend to be more reliable than earnings or book value, which is why many professional money managers like the PSR. Value investors in particular use the PSR to scan the market for bargains.

Not all value investors agree that the PSR is a good tool. And it does have some shortcomings which will be covered later in this chapter. But the PSR clearly has many advantages over the other tools used to find underpriced securities. Not only does it cut through the accounting tricks used to embellish earnings, but it also offers the following insights or benefits.

USING THE PRICE TO SALES RATIO

The PSR helps you value stocks that have no earnings. When a company is losing money, it will have a negative p/e. This is meaningless. But since a lot of companies in the red are still worthwhile investments, you will need some way to value them. The classic example is a new start-up that takes a few years to turn a profit–like most of the Internet companies in the late 1990s. If that company has sales, you can use the PSR to get a sense of how valuable the market thinks the company is. These are not the only examples. "At the bottom of a recession, typically 35% of public companies will have no earnings," notes Fisher. "In times like these, you can't screen for value with a p/e ratio."

Even when companies have earnings, the p/e can be deceptive. Let's take an extreme example to demonstrate the point. Suppose a company is selling at $10 a share and it has earnings of $1. That means it has a p/e of 10. Now, let's say earnings fall to a penny and the stock loses most of its value and drops to $1. Now it has a p/e of 100. Does the market think more of this stock? Given the "higher" valuation, it might seem so. "But in reality, we know the market actually thinks less of this stock," notes Fisher. "This is why the price earnings ratio is often misleading." The PSR, on the other hand, can show you what is unpopular and what the market likes, regardless of a company's profitability.

The PSR is great for valuations of cyclical companies, where the p/e is very unreliable. The p/e can be particularly deceptive when valuing cyclical stocks. In fact, it tells you to buy these stocks just when you should be selling. And it sends off a sell signal exactly at the point in the business cycle when you should be buying. Here's why. Auto, paper, or home building companies make very little during a recession, but they make a lot when the economy is booming. So at economic peaks, their earnings are high and their p/e's are low (earnings go up more than the stock price), even though this is exactly when you should be trimming positions because the economy is about to slow down. During recessions the p/e ratios of cyclical companies are very high because their earnings are weak (earnings fall more than the stock price). But this is precisely when you would want to buy these kinds of stocks.

"With cyclical companies, if you just looked at the price to earnings ratio, you would buy them and sell them at exactly the wrong time," says David Nelson, a portfolio manager at Legg Mason in Baltimore. "Sometimes earnings don't give you the right signal because earnings streams are volatile." Earnings will be more volatile than sales whenever a company has big fixed costs (known as "operating leverage"). This is the case with many of the cyclical companies. When sales drop (which happens because the business is cyclical), these companies simply can't cut costs as much as other types of firms. Therefore, their earnings fall a lot more than their sales, whenever their sales start to slip.

Because of this situation, it makes sense to value these kinds of companies using the PSR. Their sales are a lot more stable than their earnings. So the PSR lets you make a better historical comparison than the p/e ratio, which jumps all over the place and gives you wacky readings. As a general rule of thumb, the less stable earnings are, the more information you get from the PSR.

The PSR is a good instrument for telling you what a stock might trade at "If only…" A lot of investors prefer to use the PSR as a tool for determining what the price of an undervalued stock would be if it fixed its problems. In many ways, it is a cleaner device for this kind of analysis than either the p/e or price to book ratio. It helps cut through the accounting mystery involved in putting values on assets and liabilities, and calculating earnings. The PSR is especially handy when p/e ratios become meaningless as earnings approach zero.

Value investors, for example, often like to look at companies that have a PSR and profit margins below the industry average. Using the two numbers, they can get a good sense of how much the company's stock would trade for if management got its act together. "The price to sales ratio captures your imagination," says Edward Bousa, the portfolio manager of the Putnam Equity Income Fund. "It gives you a clue about how cheap the company is relative to other companies in the industry. It tells you what an underperforming company would be worth if it got its margins up."

The PSR, in other words, highlights companies that have high sales and low earnings. "So you might say it highlights ineffective management," says Ron Muhlenkamp, portfolio manager at the Muhlenkamp Fund. "This means that as management improves, and margins improve, earnings should improve. The assumption, with low PSR stocks, is that the company is not going out of business but will at some point get effective management."

Value investors like to look at companies with compressed profit margins along with a low PSR because small improvements in those margins have a bigger impact on earnings and the stock price than they would at healthier companies. Just remember that low margins cut both ways. A relatively small decline also hurts more. Indeed, profits generally tend to be more volatile at a low-margin business because a small change in margins has a bigger impact on earnings. "The low-margin business does not allow you to make many mistakes," points out Nelson. "If you have high margins because you are Microsoft and you lose a little margin, it isn't a problem. If you are a company with low margins, a small contraction can mean a big loss in earnings."

The price to sales ratio can also help you determine what to avoid because it is overpriced. "The highest PSR stocks are toxic," says O'Shaughnessy. In his book *What Works on Wall Street,* he presented his research on the factors that make for the best investment strategies. As part of his study, O'Shaughnessy calculated what would happen if you invested in the 50 highest PSR stocks each year over a 41-year period starting in 1953. His findings: Your returns would be worse than T-bills, with much more volatility. "Many of the high PSR stocks are all fine corporations. But fine corporations do not always make fine investments."

You have to be careful when using the PSR to screen out overpriced stocks, however. A company might simply be so good at what it does that it deserves an above-average PSR. Generally speaking, be wary of any company with a PSR above two, but a lot depends on market conditions and the sector. (See the following box.) For example, for years professional money managers pointed to Microsoft's extraordinary PSR of 12 or more and said the company was way overvalued. Their reasoning made sense. The Microsoft premium seemed to grossly overstate the company's growth prospects. Nevertheless, the stock kept going up and up.

WHAT IS AN ACCEPTABLE PRICE TO SALES RATIO?

To put things in perspective, first of all you should keep in mind that the PSR for the Standard & Poor's 500 index between 1951 and 1999 fluctuated between a low of .45 and a high of 2.45. Value investors typically focus on companies with a PSR of less than 1. They think a company with a PSR above 2 is beginning to get pricey. But a lot depends on the sector. Companies with low margins and high volume, like supermarkets, will naturally have a low PSR. For companies that have high profit margins and a franchise, a high PSR is acceptable. The PSR for an extremely successful company with a strong franchise can go as high as 12 or so. That is the PSR for Microsoft, and it has not exactly been a bad investment.

In short, some companies have a high PSR because they have earned it. Typically, they will have either a good franchise or a strong leadership position in their field. You see this often with firms that make software and popular consumer products. Coke and Gillette are examples. Companies that make pharmaceutical products and medical devices may also carry a justifiably high PSR. After all, they have patent protection for their products. "Effectively they have a moat around them," says Nelson. "So people believe their growth rates are going to remain good."

Like O'Shaughnessy, however, Nelson cautions against venturing into the high PSR waters. "By avoiding the high PSR stocks, you miss the Microsofts of the world. But you also miss the Microsoft wannabes. Their high margins eventually evaporate, they lose their premium valuation, and they go down. That is the risk of buying the prettiest companies in the world. You do get the Microsofts that go up 100 times. But you get all the other ones that break your heart."

"Stocks with high price to sales ratios are the ones that have great pasts," agrees Fisher. "They have people mesmerized into paying high valuations. They are companies that have been doing so well for so long, people think they can't do anything wrong. People can't envision any shortfall."

Companies in some industries naturally have a low PSR. This does not mean they are good buys. When you are looking at the results of a PSR screen in search of cheap stocks, remember that many companies deserve to have a low PSR because of the kind of business they are in. This is the case with businesses that have narrow profit margins like supermarkets or discount retailers. When profit margins are so thin that only a few cents drop through to the bottom line, investors naturally pay less for a dollar of sales. So don't confuse these firms with companies that make good value plays because they have a low PSR due to a problem that can be fixed.

Be aware of the shortcomings of the PSR. You also have to remember that the PSR is no magic bullet. Indeed, it has several shortcomings. Critics like to point out that the PSR tells you little about a company's all-important cost structure. They also note that, like earnings, sales figures may be manipulated by aggressive accounting practices (though this is not as easy to do as manipulating earnings or book value). What's more, the PSR does not work well with banks. For one thing, banks don't really have "sales." And they are valued on the basis of a lot more than just their income from interest and fees. Other factors, like credit quality and the interest rate sensitivity of their loan book, are important as well.

One of the biggest problems with the PSR is a weakness it has in common with any valuation tool used to screen for cheap companies. It dregs up firms that are priced cheaply because they deserve to be because they are bad investments. The trick, then, to using any value screen is to find a way to identify and avoid stocks that are cheap because of serious trouble that won't go away.

O'Shaughnessy, who uses the PSR as part of his screen to select stocks for his Cornerstone Growth Fund, solves the problem by looking for a combination of value and growth. He does so in this manner. First, he screens for all the stocks that have a market capitalization greater than $150 million and a price to sales ratio of less than 1.5. Then he screens those stocks to find those that have higher earnings than they did the year before. From that group, he buys the 50 stocks with the highest one-year price gains over the past 12 months.

"This produces an excellent marriage of growth and value," says O'Shaughnessy. "It helps you find cheap companies that are on the rebound. If you just buy the stocks with the lowest price to sales ratio, you'll always end up with dog meat companies." O'Shaughnessy's system often leads him to companies in the midst of turnarounds. When a company is improving but it still has a low PSR, "there is a tremendous amount of room for the stock to go up. To me it makes a lot of sense to buy really cheap companies that are rebounding."

HOW TO CALCULATE THE PRICE
TO SALES RATIO

Unlike the price to earnings ratio, the price to sales ratio (PSR) is not published regularly anywhere. So you have to figure it out yourself. But this is not hard. To calculate the PSR, divide the current share price by the sales per share. Sales per share is calculated by dividing total sales (or revenue) by the number of shares outstanding. You can also get at the PSR by simply dividing the market capitalization of a company by its annual sales. All of these numbers are available in the quarterly and annual statements companies file with the Securities and Exchange Commission. It is better to use sales from the latest four quarters, as opposed to the annual sales numbers you find in the most recent annual report. That number may not include the most recent quarters.

COOKING THE BOOKS: SOME FAVORITE
RECIPES THAT HELP EXPLAIN WHY
INVESTMENT ANALYSTS OFTEN PREFER TO
LOOK AT SALES RATHER THAN EARNINGS

It's not a book you will find on the shelves at your local Barnes & Noble. But a list of the accounting tricks that tick off the SEC the most might as well be called "101 Ways to Prepare the Corporate Accounts." The SEC compiled the list of recipes in the late 1990s because of its concern about the growing use of dodgy accounting practices. It said these favorite corporate formulas for cooked books "threaten the preeminent position of U.S. markets because they cause investors to question the reliability and transparency of the financial statements."

Maybe so. One thing is sure: from time to time companies do use creative accounting to meet consensus earnings expectations, smooth out long-term profit trends, or commit fraud. These practices help explain why many investors simply don't trust the price to earnings or price to book ratios and prefer to use the price to sales ratio instead.

Many investors and analysts try to get a cleaner earnings number by simply ignoring net income, or the bottom line, and moving up the income statement (see box) several lines to operating income. Operating income is the bottom line, with depreciation and amortization (the noncash costs), interest, and taxes added back in. Put another way, it is sales minus cost of goods sold and general overhead. It is also called

EBITDA (for earnings before interest, taxes, depreciation and amortization). This is a good proxy for cash flow. It makes sense to use this number because it allows you to focus on the fundamental trends. A good tip is to remember that whenever cash flow is lower than reported earnings, it's a sign profits are coming from items other than cash—including possible accounting tricks.

But even focusing on cash flow won't neutralize many of the accounting tricks that get put to use. Here are some of the most common techniques companies employ to fudge earnings. Aside from demonstrating how companies play with earnings, this list is useful because it shows you many of the dodges you should look for when examining company financials. If you see signs of any of these tricks being carried out, think twice about owning the stock.

Companies prepare "cookie jar" reserves. Companies regularly set up reserve accounts to cover anticipated expenses like the debts they figure they won't be able to collect. This is responsible accounting. But some companies deliberately overestimate the expected expenses during good times. This lets them load more money into the reserve account than is necessary. Then, whenever a quarter comes in a few cents shy of analysts' estimates, they simply reach into the cookie jar to make up the difference.

Companies change the estimated useful lives of assets. In this gimmick, they spread out the number of years over which an asset gets depreciated. This decreases the hit to earnings from that cost each quarter.

When companies make acquisitions, they overestimate the value of research and development being carried out by the firms they buy. In a process called "creative acquisition accounting," buyers assign research projects a richer valuation than they deserve. They might also put a value on follow-up research that is not even in the pipeline. The reason is simple. By assigning more of the purchase price to things that can be written off immediately (like R&D), they can understate the value of assets that gets capitalized and amortized.

Mainly this means "good will." Good will is anything the buyer spends over the fair market value of the assets, that is not written off. The problem with good will is that it gets spread out over a number of years (amortized) and continues to eat into earnings. In acquisitions, buyers prefer to write down as much of the cost of the purchase now. This way, a smaller percentage of the purchase price gets amortized as good will. Future earnings look all that much brighter. With this dynamic at work, it is no wonder that R&D projects are given high valuations. They are an acquisition-related cost that can be written off immediately.

Companies falsely describe certain costs as "immaterial" to keep them off the books. Accounting rules allow certain transactions to be classified as immaterial so that the job of keeping the books does not become onerous. The question is, what is immaterial? Traditionally, the cutoff has been any matter involving less than 5% of pretax income. But in an environment where stocks get taken out and shot for missing estimates by even a penny, this may leave too much wiggle room to ignore costs that would blow a hole in earnings. So the SEC prefers a different definition. Accountants must ask whether the information would be considered "material" by investors.

Companies say they are going to get rid of an asset even though they don't plan to, so they can suspend the depreciation cost of that asset. Eliminating the depreciation immediately lifts earnings. The problem is that many companies classify assets as "held for disposal" (in the jargon of accounting) way before their time. For a disposal plan to meet SEC approval, the company has to spell out what steps will be taken to get rid of the asset, and give an expected completion date. It must have an "active" plan to find a buyer or get rid of the asset, and it must start doing so as soon as possible. The plan has to be firm enough that significant changes are unlikely. If a lot of time passes since the depreciation was suspended and the company still does not seem to be getting rid of the asset, you should start getting suspicious. Other investors are also suspicious, and they will probably start selling the stock.

Companies change the actuarial assumptions in pension accounting. Companies can boost earnings by changing the assumptions in a manner that reduces regular pension expenses.

Sales get fudged, too. Companies puff up sales mainly through a technique formally known as "premature revenue recognition". It is more commonly called "stuffing the channel". This happens whenever a company books revenue before a sale is really complete. There are many ways to pull this off. One is to declare a done deal, even though the customer still has the option to cancel the sale and return the product. In more egregious cases, the product has not even been shipped. Or it has been shipped, but the customer didn't really order it. For more complex deals, the seller's accountants recognize up-front fees even though significant aspects of the sales agreement have yet to be fulfilled. All of these things are considered a no-no. But they are difficult to detect from the outside. One red flag to watch for is a buildup in accounts receivable. Look for amounts above industry standards, current sales, or historic levels for the company.

According to the SEC, a deal is a deal when (1) delivery has occurred, (2) the risk of ownership has passed to the buyer, (3) the customer has a "fixed commitment," (4) the seller no longer has a "performance obligation," and (5) collection of the payment is probable. Once all of these conditions apply, the sale is complete.

When looking for cooked books, keep in mind that accounting rules are flexible. So companies in the same industry may have dramatically different reporting practices. Just because you notice a more liberal approach does not mean funny business is going on. But it does mean that you should be careful about investing in the company. More conservative accounting practices leave a lot more cushion in the accounts for those times when surprise revenue shortfalls crop up. And investors in general feel more comfortable with conservative accounting. So more money is likely to flow into the stocks of companies that are more cautious when preparing the books.

THE TYPICAL CORPORATE INCOME STATEMENT

Sales

−Cost of goods

Gross profit

−SG&A (overhead)

Operating income

−Depreciation and amortization

EBIT

−Interest expense

Pretax income

−Income taxes

Net income

CHAPTER 7

CASH ON THE
BALANCE SHEET

If you invest regularly, you are probably pretty familiar with the implications of debt for a company. Like alcohol, it can make the good times better and the bad times worse. By this, money managers mean that debt is a relatively cheap form of finance that helps companies really gear up return on equity—as long as things go well.

Debt financing is good for shareholders because it does not dilute earnings the way issuing new stock does. If used well, debt boosts earnings, but at the same time it allows companies to avoid increasing the number of shares among which profits must be split. Debt, in other words, makes the good times better. On the downside, when things go poorly, a company with a lot of debt might have trouble meeting interest payments and go bankrupt. Debt makes the bad times worse. This is a problem that equity financing does not cause.

Too much debt can put another constraint on a stock price. Once a firm has borrowed a lot, investors know there is no more room to use leverage to boost growth. This reduces the valuation investors are willing to assign the shares. The cutoff point varies by industry, but when debt starts to exceed equity, meaning it is more than 50% of capital, investors begin to get nervous. Companies whose debt is only a small fraction of their capital still have a lot of room left to use debt to fuel growth.

But what about cash? If too much debt is bad, does that mean that a lot of cash is good? Intuitively, you might think so. After all, in our personal lives we feel more comfortable when we have more money saved up. Likewise, companies with a pile of cash in the vault seem to have insurance against hard times. You have a vague sense that they have more options open to them for the future.

Unfortunately, understanding the significance of cash on the balance sheet is a bit more complicated than this. The truth is, a cash hoard can mean many things. It depends a lot on how the cash got there, what management plans to do with it, and what business the company is in. What's more, cash in the wrong hands for the wrong reasons can be almost as lethal as too much leverage. The bottom line is that when analyzing a company, you have to consider the cash position carefully to understand exactly why it is there and what it means.

First, let's look at some of the reassuring reasons for cash to be on the balance sheet. As you research companies, you are bound to come across many that have a lot of cash simply *because they are doing extremely well.* Their product cycles are peaking and the money is rolling in. Indeed, the cash might be building up so fast that management has trouble putting it back to work right away. Obviously, this is a great reason for a company to be flush with money. "We love cash," says Seth Glickenhaus, of Glickenhaus & Co., a New York money management firm. "It's a sign that a company is generating money so rapidly that it does not know what to do with it."

This will often be the case with the highly successful technology companies. Microsoft is one of the best examples. It has done so well that for much of its history the company has been the reigning king of cash. "It would be hard to say that cash is a bad sign in the case of a company like Microsoft," notes Ralph Wanger, a portfolio manager at the Acorn funds run by Wanger Asset Management. "If a company is highly profitable and it has little need for capital, then cash is not a negative thing." Indeed, Microsoft's trouble in the late 1990s might have been that its cash hoard got so large it had difficulty finding big new investments without annoying the antitrust authorities.

Aside from astonishing success, some companies build up a lot of cash simply because they don't use it that much. Firms in fields like computer software, biotechnology, or the entertainment business, for example, don't have the kind of big, recurring expenses that capital-intensive companies have. Their cash builds up.

In contrast, companies in the heavy industries, like steel producers, have to regularly invest a lot of money in expensive capital equipment that sooner or later wears out and must be replaced again. Utilities are another example. They typically have a lot of debt, since they can borrow at favorable interest rates because their revenue is so predictable. Many retailers are capital intensive, although it may not seem that way since they have no expensive plants to maintain. But they have inventory to carry, and they provide credit to their customers, notes James Giblin, a portfolio manager at Bankers Trust.

One way of looking at it is to remember that companies producing income from intellectual property are more likely to have cash on hand. "These companies may have high returns on invested capital, but they do not need to plow money into building plants," notes Alan Kahn, a New York-based money manager. "Because what they sell does not come out of the factory but out of the brains of someone's head." These brains, and the big stars at the entertainment companies, may be expensive. But they are still not as costly as the heavy equipment that eats into cash flow in capital-intensive industries. In short, it's not a warning sign when companies that don't have big capital expenses build up cash.

Another acceptable reason to build up cash is when companies in cyclical businesses, like aircraft or manufacturing, want to keep some of it on hand for the expenses or hard times they know are ahead. "When your outlays are in big, discrete pieces or your demand is seasonal, then you have to keep cash aside," notes Ron Muhlenkamp, a portfolio manager with the Muhlenkamp Fund. "A farmer would be crazy not to stockpile cash." Certain kinds of companies are in the same boat. Firms like Boeing or General Motors might have a lot of orders at one point in the business cycle and then go through a period when revenue and cash flow dry up. In contrast, a noncyclical company like Coca-Cola does not need to stockpile cash.

Even technology companies go through product cycles. This means it can be useful for them to have some cash on hand even though they don't have big capital outlays. Firms like Dell, Compaq, or Intel might want to stash a little away so that they can cut prices when they must to stay competitive, points out John Church, a portfolio manager at Glenmede Equity.

"Technology companies have somewhat less visibility in terms of their future because of the constant competition, change, and obsolescence of their product lines," says Will Browne, a value fund manager at Tweedy Browne. "They may not want to have leverage in their balance sheet, so that they can have a margin of safety, because their earning position is more volatile and difficult to predict." If this explains why a company has some cash on hand, give it a break.

At the opposite extreme, predictable businesses like water or electrical utilities will usually have a lot of debt. "They have steady cash flow and operating income from a very predictable business, so they can leverage their capital structure," says Browne. "They are required by law to have a leveraged structure because it is cheaper than equity and it benefits consumers with lower rates."

Another reason you might find a company with a lot of cash on the balance sheet is that the firm just did an equity offering or it recently issued debt. Be a little suspicious in these cases. Management may be able to put that money to good use, but that still remains to be seen. Generally, if the company has a good track record, then the money will probably be used well. At the other extreme are money-losing companies that have to issue debt or stock just to cover expenses. Beware of these.

When considering whether cash is a warning sign, know what the plan is. The worst explanation you want to hear is that management has let cash build up because it does not know what to do with it. Believe it or not, as much money as top managers make, this might be the case. "The cash could be there because management has run out of investment opportunities or is too short sighted and does not know what to do with the cash," notes Kahn.

Your job is to find out whether or not this is the case. If you do some checking around, you might learn that the cash hoard is there because management has been wisely accumulating money for a new investment opportunity. "It depends on what the opportunities for investment are," says Muhlenkamp. "If a company can get 20% return on equity in a new project or by expanding the current business, it is a mistake to give the cash back to shareholders. If it gets only 8%, it is a mistake not to return the money."

And you can hardly fault management if it is building up a war chest for a sensible takeover or because it knows it must build a more competitive plant. The company may even be planning to give it back to shareholders in the form of a dividend or share buyback. These are good explanations for the presence of cash on the balance sheet.

But when management does not seem to have a sensible plan for the cash, you have to start thinking the money might be a red flag. "If the cash is a temporary blip, as an investor you may want to make a bet as to how it will be used in the near term," notes James Solloway, the director of research at Argus Research. "If cash is more or less a permanent feature of that company's balance sheet, you have to question how come those managers are being so lazy."

VALUE VS. GROWTH MANAGERS

In the world of investing, not all professional money managers agree about what cash on the balance sheet really means. To a large degree, how the pros react to cash depends on their investing style. There are basically two camps: the value investors and the growth investors.

Value investors generally like cash because they see it as a form of protection against hard times. In fact, value investors are likely to own many companies with lots of cash because the tools they use to find stocks naturally lead them in that direction. (More on that soon.) Growth investors, on the other hand, often consider cash a waste of resources—and possibly a sign that management is spending too much time on the golf course.

First, the value investors. They usually welcome a big cash position in any company—cyclical or not—since they think cash serves as a form of insurance. If revenues dry up because the economy turns sour or there are other problems, the cash on hand will be useful for covering expenses and keeping these companies out of trouble. "We don't invest in common stocks unless they have superb balance sheets," said Martin Whitman, the portfolio manager of the Third Avenue Value fund. "We want a big margin of safety because if something goes wrong, the business will have staying power." Many of the stocks Whitman owns have a cash position greater than total liabilities. "This is the first criterion. We screen for cash that is 90% of book liabilities."

It is important to point out, however, that having a lot of cash is not always a sign that a company is a safe investment. King World Productions, which supplies television programs, often had as much as a third of its share price backed by cash. But that did not always mean it was a safe bet. The reason: A big chunk of the company's revenue came from one single program, the "Oprah Winfrey Show." At any point, this popular star could have decided not to renew her contract. If she did not renew, King World stock would probably have dropped quickly, regardless of the company's cash hoard. This threat is one of the reasons why King World Productions stock often seemed undervalued. In general, whenever a stock trading at a very high multiple runs into a little trouble, don't count on the cash on the balance sheet to protect it from a sharp fall.

Despite the exceptions, value managers usually find safety in cash on the balance sheet. They don't view it as a reason to lose respect for management. According to Whitman, saying that lots of cash on the balance sheet is a sign of poor management "is roughly the equivalent of saying you wasted your money on fire insurance last year because your house never burned down."

Many value managers also like cash because of the promise it holds. Wanger borrows a metaphor from physicists, who distinguish between potential and kinetic energy. "Cash is potential energy. It is stored-up energy that is available to be used on something in the future like making acquisitions, expanding your business, or paying a dividend. It is a form of power that you can use. Cash represents future opportunities."

Value managers rightly point out that this value of cash often goes unrecognized in the stock market. The result is that cash can actually depress the price of a stock, which is part of the reason why value managers are drawn to them in the first place.

How can Wall Street analysts misjudge the value of something as simple as cash? The reason has to do with the traditional method used by the Street analysts to value a company. Typically, analysts first project out all expected earnings into the future. As anyone who has taken a finance class knows, they then use a "discount rate" to adjust those future earnings for the time value of money. Doing so allows them to figure out what those future earnings are worth today.

This technique makes sense for the earnings from most business activities. But when it comes to cash, it leads to big valuation errors. For cash to be valued dollar for dollar in the stock market, its interest income would have to carry a very high price earnings ratio, but it does not.

Let's take an extreme example to demonstrate the point. Suppose interest on cash pays just 0.5% after taxes, as was the case in Japan for much of the late 1990s. That means $100 pays 50 cents in interest each year. For that $100 to be valued as $100 in the market based on the interest it earns, it would have to carry a price earnings ratio of 200. This is because 0.5 (the 50 cents) times 200 equals $100. Even in Japan, where stocks tend to carry higher price earnings ratios, that is high. In the United States, where money earned 3% after taxes when the money market interest rate was 5% in the late 1990s, the price earnings ratio had to be 33, for a dollar of cash to be valued as a dollar. Not sky high, but that was still a level way above the market price earnings ratio most of the time.

If you don't want to follow the math, just think of it this way. By focusing on the paltry income that cash produces, analysts overlook the gains that the money could bring in if it were used more wisely–if it were a more effective asset producing higher returns. Just re-deploy the money, value managers argue, and it will generate a lot more revenue than when it is simply earning interest. This extra income will push up the value of the stock. At the very least, a company with a lot of cash could buy in their own shares. This would lower the price earnings multiple or increase the stock price because there would be fewer shares among which to spread the earnings.

"Investors often overlook the fact that cash is an asset that can be redeployed in an effective manner," notes Browne. "Since this potential value of the cash is not fully taken into account, the stock itself ends up undervalued. When people value stocks based on earnings without looking at balance sheets, that can lead to a $30 valuation on a hundred dollars in cash." In other words, cash on the balance sheet depresses the value of a stock. "That in turn can attract value investors like Tweedy Browne. But it doesn't necessarily mean that it will be a good investment."

There is another reason why cash pushes down the value of a stock. Companies with lots of it lose out on the advantages of debt–which can increase earnings potential because it tends to be a cheaper way to raise money than equity. This means that companies with a lot of cash have a lower return on equity and probably a lower stock price as a result. "They are not using leverage on the right-hand side of the balance sheet. But that is the kind of company we like, one with a big margin of safety," says Whitman. "We get in bed with managers who will sacrifice return on equity for safety. If something goes wrong, the business has staying power. The key to investing is staying power. You can make forecasts, but they will be wrong."

This view of the value investors makes a lot of sense. But not to growth investors–who disagree with value managers about a lot of things. Growth fund managers generally think that a lot of cash is often a good reason to be highly suspicious of management. Neil Hokanson, the president of Hokanson Financial Management in Solana Beach, California, considers a large amount of cash to be a contrary indicator.

"The average investor might view cash on the balance sheet as a plus," says Hokanson. "But we don't because we feel it is management's job to manage resources efficiently. And the return on cash is very low. If they have too much cash, you have to ask yourself, 'Why aren't they putting it to work? Is management going and playing golf?' So when we see a lot of cash, unless there is a pending acquisition, we begin to wonder what management is up to."

Hokanson rejects the reasoning that having cash is a good way to be defensive. "If cash flow is managed well, that should be enough. In a well-run company, earnings don't just suddenly dry up." And value investors who buy shares in companies hoping to exploit their cash position won't be successful unless they get management to use it well—not always an easy task. "Otherwise, as a fund manager you end up owning a lot of undermanaged companies, which is a polite way of saying poorly managed companies."

"There is relatively little excuse for sitting around with idle cash on the balance sheet," agrees David Beim, a finance professor at Columbia Business School. "Anything above 1% of sales is excessive. Anything above 2% is really suspect. There are very few businesses that need more than that. It is almost always wasteful. The academics would say: `Buy your own stock in.'" Sometimes companies argue that keeping cash is convenient because it saves them the trouble of paying it out only to raise it again later if they need it. "But this is a poor reason to lower your overall performance—because you can't be bothered to raise cash again."

Finally, there is another problem with a big cash hoard. It can get companies into trouble for a very simple reason, and both value and growth managers agree on this. "The risk of having a lot of cash is that managers might do dumb things," says Church. Above all, cash can tempt management into the dangerous waters of empire building. Acquisitions can be a good thing, but too often they don't work out. Managers often pay too much for a company in a takeover. The result is just a transfer of wealth from the shareholders of the purchasing company to shareholders of the target. Managers also buy businesses they don't know how to run. Or else the promised synergies never develop.

At its worst, empire building and poorly thought out mergers and acquisitions lead to consequences such as the conglomerate craze of the 1960s. During that time, many companies squandered corporate assets by piecing together too many unrelated businesses in vast corporate empires that were later dismantled.

Generally, an acquisition, and any project for that matter, should offer a better return than the current line of business. In other words, it should produce a return that is greater than what managers would get if they bought their own stock back. If not, then the managers should do just that: Buy their own stock back. "You are better off giving the money back to the shareholders so they can earn the kind of return they are looking for on their money," says Beim. "Giving it back is better than simply earning the money market rate for investors by carrying the cash on the balance sheet."

One other factor can influence how investors look at cash. When the market is in the greed phase of the investing cycle, investors are not thinking about cash as a defense but about how much better the company could be doing if the cash were well invested. When fear reigns, investors look to cash as a defense. This is just another way of saying that even something as simple as cash can mean different things to different investors, at different times.

THE DEFINITION OF CASH

Like the meaning of cash on the balance sheet, the definition of cash itself depends a lot on whether you are a value or a growth investor.

First the value investors. A simple definition of a value investor is someone who tries to buy a dollar's worth of assets for 50 cents. How the value investor defines that 50 cents is a little more complicated. When valuing companies, for example, they use several different definitions of cash, depending on their objective. At their most cautious, they look for companies whose stocks are trading below the value of what they call *net, net cash* per share—the most conservative definition of cash. Net, net cash is cash and cash equivalents minus all long-term and current liabilities. Cash equivalents are money market instruments, like certificates of deposit. Current liabilities means any obligation that must be paid within a year, like short-term debt and accounts payable. Finding companies that trade below net, net cash is like nirvana for value investors.

The next best thing for a value investor is to buy companies whose stocks are trading below *net, net working capital.* This is a slightly less conservative definition of cash. It is current assets minus current liabilities and long-term liabilities. Current assets means cash and cash equivalents, accounts receivables, and inventories. Ben Graham, one of the gurus of value investing, wrote in the 1930s that if you buy a large enough selection of stocks selling below net, net working capital, you almost can't help but make money. Value investors believe that to this day.

Value investors might also define cash as *net working capital,* when they want to get a sense of a company's strength in the short term. This is current assets minus current liabilities. But if you are interested in cash as a measure of safety or potential earnings, just like the value investor, then follow one of the first two definitions above.

If you want to use the cash position as a gauge of whether managers are asleep on the job, take a page out of the growth investors' book. Look at cash as *ready cash,* or cash and cash equivalents. Like the growth investor, you don't want to see much. Many growth investors expect managers to be adept enough to finance expenses out of cash flow. One rule of thumb is to be wary of cash positions that exceed 1% of sales. However, many growth managers shy away from hard and fast ratios. Instead, they talk with the company when cash starts to build up. If management does not have a good plan for the money that sounds like it will add value for shareholders, they sell.

CHAPTER 8

WHAT THE ECONOMIC
INDICATORS REALLY
MEAN

Professional investors know that interest rates are one of the two factors that have the biggest impact on stock prices. (The other is earnings.) When rates go up, stocks tumble. In contrast, a decline in interest rates can kick off a sustained stock market rally. So you obviously want to try to figure out what the trend is regarding interest rates and buy stocks accordingly.

Like a lot of things in investing, however, this is not so easy. Understanding what affects interest rates is a complex matter. But it often comes down to two factors. One is the perception investors have about where the economy is headed. The other is the Federal Reserve Board. Both are influenced by the steady flow of economic indicators that come out each month. So if you invest in stocks, you need to understand these numbers and how to interpret them.

The indicators, which measure things like employment or retail sales, have an impact on interest rates because they tell investors where the economy is headed. And expectations about economic growth determine where interest rates are set in the bond markets. If bond investors think the economy is heating up, they worry that excess demand may lead to shortages of goods and labor—and cause inflation. So they demand higher interest rates on bonds as a hedge against the chance that higher inflation may soon be eating into bond returns.

The other big factor is the Fed, since it has the power to change key interest rates. Why would the Fed do this? Because it's one of the most effective ways it can perform its job. By law, the Fed is supposed to maintain stable prices and full employment. When the economy heats up too much, it raises rates to cool things off. If the economy sags and unemployment moves up, it cuts rates to stimulate growth. This is a tricky job. The central bank has to walk the line between slowing the economy too much and overstimulating it. Every recession since World War II has been caused by the Fed putting on the brakes too hard.

Meanwhile, professional investors are constantly on the lookout for signs of a slowdown or excessive growth. They are trying to predict the Fed's next move, so they can know what kind of stocks to hold. The tea leaves they use are the economic indicators that come out during the course of each month. Many investors take positions ahead of these economic releases, playing the expectations game. It goes like this. First, the market develops an opinion about the numbers that are about to come out. Then traders take positions based on their outlook. The most widely accepted expectations get "priced into" the market—meaning traders have already bid bonds up (or down) as if the anticipated level for the next indicator were reality.

The financial markets then react strongly if the fresh data show the markets got it wrong about the indicator. This happens a lot. It is hard for economists to make accurate predictions because the economy is so big and complicated. Another problem is that each business cycle is different, so lessons learned in the past may no longer apply. For whatever reason, forecasters often blow it, and the markets react sharply when investors are surprised by the data.

Instead of trying to make bets on whether this will occur, it is better to use the economic indicators to develop an overall sense of the interest rate trends, and make your investment decisions accordingly. If it looks like interest rates are going to come down in the next year or two, tilt your portfolio toward securities that would benefit. These include bonds and any of the interest rate-sensitive stocks—like banks and utilities or cyclical stocks in areas like housing and auto making. Generally, though *most* stocks do better when interest rates decline, unless earnings are extremely weak because of recession. If it looks like interest rates are headed up, lighten up on stocks, particularly the interest rate-sensitive issues. Stock become vulnerable when rates are rising, unless earnings are very strong.

Sometimes you can take advantage of short-term moves that occur in the markets when investors get faked out by an economic release and momentarily lose sight of the long-term trend. Suppose there is a bigger-than-expected employment number. This might create doubts about whether an expected long-term decline in interest rates will really happen. Investors will sell stocks because of new fears that there will be a rate hike. If you have done your homework and are pretty convinced the long-term trend is really still in place, you can take advantage of what will turn out to have been a good buying opportunity. This happens often. As smart as investors and traders are, they get fooled by short-term blips in the economic releases, which are notoriously volatile. Indeed, one of the first rules of economic analysis is to draw conclusions from trends in the data, not just one month's numbers.

To get you started, here are some basic tips from economists and Fed watchers who have been at the game for years. This advice is followed by an explanation of how to interpret the most important economic indicators.

TIPS ON INTERPRETING THE ECONOMIC INDICATORS

Examine the indicators for signs of how prices will behave. Evidence that inflation is under control soothes the markets because it dispels the fear that the Fed will raise rates. On the other hand, signs that inflation is building will spark fears that the Fed will hike rates. This makes stock investors jittery because higher rates generally hurt stocks. Monetary tightening usually comes in waves that last many months and bring more than one rate increase. But this is not always the case.

Know the Fed. It is crucial to understand what factors are important to the Fed. If the Fed is watching a certain indicator closely, the markets are, too. Remember that the indicators which move the markets will change over time. What makes the list depends on what is going on in the economy. If the labor markets are tight, the Fed may be looking for signs of wage-led inflation—in indicators like the employment cost index, productivity, and employment. Does it look like there may be bottlenecks shaping up on the production side? Then the Fed may be watching the indicators on orders, capacity utilization, and production.

One of the best ways to find out what is bugging the Fed chairman—the most important person to watch—is to read the dense testimony he presents to Congress twice a year in sessions known as the Humphrey Hawkins hearings. Speeches by the chairman outside of Congress are important, as well. Economists also like to follow speeches by the other Fed board governors. But the Fed chairman matters most. "The chairman is really the dominant player," says Leonard Santow, of Griggs and Santow, a firm that forecasts interest rates. "Unless circumstances are unusual, the chairman gets his way."

Don't fight the Fed. Once the Fed is on a campaign to change monetary policy, go with the flow. The Fed always wins. Usually, it changes policy in several steps over the course of many months. One move on interest rates, after a period of inactivity, is normally followed by a few more moves.

Look at the trend, not just one month's worth of data. The economic indicators are volatile, and they contain a lot of noise. So be careful about drawing conclusions on the basis of one month's release. Instead, look for the long-term trends.

Be alert for false signals. The numbers are complex, and the first read may be wrong. Sometimes this happens because an important subcomponent of the data goes unnoticed during the initial rush of headlines. Financial journalists get the numbers before the economists, and they start their reporting by dolloping out headlines. Once economists get copies of the economic releases and begin poking around, they may notice trends that conflict with the headlines. If so, the markets will turn on a dime. "The first knee-jerk reaction can be wrong," says Stan Shipley, an economist with Merrill Lynch. "But within an hour or two they have it right."

The indicators won't always take center stage. There can be long stretches of time when the markets don't seem to care at all about the economic indicators. Usually, it is because investors are pretty sure the Fed is in a holding pattern. Or maybe some other matter, like corporate earnings, is getting most of the market's attention. But the economic data are never far off the radar screen.

THE BIG FIVE

Just about all of the indicators that come out during the course of the month are important because they provide pieces of the puzzle that is economic growth. But five of them stand out. Some of these have a bigger impact simply because they are released early in the monthly cycle. They set the tone for the rest of the indicators. Others predominate because they directly address important issues like prices and employment levels, or they reveal trends in the most important sections of the economy. "If you understand these five numbers, you are usually in pretty good shape," says Shipley.

WHY INTEREST RATES MATTER TO STOCKS

Stocks go down when interest rates go up for the following reasons:

- Higher interest rates increase the "discount rate" used by Wall Street analysts in the models they use to put a value today on future earnings. When future earnings streams are "discounted"– or adjusted to their present value–using a higher interest rate, their present value goes down. And if expected earnings are suddenly worth less because interest rates go up, then so is the stock in the company generating those earnings. Its price drops.

- Higher interest rates are especially hard on the "interest rate-sensitive" stocks–or those for which interest rates are a big piece of the cost structure. These include banks, which have to borrow a lot of money, and utilities and heavy industry–sectors where companies borrow heavily for big-ticket capital spending. Home building companies and firms that supply things that go into homes also get hurt, since higher rates make home buying less desirable.

- Higher interest rates make the returns from competing assets– namely bonds–more attractive. So investors move money in that direction, driving down stock prices.

- Higher interest rates mean companies and consumers have to pay more for loans. So they borrow and spend less, gradually slowing down the economy. This effect is offset somewhat by the fact that an increase in interest rates drives up the value of bonds, giving bondholders more spending power.

- Higher interest rates increase the value of the dollar by attracting foreign investment, thereby driving up demand for the U.S. currency. A stronger dollar makes it harder for U.S. companies to sell abroad. It also cuts into the value of profits earned in foreign currencies.

NONFARM PAYROLLS, UNEMPLOYMENT RATE, HOURLY EARNINGS, AVERAGE WORKWEEK

Released as a package at the start of each month, these indicators are always closely watched–but even more so when the market's afraid that the Fed may increase interest rates. There are four reasons why.

First, the release gives you a good sense of the strength of consumer demand. After all, the number of people working—and how much they work and earn—can tell you a lot about how much they are going to spend. And consumer spending accounts for about two-thirds of U.S. gross domestic product (GDP). Second, the unemployment rate gives you a sense of labor market pressures. It tells you whether workers feel confident enough to ask for a raise because the job market is getting tight.

The third reason this release matters is simply because it comes out at the beginning of the month. With this report and a calculator in hand, economists can do some quick math and get a sense of how other indicators for the month will shape up. By multiplying the number of people working by the number of hours they worked and how much they earned, economists can begin to predict personal income, industrial production, and GDP. In a sense, once this report is out, a lot of the key numbers for the month begin to fall into place. Finally, this release is important because the Fed is watching it as closely as the economists. Aside from making the same calculations, and a few of its own, the Fed also has an idea of how low it thinks unemployment can go before it causes wage-led inflation—hence its interest in this economic release.

When interpreting the employment data, remember that the level of unemployment can be affected by the growth of the labor force as well as job growth. If unemployment goes up because the labor force has expanded, it does not mean that job growth is declining and the economy is getting weaker. Indeed, economists like to look at things like the change in the amount of overtime or the number of shifts worked to get an idea of where employment is headed. That's because when business picks up, firms typically add overtime instead of hiring new people at first. The actual employment numbers tend to be a lagging indicator of economic trends. Companies usually don't bother laying off workers until they have a sense that business really has deteriorated. Likewise, they don't hire until they know for sure that business is a lot stronger. These numbers, released by the Labor Department, usually come out on the first Friday of the month.

NATIONAL ASSOCIATION OF PURCHASING MANAGERS INDEX (NAPM)

Some economists don't take this survey of manufacturing activity too seriously as a forecasting tool, but the markets react to it. That's mainly because the release comes out early in the month. So investors believe they can use it to figure out how important indicators will size up later in the month–like the employment and industrial production numbers released by the government. The NAPM index can be misleading, though. For one thing, it is based on responses from over 350 companies. In contrast, the government's production index surveys over 60,000. The survey can also be volatile. Despite its shortcomings, NAPM moves markets, so it is worth watching.

The most important thing to know about the NAPM index is that readings below 50 suggest the manufacturing sector is shrinking. This number is derived from responses by NAPM members to questions about whether conditions are "better, worse, or the same" for the month at issue. This means the index is not a measure of overall activity, but rather the perceived change in conditions in the manufacturing sector.

While the media focus on whether the overall index was above or below 50, economists are busy digging into the details for the real clues. Here's what they are looking at. The survey sounds out how conditions are changing in six areas: domestic orders, export orders, production, employment, prices, and how fast suppliers deliver. Orders are the key leading indicator in the survey, says Rosanne Cahn of Credit Suisse First Boston. Production is less useful because it often lags changes in orders. Economists look at the layoffs component to get a feel for where the official employment numbers will come in later in the month. "Prices paid" gives a good handle on where inflation is going. About half the change in prices paid shows up in inflation six months later. The full impact then takes two years. "Supplier delivery," also called vendor performance, is a good leading indicator of inflation since it tells you something about capacity usage, notes John Silvia, the chief economist at Scudder Kemper Investments. If vendors are taking longer to deliver, it probably means that capacity is more stretched–which could mean there are bottlenecks and price increases.

CONSUMER PRICE INDEX (CPI)

This number matters because the Fed is always concerned about inflation. Although some economists claim other tools pick up the scent of inflation a lot earlier than this one, the CPI can be a major market mover–especially when investors are worried that inflation may lead to higher interest rates. When that is the case, an increase in the CPI can spark selling in the stock market and drive bond prices down on fears that the potential for higher inflation makes it more likely the Fed will raise rates. During times when the market focus is not on the Fed, this number may have less of an impact.

Economists and the markets prefer to look at the so-called core rate, which takes out the more volatile food and energy prices. Even with those stripped out, the CPI is a fairly broad measure of inflation. Originally developed during World War I to help keep wages in line in areas hard hit by wartime inflation, the CPI measures the average change in prices paid by urban consumers for a fixed basket of goods and services. The Bureau of Labor collects information on more than 360 categories of items in over 80 urban areas.

Critics say this basket of goods is not updated often enough to reflect changes in consumer spending habits. They also claim the CPI overstates inflation by failing to fully take into account technological improvements in the products we buy. If you get more options on a refrigerator or VCR for the same amount of money, then the prices of those goods have really gone down. The Bureau of Labor tries to adjust for this but does not capture the whole impact, critics say. Another shortcoming is that the CPI does not take into account the fact that consumers alter their buying patterns when price changes. If prices go up, they often buy cheaper, substitute brands. All told, the CPI may overstate inflation by as much as 1% because of these factors.

Many economists believe that signs of impending inflation are picked up much better by upstream indicators like the prices of commodities. These prices are measured by the Commodity Research Bureau's Futures Price Index (known as the CRB Index) or the prices of futures for individual commodities. Economists also look at the *Journal of Commerce* industrial material prices. Increases in the prices of these input items eventually work through to finished goods and change the CPI. For stocks, an increase in the CPI can be a double-edged sword. On the one hand, it's probably a sign that profits are going to go up because companies will be able to get more for their goods. On the other hand, it increases the odds that the Fed may raise rates, which is bad for stocks.

RETAIL SALES

These numbers are important because two-thirds of the economy is driven by consumer spending. "If retail sales are too strong, it suggests that the economy is too strong and the Fed may tighten," says Shipley. When using these numbers, economists like to take out auto sales and building materials to reduce the impact of the volatility of those figures. Sales or rebates on cars can increase the volume of auto sales, for example, which can move the overall retail sales number quite a bit. Sales on clothing, the volatility of gasoline prices, and the unusual weather can have the same effect.

Keep in mind that the government's definition of "retail sales" is probably not what you have in mind. The Commerce Department includes things like grocery stores, restaurants, and bars—which make up a good part of the overall figure. Actual department store sales are only a small portion. Although consumer spending is important to follow, remember that the retail sales numbers in this report are just a small part of overall consumer spending. Only about 28% of the GDP is driven by retail sales. Spending on services accounts for about 40% of GDP, while capital spending, government spending, and trade are behind the rest.

The retail sales numbers usually come out in the middle of the month. Like the GDP figures, these are revised twice, in the two months after the numbers come out. There is often a big difference between the advance number and the following revisions.

DURABLE GOODS ORDERS

Economists view this as a good leading indicator, and so do investors. Therefore, the release can have a big impact on the markets. Economists define "durable goods" as products meant to last more than three years. These are essentially big-ticket items like home appliances and business equipment.

This is a handy indicator for a number of reasons. First, a change in the business cycle often shows up first in the demand for durable goods. A downturn in spending on durable goods usually occurs well in advance of business cycle peaks, while upturns usually happen ahead of the end of a recession. The demand for these products is highly sensitive to changes in interest rates and consumer confidence. So these are the things people cut out first when conditions weaken—or begin buying first when things get better.

Second, there is a knock-on effect with durable goods. An increase in this number indicates that overall growth may soon get a boost from the extra money companies may have to spend to increase capacity. This release is also important because, even though manufacturing is a relatively small part of the economy, it is more variable than the bigger services sector. Changes in the demand for manufactured goods are often what lie behind a slowdown or an increase in growth. The demand for services does not change that much over the course of the economic cycle.

Keep in mind that durable goods orders bounce around a lot. To dampen the volatility, analysts like to strip out aircraft because orders for them can bunch up. To exclude aircraft, economists focus on the "nondefense capital goods" part of the report. The markets, however, often overlook the inherent volatility in this release. Traders may react badly to a big upswing (suggesting higher growth, inflation, and interest rates), even though the increase was obviously caused by one-off, big-ticket orders. Even if you adjust the data by taking out aircraft, the numbers can move around a lot month to month, giving misleading signals. The figures are released by the Commerce Department.

OTHER IMPORTANT INDICATORS

AUTO AND TRUCK SALES

Since consumer spending is such an important factor in the U.S. economy, any numbers that tell us what households are doing with their money offer a good glimpse of the future. Spending on cars, like spending on all consumer durable goods and housing, often signals a major business cycle turning point long before other indicators. Within the durable goods group, car purchases are often the leading edge. They tend to be the most cyclical.

You have to be careful when interpreting trends in the car and truck sales data, notes Frederick Breimeyer, chief economist with State Street Bank. Ward's Automotive Reports, which supplies the numbers used by the government in preparing this release, only compiles the number of units sold each month, not the cash value of the sales. So if more expensive cars and trucks are sold, consumers could be spending a lot more, even though the same number of vehicles changed hands. But you wouldn't know that from these numbers.

BUSINESS INVENTORIES

Investors and economists like to use this number to predict changes in industrial production–which can have a big influence on overall economic growth. Rather than simply look at the change in inventory levels, economists focus on the ratio of inventory to sales. Did inventories shrink while sales increased, causing the ratio to drop? If so, companies may have underestimated the strength of demand. They may have to increase production to keep up. Are inventories building up in relation to sales? Maybe consumers are buying less, and the economy is headed for a recession. Companies may soon have to cut production.

CHICAGO PURCHASING MANAGERS' INDEX

Because this number comes out at the beginning of the monthly cycle of economic reports, it takes on more importance than it might otherwise deserve. Coming out first, it can be used to forecast how other key indicators will shape up–and how they may move the markets–during the month. Investors don't really care that much about what is happening in Chicago. But there is a loose correlation between the Chicago report and the National Association of Purchasing Managers' (NAPM) report which is released the next day, points out James Paulsen, the chief investment officer at Wells Capital Management. And there is a strong correlation between those national NAPM results and the market-moving payroll and wage numbers that come out a few days later, on the first Friday of every month.

EMPLOYMENT COST INDEX (ECI)

This number is sure to attract a lot of attention when the markets are focused on the risk of a Fed rate hike because the labor markets are tight. If that's the case, investors examine this report to figure out the extent to which tight conditions in the labor market may contribute to wage pressures and inflation. At some point, employers have to pass higher labor costs on by raising prices, or profits will fall. The two most popular wage measures are the ECI and the hourly earnings component of the nonfarm payroll report. But economists like the ECI better. For one thing, it measures more than just wages and salaries, a shortcoming of the hourly wages component of the payroll report. It also captures the cost of benefits like health insurance, as well as commissions and bonuses. Critics point out the ECI does not include stock options, a big part of many pay packages.

GROSS DOMESTIC PRODUCT

Although this release is a broad measure of the health of the U.S. economy for the most recent quarter, it usually does not have a big impact on the markets. That's because much of the information has already come out by the time this report is released. Sometimes, however, it contains surprises that have an impact on the markets. An attempt to offer a snapshot of growth for the previous three months, the GDP report comes out in the month after the quarter's close. It draws on real data from the first two months of the quarter and estimates for the third month. The report is released in three phases: advance, preliminary, and final. Each one is more accurate than the last but less influential as far as the markets go. The GDP report measures the total output of goods and services in the economy. It contains detailed sections on the four main components of GDP: consumption, investment, government spending, and net exports.

HOUSING STARTS, BUILDING PERMITS

These numbers do not usually have a major impact on the market. But since consumer spending is so important to U.S. economic growth, an economic release that reveals what households are doing with their money is of interest. Economists know these numbers are important because the housing sector tends to be a very good leading indicator. Housing starts almost always signal a major business cycle turning point way before other indicators, notes Silvia. Downturns in housing starts usually occur well in advance of business cycle peaks, while upturns usually happen ahead of the end of a recession.

INDUSTRIAL PRODUCTION AND CAPACITY UTILIZATION

Economists and the Fed look at these closely for clues about where the economy and inflation are headed. The production figures cover manufacturing, mining, and utilities, but economists prefer the part on manufacturing when trying to get a handle on big-picture growth trends. (Utilities tend to simply grow in line with the economy, whereas mining is affected too much by energy prices.) As a rule of thumb, manufacturing growth needs to be faster than the overall growth of the economy for an expansion to continue, but this is not always the case. The index measures changes in production relative to a base year. An index value of 130 means production was 30% higher than in that base year.

Capacity usage tells you whether the economy has room to grow faster without sparking an increase in inflation. Historically, capacity usage greater than 82% to 84% has meant that inflation may be on the way because at these levels there are supply shortages and production bottlenecks. If you combine the production and capacity usage numbers, you can get a feel for trends in the level of capital investment by firms, an important force in the economy. If production is strong and capacity usage goes down, then you know businesses are adding capacity—a possible leading economic indicator. Likewise, if both production and capacity usage are going down, businesses may soon be cutting back on capital spending.

INITIAL JOBLESS CLAIMS

Since it is a weekly number, this indicator contains even more noise than the monthly employment data, which can move around so much on a short-term basis that it is risky to draw conclusions from an individual release, notes Gordon Richards, the economist for the National Association of Manufacturers. Nevertheless, the markets are keen on this figure, which tells how many people applied for unemployment insurance. When the number comes in low, it suggests job growth is strong. Economists use this release as an early indicator of how the all-important monthly employment data will shake out.

PERSONAL INCOME, SPENDING, AND SAVINGS

Put together by the Commerce Department, these numbers are an attempt to capture how much people earned, spent, and saved. Income includes money that comes in from wages, many investments, and payments made by Uncle Sam. Spending is estimated from retail sales data. Savings is calculated as the difference between the two, minus new debt taken on in the same period. Since personal income and spending are crucial to the economy, you might think these releases move the markets. They usually don't. It isn't because they are not important. It's just that these indicators can be predicted fairly accurately by using numbers that come out before this report.

PRODUCER PRICE INDEX (PPI)

This is an important indicator to watch when the markets are worried that the Fed may be thinking about changing interest rates because of potential inflation. Otherwise, it is not a market mover. Delivered in three pieces, this index measures (1) the price of raw materials like basic steel; (2) the price of semifinished goods like galvanized steel; and (3) the prices of finished goods that are sold to other businesses, like machines made from that galvanized steel. Producer prices can have an impact on the cost of goods, reflected in the Consumer Price Index (CPI), but the direct link between producer prices and consumer prices that existed during the 1970s has broken down. During that era of high inflation, it was easy for manufacturers to simply pass price hikes along, although the ability to do this varied from sector to sector. Since then, most companies have lost the power to pass on price increases. Besides, over half of the CPI is made up of services, and the PPI has no services component. While the PPI is important, there are other ways to get a feel for upstream or producer inflation. In addition to commodity prices, economists like to look at the Baltic Freight Rate Index, a measure of international shipping rates. The PPI, produced by the Bureau of Labor Statistics in the Department of Labor, usually comes out in the middle of the month, just ahead of the CPI.

PRODUCTIVITY

Defined as the amount of output per hour of labor, this number is useful for predicting inflation and growth. If labor cost increases are matched by increases in productivity, then those higher labor costs are less likely to cause inflation. That's because even though firms have to pay employees more, companies are also producing and earning more, so there is less pressure to raise prices. In other words, if you take the increase in labor costs and subtract the increase in productivity, the difference should be the pressure on producers to raise prices. This number is usually not a big market mover because it really does not contain much new information. Once economists have GDP and the number of hours worked (available from the employment report), they can figure out productivity growth, which is output per hour worked. Don't make the mistake of thinking that changes in productivity reflect how hard people are working. Productivity numbers have more to do with the level of efficiency in a company overall. Better technology and equipment, and more capital spending, are what increase productivity. In addition to giving a read on whether there is pressure on prices, productivity tells you a lot about corporate profits. If productivity is going up, profits probably will, too.

KEY EVENTS TO WATCH

FEDERAL OPEN MARKET COMMITTEE (FMOC) MEETING

This meeting can really shake up the markets because it is where the Federal Reserve decides whether or not to change interest rates. If there are doubts about what the Fed will do, the level of uncertainty increases as the meeting approaches, building sharply a day or two before. When there are fears that the Fed will raise rates (or won't cut rates as previously expected), investors will head for the sidelines to wait it out, selling off both the bond and the stock markets. This can be a buying opportunity if the Fed then acts in a market-friendly way, proving that the fears were misplaced. If everyone fully expects the Fed to do something, like cut rates, and it does just that, don't be surprised if the market does not react. Since the move was widely expected, it was probably already priced into the market. But if the rate cut looks like it is part of a series of cuts that will be carried out by the Fed, the stock market will rally. Usually the Fed will send several signals to the market about what it plans to do, before it actually moves.

Remember that the Fed can change rates at any time—not just during an FMOC meeting. The trend in recent years, however, has been to act only during the regular, scheduled meeting. The meeting is usually a two-day affair. The FMOC is made up of the seven governors of the Federal Reserve Board and the presidents of five of the twelve regional Federal Reserve Banks. The seven Federal Reserve Board governors include the chairman—who is the most important person to watch. "This is an organization that really is run by the chairman, who sets the tone of the agenda and policy," says Breimeyer. "What the chairman wants, the chairman gets. The chairman rules."

By law, the main goals of the FMOC are to foster economic growth and job creation, and keep inflation in line. It controls two short-term interest rates. One is the "federal funds rate," or the interest rate banks charge each other for overnight loans. The FMOC sets targets for this rate and then guides the rate with activities in the open market. The rate is also influenced by the level of demand for money by banks. The FMOC also controls the "discount rate." This is the interest the Fed charges banks when they borrow money backed by government securities they own.

THE HUMPHREY HAWKINS HEARINGS

A good place to figure out what's on the central bank's agenda is the Fed chairman's Humphrey Hawkins testimony before Congress. The testimony, which happens twice a year (in July and February), can tell you what is bugging the chairman about trends in the economy. Don't rely on media reports and analysis to understand what is going on. Instead, get a copy of the testimony (available at the Fed website) and follow the Fed chairman's reasoning yourself. The question and answer session during the hearing can also be important. But most of what you will need is in the testimony. "If you are trying to get a feel for where the Fed sees the economy and inflation going, you really do have to read the documents," says Santow.

Pay attention to what bothers the chairman and what would make him happy. The markets, whose sharpest minds have also read the testimony, are likely to react to events the same way the Fed chairman says he does. The testimony is a place where the Fed applies one of its favorite tools: jawboning the market. But the hearings are important for another reason. When the Fed is close to moving on interest rates, it normally signals the markets beforehand. This testimony is often a place where this is done.

To gather all the clues, however, you need to pay attention to the Fed chairman's testimony at other hearings. The chairman can speak a dozen times or more before various committees during the year.

You also have to follow public speeches by the chairman and the other FMOC members. Don't ignore them just because they are college commencement addresses. Pay close attention to the more important FMOC members. Their rank can be determined by following press reports, checking who is on the more significant Fed committees (like the one that covers banking regulation), and reading the minutes from Fed meetings for clues.

Two notes of caution on the Humphrey Hawkins testimony. First, it contains elliptical, sometimes impenetrable language known as "Fed-speak." This is excruciatingly careful phrasing used by the chairman to avoid sending false signals. Since the language is often unclear, it can have the opposite effect. At the end of 1998, the Fed decided to do something about this. It said it would simplify the wording of "directives" used to summarize the thinking at Fed meetings. The Fed also began issuing occasional statements when its views change about the direction of policy or risks in the economy. The second thing to be cautious about when following the Humphrey Hawkins testimony is that the initial headlines from the hearings may be misleading. Journalists get the testimony first, and their interpretations may be different from those of the trained economic analysts who see it later.

PART TWO

PROFITABLE STOCK MARKET PATTERNS

CHAPTER 9

THE EARNINGS "CONFESSION" SEASON

Most people love a sale. If you do too and you invest in stocks, you are in luck. Because you can pretty much count on a "blue-light special" four times a year. It isn't *exactly* clockwork, but each quarter companies go through a ritual that temporarily brings down stock prices in a sector, or better yet–the whole market. If you understand what is going on while this is happening and you resist losing your head like most other investors, you can take advantage of these short-lived market declines to pick up some real bargains among your favorite stocks. Here's why this happens and how it works.

FOCUS ON THE SHORT TERM

Years ago, the markets were more or less dominated by professional investors who had a long-term view about stocks. They weren't anything like a lot of money managers today. Typically, the old timers would buy and hold for at least one to three years. To them, annual results were the real read on how a company was doing. Quarterly numbers were just minor progress reports along the way.

Now things are different. Many more people are responsible for managing their own retirement money. They are constantly shopping around for the fund manager with the best performance. Or their advisors are doing it for them. The report card they turn to–rightly or wrongly–is the manager's performance in the most recent quarter. This puts a lot of pressure on the fund managers to produce decent gains every three months. After all, a big part of their pay is a percentage of the assets under their management.

"Almost all of the money that comes in ends up going to the top-rated funds," notes Robert Froehlich, the chief investment strategist at Scudder Kemper Funds Group. "If your fund is marketed through a sales network and you slip from a four-star to a three-star ranking, that is like going out of business. As a fund manager, you get your score card every quarter. If the fund flows drop, you don't earn as much money."

In other words, money managers can't always get away with shrugging off a bad quarter, just because they have a good long-term record. "Having a bad quarter did not matter a whole lot 25 years ago," says Al Kugel, a former portfolio manager and now the senior investment strategist at Stein Roe & Farnham. "Now managers get paid for short-term performance. They are the day traders, even though it is hard to make money by trading and moving it around quickly." This focus on the short term by mutual fund investors and money managers is not necessarily right. And you don't have to like it. It is just the way it is. Rather than preach, this chapter is meant to show you how to use it to your advantage.

EARNINGS SURPRISE AND REVISION ANALYSIS

The second factor that explains the markdowns on stocks that occur four times a year is the technology revolution, which brought the "information age" to investing. Advances during the 1980s meant that the latest earnings news about a company could be zapped onto the computer screens of money managers around the world in a matter of seconds. Not only that. Once professional investors got the news, they had the computing power to manipulate the numbers and reach instant conclusions about what they meant for the future of the stock.

As the head of quantitative equity research at Drexel Burnham Lambert, Robert Butman was one of the pioneers in the use of computers to analyze quarterly results and earnings estimate revisions to predict stock price movements. "When we started the quant group at Drexel in the mid-1980s, we were a novelty. We had a big Vax computer and clients would get on with their personal computers," says Butman, who is now the president of a hedge fund company named TQA Investors LLC.

Then technology evolved. Soon money managers could afford to put some serious computing horsepower right in their own shops. At about the same time, new companies like IBES International, Zacks Investment Research, and First Call were beginning to offer comprehensive earnings-related numbers to crunch. "So you had a way for investors to exploit this data," says Butman. Laying the groundwork for what later became the most effective and popular investment tool among professionals–earnings surprise and revision analysis–investors like Butman, Langdon Wheeler of Numeric Investors, and others figured out how to draw conclusions from trends in the flow of earnings numbers and earnings revisions. Their systems told them with pretty good certainty how a stock would perform. "We began to promote the concept and during the second half of the 1980s it really took off like wildfire," says Butman. "Now there is tons and tons of money pursuing these things."

THE CONFESSION SEASON

The result of all this was that quarterly earnings performance at companies became much more important for money managers. It has gotten to the point where firms that miss their earnings estimates even slightly get taken out and shot. "At one time we talked about what the trailing earnings were and what they are going to be this year," says Hugh Johnson, a market strategist for the brokerage First Albany. "We only had a passing interest in the earnings for any given quarter. Now everyone not only cares about the earnings for a given quarter, but they also care about whether they will be one or two cents off."

Often, if companies disappoint by coming in just one penny below estimates, investors flee the stock. "That is ridiculous," says Kugel. "You can't know these things that closely." Ridiculous or not, company managers don't like to see this happen to their stocks. Increasingly, managers are paid for how well their company stock does, not only how well the company does. The result is that corporations are more focused on short-term results as well.

By now you can see where all this is going. Focus on quarterly fund results. Corporate managers feeling pain when their shares go down, because their pay is linked to stock performance. At some point in the early 1990s, managers started doing something to ease that pain a bit, when it looked like a quarter would end up weaker then expected. Instead of waiting for their scheduled earnings announcement to lay out the bad news, they began to "preannounce" the news, or warn that they were going to miss their quarter.

Although it's not clear that it always works, managers do this to maintain credibility and curry favor among analysts and professional investors. "It is a way of cushioning the blow," says Johnson. "Companies have learned that if they guide analysts to earnings estimates that are too high and then miss the numbers, investors and analysts won't trust the company. It is very hard to regain their confidence. So companies do their very best to guide analysts to forecasts that are reasonable, if not low."

"If you say things are not so good before the quarter is over, it appears that you are letting investors and analysts know the news when you heard it," notes Vernon Winters, the chief investment officer at Mellon Private Asset Management. "This provides better support for the stock in the long term."

The upshot of all this is that the markets now go through a quarterly ritual known as the confession season. Toward the end of each quarter, managers bring out the bad news in the hopes of atonement. The ritual has become more and more popular. When analysts began collecting numbers on this trend as it started gathering steam in 1995, about 300 companies were preannouncing. Three years later, over 1,000 companies were fessing up each quarter. (See Figure 9.1.) Typically about 60% to 80% of those preannouncements bring bad news.

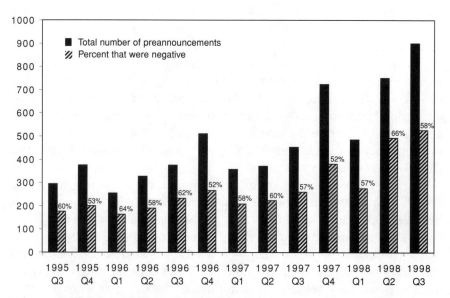

Figure 1. More and More Confessions.

Source: First Call.

These confessions tend to be concentrated in the four weeks spanning the end of a quarter and the start of the new one. When such a heavy flow of bad news takes place in a small space of time, investors focus on that and neglect everything else. As a result, the confession season usually puts investors into a bad mood, and the market goes into a funk. In the confusion, a lot of decent stocks get hit, and some great stocks go on sale. This is your chance to pick them up cheap. "I look forward to this stuff because it presents a pretty good opportunity," says Johnson.

The deals are especially attractive because of what happens next. Once the preannouncements are out of the way, earnings begin coming out fast and furious. At this point, companies typically beat the estimates. This lifts the spirits of the markets–and the stocks you just bought at a discount during the gloom of the confession season. "The market gets thrown for a loop by a few bad announcements, then the market comes roaring back," says Winters.

It is true that some companies beat the estimates merely because they just "talked the numbers down" to make them more beatable. During the confession season, you will hear commentators making a big deal out of this point. Ignore it. What really matters is a completely different group of companies that are busy beating estimates. These are the firms that never "talked down" the numbers or warned in the first place, because they were not having any problems. They produce solid results, and Wall Street throws a party.

But wait a minute. If these winners that come in and save the day were never really in any trouble to begin with, then why did the markets get so upset during the confession season? Why did Wall Street sell down the stocks of companies that were doing well all along? If you find yourself asking this question, it is probably because you make the mistake of thinking that professional investors are rational. As many well-written books on investor psychology point out,[1] investors are often slaves to crowd psychology. Like members of many large groups, investors in a crowd often do things that make no sense at all. You should use this to your advantage whenever you can.

The confession season often gives you a great opportunity to do just that. During the preannouncement season, the crowd focuses on the

---

[1] Martin Pring, *Investment Psychology Explained* (New York: John Wiley & Sons, 1993) and Charles Mackay, *Extraordinary Popular Delusion & the Madness of Crowds* (New York: Random House, 1995).

small group of companies warning they won't meet earnings estimates. The market sells off. Then, during the earnings reporting season, the herd focuses on the winners who are coming in ahead of their numbers. The crowd becomes happy and buys stocks, pushing up the market. You don't have to agree that this behavior makes sense. Just take advantage of it when you see it happening, which should be every quarter.

As annoying as it may seem if you hold a stock that tanks because of a confession, be thankful that more companies are preannouncing. This is a big improvement over the old days of releasing news in closed-door meetings with a few favored analysts. With preannouncements, individual investors are getting news earlier. Unfortunately, many firms still leak bad news to a handful of favored analysts and investors first, even though the Securities and Exchange Commission discourages this practice, known as "selective disclosure." By law, of course, companies are supposed to make "material information" public to everyone at the same time by means of a press release.

Here are some tips on how to make the preannouncement panic work for you.

- Have a list of stocks you like according to your system, whatever it is. Wait for earnings warnings to cause a general market selloff. This will occur during the last two or three weeks of the quarter and the first 10 days or so of the next quarter—the time when most companies confess. (For the first quarter, for example, preannouncements will happen during the end of March and early April.) Buy stocks that get taken down with the whole market, even though you know they are good companies, based on your research. "Everything will tend to sag in sympathy, and it will be a good buying opportunity," says Louis Navellier, of Navellier Securities. This strategy usually works best with the more volatile stocks in sectors like technology, health care, and specialty retailers.
- Sometimes, however, there won't be any general market turbulence. Instead, the confessions will make only a couple of sectors sink. If this is the case, you can still look for collateral hits among firms you like in these groups. Often, perfectly healthy companies in the same industry will sell off, presenting an opportunity for the astute investor. But this is a trickier strategy. When looking over collateral hits inside a sector, it is more difficult to understand whether the company you like will be hurt by the same problems afflicting the company that warned about earnings. It is safer to look for bar-

gains during a general market selloff sparked by earnings confessions. The chances are greater that the problems affecting the companies that preannounce won't be hurting your company, especially if the culprits are in an entirely different sector.

- As the end of the quarter approaches, watch out for what the big bellwether companies like Intel or Microsoft are saying. If they announce early that they are going to make their numbers or beat estimates, then the confession season may have less of an impact that quarter. By the same token, bad news from one of these companies can have a big impact on the markets. Be sure to do the same with the bellwether stocks in whatever sector is providing market leadership at the moment. Those are the ones everyone else is watching.

- Toward the end of a quarter, firms that track earnings like First Call, IBES International, or Zacks will start releasing information about which sectors are getting hit the hardest by downward revisions to earnings estimates. These are the sectors in which companies are more likely to disappoint.

- Even though the confession season is fairly predictable, it is better not to use it as part of a trading strategy. Right after you put on your trade, some external shock (like an international crisis or an interest rate hike by the Fed) might bring down the whole market. What you thought would be a short-term trade will turn into a long-term hold, and you may not be ready for that, meaning you will have to sell at a loss. Besides, it is extremely difficult to make money trading, even though it looks easy. Instead, use the confession season to get a good entry into a stock you plan to hold because you like its long-term potential. Do you put money into the market several times a year? Use the dips that occur during the confession season as part of your dollar cost averaging strategy.

- It is not a good idea to buy the stocks that preannounce bad news. Even though you may be tempted to think they are a bargain because they have come down so much, this is probably not the case. Stock analysts use the "cockroach theory" to explain why. Just like that roach in your kitchen during your college days (for every one you see, there are 10 more you don't), one bad quarter or negative earnings surprise is usually followed by many more. Likewise, don't buy stocks you know little about, simply because they have been brought down by a similar company announcing bad news.

You won't know enough about them to understand whether they are being affected by the same trend.

• Remember that companies can preannounce any time, not just at the turn of a quarter. Usually, however, that is when it happens. "As soon as they have most of the quarter in, they figure out what is going on and they get the news out," says John Manley, a market strategist with Salomon Smith Barney. If 10 or 12 days of the new quarter go by and a company still has not confessed, then the previous quarter probably went well. But this is not always so. You have to keep in mind that some companies just don't preannounce. They have no legal obligation to do so.

• Strong reported earnings numbers after the confession season may lift the markets less than you expected. Negative comments from managers about the future can spook the markets despite strong earnings numbers. So can weak financial statement numbers like rising days sales outstanding or accounts receivables.

• Unlike retail merchandise, stocks are less likely to go on sale during the holiday season. Usually, the confessions are lightest for the fourth quarter. Between 1995 and 1998, only 53% of these preannouncements were negative for the last quarter of the year, compared with 59% to 62% for the other three quarters. But remember that the rush of money that comes into the market right at the end of the year and in the first week or so of the new year means that a purchase on even a minor dip may turn out to be a good buy.

CHAPTER 10

THE LOCKUP RELEASE

If you invest in stocks, you know that they can often decline a lot on big volume even though there is no news. This leaves you wondering whether you should hold, give up and sell too, or buy more.

In many cases, not even the pros have the answers to these questions. They can call their traders or other Wall Street contacts and get a theory or two, but in the end they are left guessing, too.

With a modem and a little detective work, however, you can anticipate some of these sudden drops in a stock price and capitalize on them as buying opportunities. Indeed, certain kinds of stocks–those recently brought public and companies that have returned to the market with a secondary offering[1]–are quite likely to go on sale by 10% or more in a very predictable manner. And it is not that hard to find out about these bargains in advance. All the information you need is available for free on the Internet. All you have to do is know how to look for it.

Stocks go on sale like this because of the way investment bankers manage initial public offerings (IPOs) and secondary or follow-on issues. They know that after fresh shares are issued, the market for a stock can be volatile for several months. It's not in the investment bankers' interest for a stock that they have recently underwritten to lose too much value. This does not make investors happy. To limit this turbulence and make sure the process goes more smoothly, the bankers try to control the aftermarket for shares in companies that just issued stock.

They do this by putting some restrictions on big shareholders in the company, people like the venture capitalists who helped start the firm,

---

[1] Strictly speaking, this is called a follow-on offering. But in practice, many investors use the phrase "secondary offering."

private owners who have a big stake, and top managers. The investment bankers will often get these shareholders to sign what is called a lockup agreement whenever there is a public offering of shares. The agreement says that these big shareholders—who may own up to a quarter or half of the company—can't sell their shares for a specified amount of time after the offering. Their shares, in other words, are "locked up," usually for three to six months after the IPO or the secondary.

When the lockup expires and these shares are allowed out, there is often a flood of selling that drives down the price of the stock. But since nothing has really changed about the fundamentals of the company, the decline in the price is a buying opportunity. "This is a very reliable way of predicting a drop in a stock price ahead of time," says Marc Strausberg of Edgar Online, a private Web site (http://www.edgar-online.com) that offers access to company documents filed with the Securities and Exchange Commission (SEC).

Don't make the mistake of thinking that just because these shares are being released onto the market they are diluting earnings, and so the stock deserves a lower price. This is not the case. Since the locked-up shares were already issued well before the lockup release, they have already been taken into account when calculating earnings per share. The fact that they can be freely traded at some point because a lockup expired has no impact on earnings per share whatsoever. It is the selling pressure that pushes the stock price down.

In most cases, in fact, the flood of new shares caused by a lockup release can actually be good news for anyone who wants to see the stock price increase. How so? "This can help the stock run up even higher because the float gets bigger," explains Bruce Rauner, of GTCR Golder Rauner LLC, a Chicago-based venture capital firm that helps take companies public. "When more shares are available, more institutions can hold the shares and there is more transaction volume."

All this does not mean that the new shares being offered in the follow-on offering itself won't dilute earnings. They probably will, at least in the short term. But if management is good, they will be able to invest the money they raised from the follow-on in a manner that increases earnings more than enough to offset the impact of the dilution caused by the new shares. "Issuing new stock is not necessarily good or bad in and of itself," says Rauner. "If the company has a good use for the cash, it won't be dilutive. If not, it will." This is a whole other debate, however, that has nothing to do with the lockup release covered here. The point to keep in mind is that the shares released from a lockup are not "new" shares, and they don't water down earnings.

One shortcoming of using lockup releases as entry points into a stock is that you have to spend time rooting around in rather drab legal documents filed with the SEC, to figure out when they will occur. To assist you with that, here is a guide that will take you through the whole process and help you wade through the legalese, so you can get what you need from the SEC documents without too much pain and suffering.

USING LOCKUP RELEASES

STEP ONE: IDENTIFY DECENT STOCKS

This sounds obvious, but remember that you should never use the lockup release to get into stocks you know little about or stocks that have poor prospects. Just because a stock goes down due to a lockup release does not mean it will go back up. So the first step, of course, is to apply whatever investment analysis system you use to identify strong companies. An obvious place to look is among companies that have recently come public. They are more likely to have lockup agreements linked to the IPO. Finding winners may be more of a challenge with recently issued stock because fewer analysts follow them. On the other hand, the best time to buy shares in a good company is before the crowd has arrived. Just be prepared for some breathtaking volatility if you invest in IPO shares.

Keep in mind that the lockup release buying opportunity is not for IPOs only. Just about any company can carry out a secondary issue of new stock at any time—and secondaries often contain lockup agreements. When hunting for targets, remember that the lockup release is more likely to have an impact on the price of stock in the smaller companies with lower trading volume, as opposed to a giant like Intel. So it is usually more fruitful to look for lockup news among stocks with a market cap of less than $1 billion and volume well below 2 or 3 million shares a day. These are just general guidelines.

STEP TWO: FIND THE RIGHT SEC FORMS

Once you have selected companies with good prospects, you need to look at the right SEC documents to see if there is a lockup release. Go to the SEC's Edgar site (http://www.sec.gov/cgi-bin/srch-edgar), which is free. Another site, Edgar Online (http://www.edgar-online.com), offers documents for free if they are more than a day old. If you use their pay service, you can get more sophisticated search capabilities and quicker access to SEC filings, but these are not necessarily for lockup research. One nice feature of this site is that it will notify paying customers by e-mail whenever a company files any SEC forms. This is a good way of keeping tabs on whether a company you like is going to carry out a secondary offering. If so, you can check whether a lockup agreement is part of the deal.

Once you are at either of the Edgar sites, type in the ticker of your favorite IPO or the company for which you want to find out if there is going to be a secondary. You will then see a list of SEC forms. Four of them will help you find out about lockup agreements. One of the best ones is called the 424B (followed by some letters and numbers, depending on what kind of a 424B it is). Named after the SEC rule that makes companies file this document, the 424B might be the preliminary prospectus for a stock offering, an amendment, or the final prospectus, before it gets put in slick packaging. This electronic version, however, has everything you need. A 424B may cover either an IPO or a secondary. If there is no 424B, look for the S-1, which is the basic registration form for a new company; the S-2, or the S-3. Use the most recent one. Finally, keep an eye out for any amended versions of these documents (the S-1/A, etc). These amendments are filed in response to SEC questions or to correct errors in the original version. Usually, they do not change the lockup agreement outlined in the first form, but you never know. So it pays to check these.

STEP THREE: WADE THROUGH THE DOCUMENTS FOR THE IMPORTANT INFORMATION

Now you have a 90-page or so document on your screen written in dense legalese. Don't fret. It won't be necessary to read the whole thing. To be sure, this document contains a lot of useful information about your company that you should know. But you don't have to read through all of it to get to the juicy parts about the lockup agreement.

Instead, use your Web browser's search tool (under Find). The key words to search for are: "shares eligible." That should take you right to the section that discusses the lockup, which is normally called *Shares Eligible for Future Sale,* though the heading may be different. This search, however, may first land you in the table of contents for the document. If it does, just search again until you find the right part. If the phrase "shares eligible" doesn't get you there, try searching on the phrases "dispose of," "180 days," and, not surprisingly, "lockup." You may want to search on the word "lock," since "lockup" may be spelled with or without a hyphen. (Put a space before the word "lock" to avoid getting hits on words like "block.")

Once you've found the right part of the document, the page or two discussing the lockup should tell you all you need to know. The section will indicate how many shares will be released and when. Typically, shares are locked up for 180 days from the prospectus date. (That date will be either at the top or the bottom of the Form 424B. It is usually the same as the date the form was filed with the SEC, but not always. If you are looking at the S1, you won't find the prospectus date there, but you can get it by looking at other SEC documents or calling the company.) While 180 days is a normal time frame, shares are often locked up for either 120 or 90 days. Take note of how many shares will be released and after how many days. Then count forward (including weekend days) from the prospectus date and mark it on your calendar. You probably should start watching for unexplained dips on big volume about a month ahead of the lockup release, since shareholders can be let out of the lockup early. So mark that date, too. Before leaving the document, you might want to search a few more times for later references to the phrase "shares eligible." It is not likely, but there may be more important information about the lockup further on.

If nothing turns up, you have what you need to know: the release date and the number of shares that will be free to trade. Here are some other important tips about investing with lockup releases.

- Tally up the number of shares in the lockup release and compare it to the total number of shares outstanding for the company. This can help you gauge the possible impact of the lockup release. Generally, a lockup release of anything under 500,000 shares is not likely to have a big effect, depending on the number of outstanding shares. You want to see a large amount of shares–in the range of several million being released against an outstanding base of 7 or 8 million shares for example. Ten or 15 percent of the total number of shares outstanding should be enough.

- Even under these conditions, you won't always see a price movement on the day of the lockup release. Lockup agreements are often the subject of gigantic battles between the venture capitalists and the underwriters. The venture capitalists want to sell their shares, and the underwriters want to keep them out of the market to limit volatility. Sometimes a shareholder will insist on selling early and won't approve the deal unless satisfied. In other cases, the investment bankers will change the agreement after it's been made and let some shareholders out early. "The underwriters have the ability to waive the lockup deadline," points out Alan Paley, a securities attorney with the securities law firm Debevois & Plimpton. "And there is no way for the investor to know." This means you have to start watching the stock price a month before the lockup is due to expire.

- Even if no one gets out of the lockup early, don't expect the flood of selling to occur on the exact target date day. Maybe the big shareholders won't rush to sell. The selling may not occur at all. It might get spread out over several days or weeks. Or it might be arranged "upstairs" at a brokerage beforehand as a series of big block transactions. In this case, the trades might not have an impact on the market price since the details were worked out in advance and the agreed on price is about the same as what the stock is going for in the market. The bottom line is there is no certainty that a lockup release will have an impact on a stock price. This is why it can be risky to count on this strategy to short stocks.

- Fairly often, the lockup release will be timed to coincide with a positive event like an earnings release or some news release. This means that the big shareholders can sell into the enthusiasm generated by the positive news event. Either they get more for their shares than they otherwise would because the stock is higher, or their selling has less of an impact on the price of the stock because of the buying pressure. If that's the case, you might not get a bargain out of the lockup release.

- It is probably better to use the decline in a stock caused by a lockup release as a way to pick an entry point into a long-term position in a stock rather than for trading—simply because it is so tough to win at trading.

- Even if you don't use lockup releases to pick an entry point for a stock, knowing that a release is under way for one of your stocks can help explain a sudden surge in volume or a price decline that would otherwise make you nervous. In fact, if you notice one of your stocks falling sharply on big volume when there is no news, there is a chance that there may be a lockup release. It pays to check, especially now that you know how to do so without too much trouble.

Plenty of web sites help you keep track of stocks that have recently come on the market through an initial public offering (IPO). Here are some of them.

Alert IPO (http://www.ostman.com)

Edgar Online (http://www.edgar-online.com)

IPO Central (http://www.ipocentral.com)

IPO Intelligence Online (http://www.ipo-fund.com)

IPO Interactive (http://www.fedfil.com/ipo/index.html)

IPO Maven (http://www.investools.com/cgi-bin/Library/mavn.pl)

USA Today's list of weekly IPOs (http://www.usatoday.com/money/mipo.htm)

Yahoo's IPO News (http://biz.yahoo.com/reports/ipo.html)

CHAPTER 11

THE RUSSELL
RESHUFFE

Each year around the end of June, a lot of small-cap stocks start bouncing around like crazy. The reason has little to do with earnings or the management behind the stocks. It has everything to do with a small company in Washington State that advises pension funds on how to pick money managers.

The firm is called the Frank Russell Company. As you might suspect from the name, it is the group behind the well-known Russell stock indexes. Although they are not quite as famous as the S&P 500 or the Dow Jones Industrial Average, the Russell indexes are probably familiar to you. They are often cited in the media when journalists are talking about stock market performance.

More importantly, for the purposes of the investment strategy outlined in this chapter, the Russell indexes are used for another end. Originally, they were designed as yardsticks for Frank Russell when deciding which funds to recommend. But over time they have become the list of stocks that many passively managed index funds use to create their portfolios. These funds mimic the Russell indexes, just as other index funds match the stocks in the S&P 500.

This means that whenever stocks are added to or deleted from the Russell groupings, index fund managers have to make the same adjustments. All that money moving in and out of the stocks over a limited number of trading days drives up the prices of stocks being added and pushes down the prices of those being taken out. The effect can be dramatic. Especially so, for the Russell 1000, which is made up of small- and mid-cap companies. But the impact on Russell 2000 stocks can be big, as well. In recent years, the stocks being added to one of these indexes outperformed those taken out by as much as 18% in the two months before the changes were made final.

One reason for the big moves is that these stocks tend to lack "liquidity." Because they are so small, there are not as many buyers or sellers compared with the market for stock in a big company like Microsoft. So when a lot of buyers or sellers actually *do* turn up, because of the annual Russell reshuffle, the stock prices of these little companies react in a big way. They get pushed up and down quite a bit.

Wouldn't it be nice to know in advance which stocks are leaving and joining the indexes? Well, you *can* find out ahead of time because the Frank Russell Company releases a rough draft of the changes in advance. However, making money off this knowledge is not easy. You can take advantage of the Russell reshuffle, but it is riskier than you might think, and you have to go about it in the right manner. It is not as simple as buying the stocks going in and shorting the ones being taken out. Before we get to the most effective strategies, it helps to know more about the annual rebalancing process, so that you can understand how best to profit from it.

First, it is easy to see why these indexes have to be modified each year. Frank Russell picks the stocks for the indexes on the basis of market capitalization. So as companies grow or shrink, they have to be put in or booted out of the indexes. The biggest 3,000 U.S. stocks go into what is called the Russell 3000 index (foreign stocks are excluded). That group is then divided into the Russell 1000, which are the biggest thousand stocks in the pool. The remaining names are the Russell 2000.

Each year, a huge amount of money flows in and out of stocks simply because they are added to or removed from the indexes. This explains the wild price moves. How much? Merrill Lynch analyst Satya Pradhuman estimates that over $100 billion in assets are indexed to the Russell benchmarks, above all the Russell 3000, and its two subcomponents, the Russell 2000 and the Russell 1000. (Russell subdivides those indexes into growth and value versions.)

Much of that money is invested in the smaller names on the lists. These are the ones that tend to move the most when they are added or deleted—because the markets for these stocks are so illiquid. Pradhuman estimates that more than $14 billion is indexed to the smaller-cap Russell 2000, either directly or indirectly through the Russell 3000. Russell 2000 stocks typically have a market cap of between about $200 million and $2 billion. (Russell 1000 stocks have a market cap of between $1.4 billion and $300 billion, about the same size as S&P 500 stocks.)

The large amount of money moving in and out of these stocks has a big effect on their prices. In 1997, stocks being added to the Russell 2000 outperformed those being taken off by 18% between the beginning of May and the end of June, when the changes are made final. The year before, the difference was 14%, says David Cushing, of ITG Research, an investment advisory firm. And in 1995 it was 12%.

THE MYTH OF SMALL COMPANY GROWTH: BIGGER MAY BE BETTER AFTER ALL

Many books on investing assure you that small-cap stocks outperform the big ones. Just look at the long-term data, they say. True, if you consider the last 40 years or so, small-cap stocks do seem to outperform. And it makes sense to look at such a big stretch of time, since investors should have a long-term horizon. Take a closer look, however, and you can see why this reasoning is misleading. The long-term comparisons are distorted by the fact that small-cap stocks beat large-cap stocks by a lot between 1973 and 1983. But most of the other years, small companies either underperformed or beat large-cap stocks by only a small margin, point out analysts at the brokerage Donaldson, Lufkin & Jenrette.

Moreover, the conditions that helped small-cap stocks do so well during their golden decade of the 1970s might not ever return. What was it about that decade that gave small-cap stocks such a boost? In a word, inflation. When prices are moving up, costs usually are, too. Managers at big companies try to trim corporate fat to take care of the problem, but this does not help enough. So to ease the pressure on the bottom line, big companies join the crowd and raise prices as well.

This is a dream come true for small companies. Why? Because they are typically better at controlling costs than big firms. So when inflation is high, the lean and mean small firms are able to make use of one of their best competitive weapons: lower prices. This helps them grab market share from the big companies, which are hamstrung by their large cost structures. That is exactly what happened in the 1970s, which explains why small-cap stocks did so well during that decade. It also explains why they have lagged in so many other years—when prices were not moving up as fast.

(continues)

Will inflation ever get as high as it was during the 1970s, bringing back the rollicking times for small companies? No one knows for sure, of course. But until inflation returns, it will remain difficult for small companies to outperform by seducing customers away with lower prices. And if prices are *stable* or there is deflation, things will be worse for many small companies. Whenever firms have a hard time raising prices, managers put even more emphasis on cost cutting to boost profits. This kind of environment gives big companies the advantage because they typically have more fat to cut out than smaller companies.

Why does the Russell effect start to take place long before the list is finalized at the end of June? Part of the reason is that companies like ITG try to predict which stocks are coming and going way in advance. This is not too hard, because the criteria Frank Russell uses are an open book. Don't worry if you can't do the work yourself. Frank Russell itself releases a preliminary list in the middle of June. Just about all those stocks end up on the final list.

Once the stocks finish moving when changes to the indexes are finalized at the end of June, most of the movement in their prices then reverses. But this is not always the case. In 1996 the entire 14% gap in performance that had opened up between adds and deletes was reversed in just 12 trading days after the end of June, according to ITG. But in 1997, only about seven percentage points of the 18% difference was reversed by the end of July.

Typically, stocks being added to the indexes are those whose share prices have come up a lot, increasing the market cap for the stock. They also tend to be initial public offerings, or firms spun off from others. Stocks being deleted are often—but not always—fallen angels. These are companies whose stock price decline shrank their market caps so much that they are no longer among the 3,000 largest companies. Just because a stock is on the delete list, however, does not mean you should sell it.

HOW TO PROFIT FROM THE RUSSELL RESHUFFLE

You don't need expensive investment advisors to help you figure out which stocks are being added and deleted. The preliminary list is available in the middle of June at Frank Russell's website at www.russell.com. Typically, about 95% of these stocks will be on the final version that comes out at the end of June.

This makes things easy enough for speculators. But the story gets better. Most of the movement in stock prices caused by the Russell reshuffle happens in the two weeks after the preliminary list is published in the middle of June, says Steve Kim, the manager of U.S. equities derivative research at Merrill Lynch. The biggest part of the change is concentrated in the last week of June. This is because the charters of mutual funds that match the Russell indexes don't allow them to make the adjustments too far in advance, even though companies like Merrill Lynch and ITG Research are fairly adept at predicting who will be on the list, weeks in advance.

Speculators have something else working in their favor. After the lists are finalized at the end of June and the stocks have finished moving, those price changes typically reverse completely over the following 10 trading days, or the first two weeks in July. All of this makes it seem like playing the Russell reshuffle would be a lay-up. Just go long stocks being added and short those being taken out. Then reverse those positions at the end of June.

Unfortunately, things are not that easy. First of all, not every stock that gets added will go up as a result. And not every stock being taken out goes down. Furthermore, since several hundred stocks move in and out each year, it is impossible to solve this problem by simply playing them all. What's more, it is hard to predict which addition will move up, because Frank Russell does not list the weighting each new stock will have in its indexes. So it is tough to know how much demand there will be from the index funds for each of the stocks being added.

There are other pitfalls to trading Russell reshuffle stocks for a quick profit. For example, suppose you buy some of the stocks being added and then the sector they are in—or the whole market—tanks. The stocks that make up your speculative position are likely to get hit worse. Why? First, the chances are good that your gamble was made on smaller-cap stocks—since many of the changes made to the Russell indexes occur at the low end of the market cap range. And you might have been attracted to smaller stocks anyway because they are less liquid, which exaggerates the Russell effect.

But precisely because those stocks are less liquid, they will probably get hammered more than most stocks if that sector or the market tanks. Suddenly, your short-term speculative play will be way under water. Even if these kinds of problems don't arise, you face other hurdles. One is that trading in and out of many of the Russell reshuffle stocks will be costly, since these small-cap stocks usually have huge bid-ask spreads. Despite these kinds of problems, you can work the Russell index reshuffle in your favor. Here are the best ways to do so.

TIPS ON USING THE RUSSELL RESHUFFLE

If you were already thinking about buying a stock that pops up on the "add" list in the middle of June, do it as soon as possible. The chances are good its price will go up, and you don't want to miss out on that part of the ride. Yes, it may come back down after the reshuffle. But maybe it won't. In any case, consider it a good omen that your stock is joining a Russell index. The stock is more likely to have decent support in the future as a result. Being part of an index draws attention to the stock. It also means that more stable owners—the index funds—will be among your fellow shareholders.

If you own a stock that turns up on the delete list and you still believe in the company, hang on to it. The chances are the stock will rebound after it gets hit by Russell reshuffle selling, although this is not always true. Trying to trade in and out around the dip probably won't make sense for tax reasons. You will also lose the difference between the bid and the ask spreads for the stock—spreads that will be high if it is a small stock. Besides, what if the company announces good news, and the stock shoots up while you are on the sidelines? "If you are a long-term investor, you should just wait it out, if you still believe in the fundamentals," says Kim. Or add to your position.

It is good to be aware that your stock is on the delete, however. This will help explain why the price is bouncing around so much. Don't forget that the fact that your stock is getting booted out of a Russell index may be a bad sign. After all, some kind of problem must have reduced the stock's price and, therefore, its market cap. But don't jump to the conclusion that something is wrong. Stocks can drift down even when there are no problems. And stocks that are down, of course, can be good turnaround candidates or value plays. Just be sure you know the story, and be sure you can see a potential catalyst that will bring the stock back.

If you were thinking about buying a stock that appears on the delete list, consider waiting until the last week of June, when it may go on sale. Presumably, you already know why the stock took the plunge that brought down the market cap and led to its exile from the Russell index. And you are also reasonably sure the stock is only suffering from temporary problems.

Although the Russell reshuffle has a bigger impact on less liquid stocks with low trading volume, this does not necessarily make them the best plays. It is often better to consider the bigger market cap stocks that are part of the reshuffle. They are more likely to be bought by an index fund trying to match the Russell universe, notes Prudential Securities small-cap analyst Claudia Mott. The charters of small-cap index funds don't always require them to buy *all* of the stocks in the Russell indexes. That being said, you should probably focus on the Russell 2000 stocks, as opposed to the Russell 1000 list. The Russell 2000 is the index that is most widely matched by index funds or benchmarked by actively managed funds. Some of the best action is among stocks being put on a Russell list for the first time, as opposed to those graduating because their market cap grew.

NEW YEAR'S IN NOVEMBER

For years, investment analysts noticed a curious thing about small-cap stocks in January. Inevitably, they did better than large-cap shares. Between 1925 and 1998, for example, small caps outperformed more than 75% of the time during the first month of the year, according to Claudia Mott at Prudential Securities. This pattern was soon dubbed the "January effect." What was behind it? Most market watchers put it down to tax-loss selling at the end of the year. Small-cap stocks got oversold in December. Then they would spring back in January.

By the end of the 1990s, however, widespread publicity about the January effect toned it down and led to a "December effect" instead. Investors trying to exploit the January effect began buying small-cap stocks in December, pushing up the prices of these shares and making them outperform in the last month of the year.

But the real play on tax-loss selling of small-cap stocks—which get hit harder by this than big caps because of their low liquidity—is actually in neither of these months. As mutual funds have grown to be such a force in the market, it's *their* tax-loss selling of small-cap stocks that really matters. Mutual funds, however, do their selling in October, the month when their fiscal year ends. Small-cap stocks recover the following month, giving rise to the "November effect."

The biggest price movements tend to occur in the two weeks before the changes are made final. This is the last two weeks in June. During that time, more of the action occurs in the second week. "That is when the spike in volume occurs," says Kim. In July, the stocks revert, as the selling and buying pressure dwindle. The price movements often start happening as early as April because investment advisory firms like ITG are making predictions about what stocks are being added and deleted.

Making an outright bet on the Russell reshuffle is risky. For all of the reasons discussed above, the Russell effect is never a sure thing for any single stock. "It is inherently risky. And it is definitely not easy to make money off of this," says ITG's Cushing. "There are a lot of moving parts. So you really have to devote a lot of time and research to getting it right." Kim, from Merrill Lynch, has the same view. "There is definitely risk. This is not easy money. But at the end of the day, it is risk that can be rewarded."

PART THREE

ADVANCED INVESTMENT TACTICS

CHAPTER 12

INVESTING IN
ROLL-UPS

$\mathbf{H}$ave you ever watched in astonishment as a stock jumped after a merger announcement–and then privately worked out the math on what you would have made *if you had only known?* Most likely, the answer is "yes." If so, you are not alone. Because of the fantastic run-ups of takeover candidates, many investors spend a lot of time trying to figure out who will be the next target. They do extensive research and scout out rumors. Then they take positions and pray their stock will be next.

This is a bad way to invest in mergers. More often than not, the stock you thought was going to be bought ends up getting passed over. Before this becomes clear, the rumors fade, the speculative money leaves, and the stock declines. The speculator is left holding a losing position in a company he doesn't really know much about.

There is a much better way to invest in mergers. While the big deals are grabbing all the headlines, a lot of much smaller companies are methodically piecing together a burgeoning empire by following a well-mapped-out strategy of consolidating a sector.

Although the much smaller deals might not grab the media attention, these are the real merger plays you want to be in on. The consolidators often put together impressive growth stories that can be quite lucrative for investors. These consolidations or roll-ups, as they are also known, won't give you a 20% return overnight. But it is not uncommon for them to double or triple in a year or two.

To get those kinds of returns, however, you can't just invest in any old consolidation play you come across. The first rule of thumb used by professional money managers is to look for something more than a company that is simply stacking up revenue streams by buying lots of smaller firms. The second thing to be aware of is that a lot of roll-ups that look good end up flaming out. To help you figure out how to find the ones that are likely to pay off, several investment bankers and analysts explained what they look for when putting together successful deals.

Before that, some background. Typically, roll-ups are spawned by a venture capital firm that lays the groundwork and then sets the process in motion. First, the financiers handpick managers to lead the fledgling company. Next, they provide some of the initial financing. "Then we go out and methodically buy and build," says Bruce Rauner of GTCR Golder Rauner LLC. GTCR is a Chicago-based venture capital firm that has designed and helped carry out scores of roll-ups since it started doing them.

"We were among the first in the very early 1980s to focus on industry consolidation, which we look at as backing especially proven management teams to acquire small companies to build a dominant competitor through acquisition, then internal growth," says Rauner. "When we go into an industry we try to be the number one, two, or three player in that sector over time. Typically, it takes about seven or eight years. We will commit $20 million to $60 million in equity for acquisitions, then the management arranges two to four times that in debt, so they have $100 million to $200 million in debt. That leaves them with a couple hundred million in total capital."

That money is used to make acquisitions. Once a company has reached critical mass, it is then taken public. While the venture capitalists may trim their position in the company at this point, they do not always sell out right away. That's because they know that a well-designed roll-up can continue to produce superior growth by buying up private mom-and-pop-type operations in their field.

Outstanding revenue and earnings growth won't occur, though, unless the roll-up has a well-thought-out plan. It has to be doing more than mere consolidation. "I want companies with a real strategy, not just a consolidator that is trying to build revenue by buying companies cheaply," says Richard Dowd, a managing director of the investment banking group at Wachovia Securities Inc. Firms that are simply accumulating business without a well-designed plan are known as "poof companies," says Dowd. Usually they are appropriately discounted in the market. This brings us to the first point you need to keep in mind about consolidation plays.

TIPS ON INVESTING IN ROLL-UPS

The roll-up must be redefining the business model in some way. "If all you are doing is playing musical chairs with the assets and stripping the costs out, it will be a limited investment opportunity," says Sheryl R. Skolnick, a BankBoston Robertson Stephens analyst who has evaluated many roll-ups. "Even if it works for a while, it won't work for long." Instead, says Skolnick, you should look for consolidation plays that redefine the company's business model in some way. "You have to change the economics of the business, not just aggregate cash flows," agrees Robert Chefitz, an investment banker who has worked on roll-ups as a partner at Patricof & Co. Ventures Inc.

Typically, a company will try to broaden its product line and branch out into related markets, notes Dowd. A common approach that often works well is to roll up companies that have similar, but slightly different, lines of products or services. The expanded portfolio of products or services then gets cross marketed throughout the new client base, which has grown because of the acquisitions. The consolidator uses the sales force or distribution channel from one company they buy to sell new products from other companies that are being rolled up. "We do that a lot with business outsourcing and information technology companies," says Rauner. "A new element of services gets sold into the new customer base. You fold it right into their system."

A good example is a company called Lason, a highly successful roll-up that Rauner's firm helped put together. The stock more than tripled in the two years after it was taken public in late 1996. The company started off as a traditional high-speed print-on-demand company. Through a series of acquisitions, it expanded into more sophisticated kinds of digital imaging, data manipulation, and printing. In essence, a roll-up like Lason that follows this strategy is building a one-stop shop. As an investor, you just want to make sure that all the new customers want to shop there. If the products and services being grouped together are too different, the one-stop shop will fail.

Another factor you want to look for when assessing a roll-up is whether the consolidation plays into a sector trend. During the 1990s many big companies were frustrated because they had to deal with dozens of small staffing services at the same time. They wanted to cut down their vendor list to simplify things, so they could negotiate with just one supplier in several regions. Companies like Corestaff or Accustaff were successful at consolidating the sector of staffing services and meeting that need.

At the same time, the roll-up might also be part of a strategy to change the business model or product mix to get higher margins. During Corestaff's roll-up, the company moved from simply providing recruiting and temporary placement services to managing teams of workers on a project basis. "They moved up the food chain to where the margins are higher and the relationship to clients are longer term," says Rauner. These are all good examples of how companies did a lot more than just piece together revenue streams.

Management is the key. This sounds like just another investing platitude. But roll-ups do require a special set of management skills that you had better see before buying shares in a consolidation play. Basically, you want to see a management team that has experience at both *negotiating* the deals and *integrating* them afterward.

"If they are only deal guys and they do not know how to grow a business, it will not work," says Skolnick. How can you tell? Look at the backgrounds of the managers and see what kind of experience they have. "If the guy at top is a deal guy and the chief operating officer is someone who has been growing businesses from scratch, that reduces the risk that there will be problems."

And make sure the team has experience in running big enough businesses. "There are people who are great entrepreneurs and good at growing a business from a standing start to $100 million in revenue a year. But they are not the same management team that can get the business from $100 million to $500 million or $1 billion." Skolnick also likes to see situations in which the operating team has a strong voice in the decisions about what gets bought, if not the final say. "It's the operating team that has to live with the potential problems in the deal."

One other thing. It is important that the managers have experience in the field. Again, this sounds obvious. But many investment bankers try to put together deals led by managers brought in from another sector. When you see this, move on to another investment opportunity.

The roll-up must be done in an appropriate sector. First, of course, the sector has to be fragmented. Ideally, it should contain a lot of mom and pop shops. But the sector also has to be big enough to make a consolidation play worthwhile.

Second, you should avoid roll-ups in sectors that don't have decent growth. It is easy to fall into this trap, since a lot of industries are consolidating precisely because there is shrinking demand. But you should stay away from roll-ups motivated by a slump in business. "You want to avoid these because you will constantly be battling the trend," notes Rauner.

Indeed, it is important to look for some kind of economic or demographic pattern that favors the roll-up. The staffing companies in the 1990s, for example, benefited from labor shortages caused by strong economic growth. Outsourcing of business services was a hot sector for much of the 1990s when downsizing and cost cutting were so important. A roll-up of pharmacies serving nursing homes would benefit from the aging population.

Because roll-ups require a lot of borrowing, avoid cyclical or recession-prone industries. The leverage will kill your investment in an economic downturn. Natural resources and auto manufacturer supply are good examples of sectors to stay away from because they are cyclical.

You should also avoid sectors where there is concentration of customers. You don't want to see one or two clients accounting for a big percentage of the revenue. Again, the auto supply business is an example. "We like to have locked in customers, but we like them to be dependent on us and not vice versa," says Rauner.

Some of the more successful roll-ups have been in the more mundane industries. The less complex a business is, the less complicated it is to integrate it. But stay away from sectors where firms do not have a franchise or decent barriers against competitors. Many parts of the retail sector fit into this category. Companies in video rental, for example, do not really have any barriers to entry because there are alternative distribution methods—and new ones will develop. This does not mean you should rule out all distribution businesses, since many of them have made for profitable roll-ups.

Steer clear of roll-ups that are consolidating a sector because companies in the group are cheap. Companies are usually cheap for a reason. "When I hear management teams come forth and say, 'I can collect these assets at a really low value,' I want to know why it is that a person who has spent the blood, sweat, and tears of his life on a business wants to sell out so cheap," says Skolnick. "If they want out, there has got to be a real good reason." On the other hand, it is true that the promoters of a roll-up can often get good business at great prices. They can take advantage of the shortage of buyers and lack of liquidity for the companies being rolled up. They sometimes even get good prices by taking advantage of the lack of sophistication of the entrepreneurs selling their businesses.

Finally, there needs to be enough homogeneity among the products and customers in the consolidation play. A GTCR roll-up of companies that make hydraulic pumps and pneumatic devices fell through in part because it could not clear this hurdle. The sector seemed like a good candidate because it was very fragmented. "And there were role models or companies in the field that were public and had grown, which we like to see," says Rauner. But the producers and customers in the roll-up were too diverse. The raw material inputs varied from firm to firm. There were different production methods and types of distribution channels. The sales forces and end users of the various products were not enough alike. "So it was difficult to integrate them and get economies of scale," says Rauner. "Finding the synergies was challenging and it distracted management. We ended up losing most of our money."

Look for the cost savings. Good old-fashioned economies of scale and cost cutting are key factors behind the success of many roll-ups, even if they should never be the raison d'être. You should look for several tactics designed to reduce costs. When you put a lot of little companies together, for example, you get increased buying power and volume discounts. Roll-ups also enjoy savings from the centralization of back-office functions and the consolidation of production. Marketing gets more efficient when you fill up the bags of salespeople with more products. In many cases it is simply a lot cheaper to buy a production facility than start one up from scratch. If distribution is involved, you can get savings when trucks going down the same street anyway make more deliveries on the same route.

Consolidations also have the advantage of being able to put a lot of managers together to "bench mark" and compare "best practices," to trot out some old management consultant phrases. This means getting them to talk about the tricks they use to motivate their staff, optimize their fleet of trucks, for example, or make improvements in other ways. When there are hot margins in one section of the company, managers examine what is going on to see where else the practices behind those margins can be applied.

Cost cutting should not be taken for granted. It takes a lot of effort, and it does not happen overnight. Sometimes it does not happen at all, and the whole thing ends up as a disaster.

"What you find is that even the best-managed consolidations have to work like heck to keep their overhead flat," says Rauner. "Without constant battling, it ends up creeping up. After an acquisition you find yourself with a new location and another set of financial reports. So you add two more accountants, an information technology person, another salesperson, and two more people for the phones. Pretty soon the overhead is a lot higher. You bought some nice small companies, but you just lay on another line of overhead. Things get more bureaucratic and bogged down, the entrepreneurial spirit gets lost, and you generally have a mess." In short, don't simply assume there will be cost savings. Managers will have to work for them.

Check to see whether the owners and managers who are getting bought out have strong incentives to perform and stay with the new company. The worst thing you can find is that the owners are given most of the payment for their business in the form of cash up front. This is an invitation to go into semi-retirement and let the business coast. "Most business owners who want to sell think this is what happens," says Patrick Boroian, a general partner in the Sprout Group, which is a venture capital division of Donaldson, Lufkin & Jenrette. "The reality is very few consolidations that are done this way actually work. The owners won't execute the plan if they are not locked in with the right incentives." Boroian says you should look for a combination of cash, stock that the managers are restricted from selling for a few years, and performance-based notes.

If unmade acquisitions are already built into the earnings estimates, move on to another investment opportunity. "Most of the time when roll-ups come public, they do so with unnamed and indeterminable acquisitions in the earnings estimates," says Skolnick. "Management, investment bankers, and analysts buy the theory that you have to have those acquisitions in the number."

This is not good, because conditions can change before the acquisition is made. The capital markets might weaken, lowering the value of the buyer's stock, which is used as part of the purchase package. Other companies bidding for the same targets drive up the prices. Or maybe management cannot integrate the previous acquisition fast enough. "For whatever reason, the company fails to make an acquisition on time," says Skolnick. Then a vicious circle develops. The stock price goes down, which makes it harder for them to make more acquisitions. And so the story falls apart.

Because of this pitfall, be sure the earnings estimates for the roll-up are based on what the company owns today. If that is the case, whenever the company makes an acquisition that adds to earnings, the stock price will eventually go up as a result. How do you know if unmade deals are in the estimates? Look in the analysts' reports. You won't find this information in the company's SEC documents.

But be wary of the Wall Street research on roll-ups. Keep in mind that consolidations consume enormous amounts of capital. This means they make use of a lot of investment banking services. Remember, too, that Wall Street analysts who write research reports have an interest in investment banking deals. They often get a percentage of the fees charged by the investment banking side of their brokerage (see Chapter 1). This means the analysts have an extra incentive to talk up consolidation plays. Not all analysts exaggerate when they write reports on companies, but they will be more tempted when they cover a roll-up. If projected growth for the company is 50% a year but its sector is only growing at 5%, something is wrong. When looking at reports on roll-ups, be familiar with the style and experience level of the analyst. Young analysts can be overly enthusiastic. They love roll-ups because they are rapidly growing companies that are fun to talk about. They have not had one blow up in their face yet.

The smarter, more experienced investor knows there is always some problem lurking that can make them collapse. The cultures of the companies being put together might not match. This causes a lot of turnover that drags the whole thing down. Maybe the roll-up is just a consolidation for the sake of consolidation, with no strategy to redefine the economics of the business. Often, what comes back to bite the consolidator is accounts receivable that turn out to be uncollectable. This and other surprises are usually the result of sloppy due diligence—which often occurs when companies are desperate to buy because they need to make the analysts' estimates. "It is a big red flag when companies start making too many acquisitions that were not in the plan, because they need to meet the numbers," says Skolnick. For every highly successful consolidation play, there are 20 that are tremendous disasters. "And when they go down, they really flame," says Skolnick.

CHAPTER 13

INVESTING IN IPOS

W ho hasn't watched in awe as an initial public offering (IPO) takes off like a bottle rocket? Consider MarketWatch.com which jumped more than 470% on its first day of trading in early 1999. Or how about eBay Inc., which came public at $18 a share and traded for over $280 within seven months?

The Internet stocks like these two stand out. As a group, they shot up more than 80% on average their first day in 1998. But IPO joyrides are not limited to stocks stricken with dot com fever. The typical IPO, which happens when a privately held company decides to raise money by selling shares to the public, moves up as much as 15% to 30% on its first day.

If you have been captivated by these kinds of returns and you want in on the action, don't get your hopes up too fast. Unless you are a high roller or an institutional investor, you aren't likely to get your hands on a lot of IPO shares. And if you *can* get easy access, the shares *are probably not worth buying.*

Brokers typically know ahead of time which IPO shares are going to rocket, and they save them for preferred customers who have a record of generating lots of commission revenue. When a new stock is destined to take off, the shares end up serving as the currency by which investment bankers and brokers pay off old favors or drum up new business.

It may not sound fair, but that's the way Wall Street works. True, you may be able to get small blocks of IPO shares if you have a brokerage account with a balance of around $50,000 to $100,000. Otherwise, you will most likely be on the outside looking in. There are a lot of reasons why that may not be such a bad place to be, however, if you are an individual investor. And keep in mind that there are many ways to successfully invest in IPOs even if you are not in on the first allotment of shares. More on that later in this chapter.

First, to understand why hot IPO shares are hard to get your hands on unless you have the right connections, it helps to know a little bit about investment banking. In IPOs, private companies are taken public by "underwriters," a syndicate of investment banks made up of a lead bank and several others who were signed up to spread the risk around.

When a company is going public, the investment bankers doing the deal face the ticklish job of determining what the shares in the new company are "worth" and then placing them in the market for that price or better. The job is risky because if the stock goes too far above where the investment banks had priced the deal, the company going public will not be happy. The issuer wanted to raise as much cash as possible, and it will think it could have gotten more money for the shares if only the bankers had done a better job of pricing the stock. Once there are too many unsatisfied customers like these, the investment bank will find it harder to get more business in the future.

On the other hand, if the market pays less than expected, or it doesn't absorb all the shares, the investment bank is stuck with the difference. It has to keep the shares and pay the new company for them out of its own pockets. Plus, the investors who bought the shares from the brokerage side of the investment bank will be disappointed.

All of this gives investment banks an incentive to lowball the price of the IPO shares—as long as they don't price them so low that they annoy the issuer. Because of this potential to err either way when setting the price, you can be sure that plenty of sleepless nights are spent worrying about how to value shares in a company that is going public. In exchange for all this trouble, investment banks believe they should have the right to distribute hot shares from juicy deals to whomever they please.

"That's what investment banking is all about," explains Richard Sylla, a professor of economics and financial history at New York University's Stern School of Business. "A key aspect of this is that the underwriters get all the shares, and they have a right to distribute the shares as they see fit. If their own clients want to buy them all, then why should they give them to someone else? The underwriters are the ones who took all the risk."

The risks can be very real. Sylla points out that investment bankers carrying out IPOs in 1979, for example, took a bath when Federal Reserve Chairman Paul Volcker raised interest rates. That sent money into the bond markets and tanked stocks, making it impossible for the banks to get what they thought they could for the shares in the companies they were taking public. But even in placid markets, pricing an IPO is tricky. So when a deal goes well, investment banks think they have a right to keep the shares in the family.

The clubby nature of all this may make you want to set up a big enough account somewhere so that you get access to IPO shares. Many investment advisors point out, however, that the real question is not how to get IPO shares, but whether you should even want to. History clearly shows that on average, IPO shares are a very risky bet.

Does this sound like sour grapes? Then consider some research. A study of 513 companies that went public in 1992 found that most of them made their highest profits ever in the year just before, or after, the IPO. From then on, it was downhill for way more than half of these companies. This should not be surprising. You would expect companies to go public at a point when they can show off their best numbers—and get the most for their shares. Profits at more than 75% of the companies in the study declined within two years of the IPO, according to the research by David L. Babson & Co. portfolio manager Peter Schliemann. And 25% of the companies went into the red at some point in the two years following the IPO.

There are other compelling reasons to think twice about getting into IPOs. Study after study shows that well more than half of them trade below their initial offering price six months to a year after they go public. And things don't necessarily get much better if you hold on and wait. The average IPO underperforms the Russell 3000 Index (the 3,000 largest market cap U.S. companies) by 30% in the three years after it comes public, according to University of Florida finance professor Jay Ritter. Another study by Ritter found that five-year returns for 4,653 IPO stocks issued between 1970 and 1990 earned just 15.7% on average, compared with 66.4% gains for similar kinds of companies that were more established. Typically, after five years more than half of all IPOs traded below their offer price. They also tend to fall faster than other stocks when the markets crash.

With results like those, why struggle to get into IPO stocks? Well, you might think, because you can sell in the first few days and profit from the initial run-up! Let some other fool worry about the poor odds for IPOs as time goes by. Unfortunately, this is not a good answer. If you do happen to get hold of an IPO that rockets out of the gate, it will surely bring you frustration rather than easy riches. Why? Because the chances are that your broker won't let you sell it.

Most brokers discourage retail investors from "flipping" IPO shares, or selling them right away. Brokers don't want a lot of selling, they say, because they want to stabilize the market for the new stock. Too much volatility can upset shareholders and executives at the issuing company, and this threatens future investment banking business. (Meanwhile, the big institutional investors, who the investment banks don't want to alienate, are allowed to dump the shares into the rally for big profits.)

ONLINE BROKERS: BRINGING IPO SHARES TO THE PEOPLE?

The Internet has been the great equalizer in many ways, but not when it comes to IPO shares.

Online brokerages like Charles Schwab, E*Trade, Fidelity, DLJ Direct, and Wit Capital have all trumpeted the offering of IPO shares to their customers. Investors who have signed up hoping to get their hands on hot IPO shares can be forgiven if it all seemed like just another marketing ploy.

For starters, you probably have to have an account worth $50,000 to $100,000 to qualify. You might also have to be an active (fee-generating) trader. Next, investors who qualify typically find that the amount of IPO shares available is so small that they disappear fast. If you end up being one of the lucky ones, you probably won't get more than a hundred shares or so. For this, you can't really fault your online broker. It only gets a small block of shares to begin with, since the lead underwriters like to hog them—especially if the deal looks good.

Finally, despite the wild and woolly ways of the Internet, the online brokers who make it their home are downright old and stodgy when it comes to IPO shares. Like their button-down brethren at the brick and mortar brokerage houses, Internet-based brokers frown on selling IPO shares for a quick profit. Most of them bar "flipping" IPO shares for 30 or 60 days. If you break the rules, you will get hit with special fees and barred from future deals.

The online brokers come down hard on IPO investors who sell too soon because they know very well that if too many of their customers do this, the brokerage itself will be shut out of future deals, too.

The cold reality for investors using online brokerage accounts is that IPO shares are hard to come by. And when they do manage to get them, it is hard to turn a quick profit because they can't sell them right away.

Normally, brokers don't let individual investors sell until about 60 days after the IPO. And the brokers take it seriously when you break the rules. They will hit you with special fees for your sales and shut you out of future IPO deals. The brokers themselves are being watched by their firms to make sure they keep their customers in line. Many brokers are ranked on the basis of how long their clients stay in IPOs. Brokers whose customers sell too early will lose their commissions for the sales, and they'll get fewer IPO shares to distribute in the future. Critics of this system claim that the rules against flipping are a form of market manipulation. When underwriters prevent shares from being traded freely, the theory goes, they can price the IPOs above their market value.

The issue has attracted a lot of public attention, and policy makers may eventually take steps to change the rules of the game. Even if they don't, you should not let the apparent unfairness in the IPO market force you to turn away and miss out on these stocks altogether. Many of them do quite well, and they are a good way to add some spark to your portfolio. Just remember that they should only be a small portion of your holdings–at most around 5% depending on your age and investment goals. IPOs, after all, are highly speculative because they are companies in the early stages of development. You can skew the odds of getting a successful one in your favor, however, if you carry out the right kind of research.

RESEARCHING AN IPO

One of the nice things about IPOs is that they are undercovered by Wall Street. This means that individual investors have a better shot at getting an edge if they are able to do a good job of understanding what is going on with the company. In some ways, figuring out an IPO can be easier than analyzing a big multinational that operates in many different sectors. At least the IPO only has a few products or services.

The first place to start is the prospectus. By law, a company going public is supposed to disclose all "material information" about itself in the prospectus. It is the most important document you can get from the company. Before a prospectus is approved by the Securities and Exchange Commission (SEC), a disclaimer stating that it has not been approved is printed in red on the cover. That's why it is called a "red herring" at this stage. Once you have the final version, you should look through the whole thing, but a few sections tend to be more important. Two of the best parts will be the sections labeled "The Company" and "The Business," which offer a description of the firm, its customers and the sector. Other parts of the prospectus called "Consolidated Financial Statements" and "Liquidity and Capital Resources" are useful because they can tell you how much cash is on hand, as well as other things you will need to judge the financial strength of the company.

Look out for the risk factors. Another part of the prospectus to check out is called "Risk Factors." Ignore the boilerplate language designed to help the company defend itself against lawsuits if its stock tanks. But look in this section, elsewhere in the prospectus, and in publicly available documents for the following most common risk factors. First, be wary of inexperienced management teams. Next, look into whether management has a clean background. This is not always easy to find out. But a search of a database like Lexis Nexis can help you see what managers have been up to in the past–and get you part of the way there. Ask around, if you have contacts.

While you're at it, check the company's background, too. You want to be careful with firms that have defaulted on debt. Any outstanding lawsuits should make you wary. Even if the company swears it is in the right, you can never really predict what a jury will do, assuming the matter will go before a jury. If the company has been losing money for five years or more, this is not a good sign. Another risk factor is excess customer concentration. There are no hard and fast rules on how much is bad, but whenever one customer accounts for more than 20% or 25% of revenue, investors start to get a little nervous. Finally, you may run into a "qualifications requirement" to invest in the company. This means the SEC thinks the stock is only suitable for high net worth individuals– another way of saying it is risky.

Look for venture capital backing. Studies have shown that IPOs which have venture capital backing perform better. When VC partners are on the board, the company will probably have better contacts in the business world. This means it is more likely to attract analyst coverage and get additional financing. Institutional investors are also more likely to put money into companies backed by venture capital partners. You should also look for big-name underwriters with a history of bringing successful deals to the market (see Tables 13.1 and 13.2)..

Get some feedback about the road show. One of the biggest disadvantages for individual investors is that they cannot attend the "road show" for an IPO. Also known as the dog and pony show, this is the series of presentations in which the banks and company managers

Table 13.1

The Top 10 Lead IPO Underwriters 1996 Through End of First Quarter, 1999

Manager	No. of Deals	Amount Raised ($bil)	Total Market Share	Change in Price from One Day After Offering to End of 1st Quarter 1999	Change in Price from Offer to End of 1st Quarter 1999
Goldman, Sachs	98	$19.2	14.58%	32.29%	91.34%
Morgan Stanley Dean Witter	99	24.0	18.27	25.73	74.05
Credit Suisse First Boston	45	5.9	4.47	15.23	36.72
Bear, Stearns	39	3.3	2.50	-3.58	33.28
BT Alex. Brown	88	4.9	3.75	3.30	25.02
Lehman Brothers	50	4.3	3.25	-2.35	19.37
Merrill Lynch, Pierce, Fenner & Smith	74	18.9	14.37	-3.43	14.24
Donaldson, Lufkin & Jenrette	66	7.0	5.33	-11.92	9.06
Bank of America Securities	80	3.4	2.60	-12.66	9.04
Salomon Smith Barney	71	7.3	5.58	-18.00	-6.86

Source: CommScan.

Table 13.2

The Top 10 Lead IPO Underwriters 1997 Through End of First Quarter, 1999

Manager	No. of Deals	Amount Raised ($bil)	Total Market Share	Change in Price from One Day After Offering to End of 1st Quarter 1999	Change in Price from Offer to End of 1st Quarter 1999
Goldman, Sachs	57	$10.4	12.21%	36.69%	106.63%
Morgan Stanley Dean Witter	62	17.0	19.85	26.80	91.95
Bear, Stearns	26	2.6	3.03	-9.67	46.95
Credit Suisse First Boston	34	4.4	5.12	11.53	37.95
Merrill Lynch, Pierce, Fenner & Smith	43	15.5	18.07	9.10	32.41
BT Alex. Brown	43	2.7	3.11	-0.95	28.33
Donaldson, Lufkin & Jenrette	43	4.8	5.6	-18.82	3.92
Prudential Securities	24	2.5	2.95	10.73	-6.69
Salomon Smith Barney	40	4.2	4.91	-21.64	-11.15
Freidman, Billings, Ramsey	17	2.9	3.32	-36.02	-32.17

Source: CommScan

pitch the new shares to institutional investors. "The prospectus is fine," says David Meese, an investment advisor with T. Rowe Price. "But it doesn't allow you to ask off-the-cuff questions and really understand management style like the road show." Fortunately for individual investors, as the Internet evolves, more and more online brokerages and companies going public are broadcasting parts of the road shows on the Web. This is no substitute for being there, but it's a step in the right direction.

Signs of a hot IPO. Several days before an IPO launches, there are a few signs to watch for that indicate it will be hot. The first is when the underwriter increases the price and number of shares in the offering. Another sign is that there are no shares available. Either of these means the company might be a big success, but they are not guarantees.

The behavior of the IPO on its first day tells you a lot about its long-term prospects. There are two basic rules: Avoid the IPOs that shoot up too much in their first day out, and stay away from those that get flipped excessively as well. IPOs with the biggest first-day price gains underperform the market by two to three percentage points a month in the following year, according to a study of 1,232 companies that came on the market between 1988 to 1995. The most heavily flipped IPOs also underperformed in the year after they came public, according to the study by Krigman, Shaw, and Womack.[1]

So the first thing to do when considering new issues is to focus on the Goldilocks IPOs–those that are "not too cold and not too hot" in their first trading day. Womack recommends zeroing in on IPOs that had gains of between 10% and 40% on their first day. Next, cut out those in which there was a lot of flipping. This is a little trickier to calculate, and you will need to have access to tick-by-tick volume data. First, add up all the large-block (10,000 shares or more) downside volume, or the blocks that traded on the bid. Then compare that to the total volume for the day. If it is greater than 30%, that is too much. This analysis is helpful because it tells you what the institutional investors were up to. "The smart investors, the institutions who have been to the road show and met with management, tend to be right," says Womack. "So it is important to observe what they do on the first day." Follow these two steps and you will double your chances of making good IPO investments, says Womack.

---

[1] Laurie Krigman, Wayne Shaw, and Kent Womack, "The Persistence of IPO Mispricing and the Predictive Power of Flipping," *Journal of Finance* (June 1999).

SOME OTHER TIPS ON GETTING INTO IPO STOCKS

It is very risky to buy an IPO on its first day. Here is the typical trajectory of an IPO. Often it will shoot up in a frenzy of trading on its first day out. Then it will hold on to those gains for anywhere from a few hours to a few months. After that, it will come back down to earth. Because of this pattern, it is generally better to wait and let the dust settle before taking a position in an IPO. If you buy during the first days of trading at a big premium over the offering price, the chances are very high that your position will be under water over the next 12 months. It often makes more sense to follow the popular IPOs and buy when they fall below a price that is 10% above the offering price. In other words, avoid getting caught up in the hoopla that surrounds an IPO. Once the hype machine is turned off, the price will often come back down to levels that match the issue price.

Beware of fad IPOs. Theme restaurants like Planet Hollywood and shops like Manhattan Bagel are two examples of companies that played on a fad but then fizzled. When analyzing an IPO, ask yourself whether there are barriers to entry that block competitors.

Avoid the smaller IPOs. While it is true that over half of all IPOs trade below their offer price five years out, you can improve your odds considerably if you avoid the smallest ones. "An awful lot of the losers are the smaller ones," says Womack. "Typically, the littlest ones are the lowest quality." Womack recommends steering clear of any IPOs that start off with a market capitalization of less than $40 million.

Use limit orders. If you do enter the fray on opening day, use limit orders. These designate the highest price you will pay for a stock. Your order won't get filled unless the stock drops below your limit price. When theglobe.com came public, many novice investors got burned placing market orders. These put the stock in your hands at whatever the prevailing price is when your order hits the market. Using this approach with IPO shares that are bouncing around like mad on the first day of trading is the investment equivalent of roulette. Do this, and you are likely to get stuck with a price that is a lot higher than what you saw on your screen when you clicked on the "send" icon. Keep in mind that once you send in a market order through an online trading system, you most likely won't be able to cancel it before it hits.

There are some serious shortcomings to limit orders. First, your order gets put in a cue behind all the other limit orders. So even if the stock dips to the price you like, you won't necessarily get a fill. A similar obstacle is that market orders have priority over marketable limit orders. This also lessens your chances of getting a fill when only a limited number of shares trade at the price you want. Despite these drawbacks, you are still better off using limit orders in frenzied first-day trading in IPO shares, given the way prices move around so much under these conditions.

Wait for the lockup release. When companies come public, most of the big inside shareholders are blocked from selling their shares for three to six months. This lockup is put in place to help stabilize the market. When the lockup is lifted, a flood of shares from the insiders can push the IPO stock price down and create a good buying opportunity. But there is no guarantee this will happen. (For more information on this strategy, see Chapter 10.)

It's a bad sign if the underwriters do not issue a strong buy after the quiet period is over. About a month after a stock comes public, analysts who work for the brokerage side of the investment banks that underwrote the deal are allowed to speak openly about the company. You can assume that they will all issue strong buy recommendations. These are pretty meaningless, given that the investment banking side of the analyst's brokerage was the underwriter. It's when they *don't* issue a strong buy rating that you are getting a meaningful message. This is a warning that something is wrong. Often, once this quiet period is lifted and the analysts and managers are allowed to promote the stock, it will shoot up again at this point.

A "firm commitment" is better than a "best effort." Underwriters carry out two types of IPOs. The one they choose can speak volumes about how much confidence they have in the company. In a firm commitment IPO, the underwriter gives the company a certain amount of money per share outright. Then the underwriter turns around and sells those shares in the market. It hopes to sell them at a higher price than it paid, because the difference is part of the underwriter's payment for the job done. These deals usually have a "green shoe" over allotment option for about 10% to 15% of the amount issued, in case there is very strong demand.

In a best effort IPO, meanwhile, the underwriter says, "I will try to sell the shares, but I am offering no guarantee." Be careful with this kind of IPO. It means that no underwriters were willing to risk their own capital on the deal. If underwriters lack the confidence to do a firm commitment offering, there may be problems. Only the smaller underwriters will do best effort offerings.

Be wary of direct public offers, too. One step below the best effort offering is the IPO carried out directly by the company–without an underwriter. These direct public offers (DPOs), as they are called, are for deals worth less than $5 million. Companies raising money through DPOs can be perfectly fine investments. But for a number of reasons, you have to be even more cautious about these deals. For one thing, the lack of an underwriter means that the due diligence and deal structuring may not have been done according to the highest standards. What's more, DPOs often turn out bad because they lack the all-important distribution channels of the underwriters. Some DPOs try to get around this by using the Internet to make the offering, but it is no substitute.

At worst, a DPO can be a fraud. Beware of inflated claims under banner headlines stating the company is "the next Microsoft." Even if the company is legitimate, DPO stock can present another problem: poor liquidity for the shares. For these reasons, it is better to stick with IPOs listed on the major exchanges like Nasdaq or the New York Stock Exchange. Unless you really know what is going on, avoid the DPOs listed on the "Bulletin Board."

Diversify, diversify, diversify. IPOs can take you on a wild ride. To protect yourself against the emotional turmoil that comes from seeing your stocks bounce around too much—and to avoid losing a lot of your money—be sure to limit your exposure to IPO shares. How much you invest in them will depend on things like your tolerance for risk and the amount of time before you actually need the money you invest. Anyone who has a low threshold for volatility or who is close to retirement needs to tread lightly into IPO land. Since many IPOs grow up to be blue chip stocks in time, you probably should not avoid them altogether. Generally, however, limit your exposure to about 5% of your portfolio in IPO shares. More than that and you risk losing too much money or sleep, or both. Your first goal in investing should be to preserve capital and stay in the game. Making wild, concentrated bets on IPOs, or any stock for that matter, almost guarantees that you will be wiped out sooner or later.

Invest in IPO mutual funds or publicly traded venture capital funds. These funds eliminate the hassle of doing the research. They also provide diversification and give you access to those hard-to-get IPO shares on the first day. Mutual funds like RS Microcap Growth, Munder Microcap Equity, and Renaissance Capital's IPO Plus Aftermarket Fund offer substantial exposure to IPO shares. Investing in companies that are essentially publicly traded venture capital funds, like CMG Information, can also be a solution. Another example of this kind of company is Safeguard Scientifics. Unlike other public venture funds, Safeguard lets its shareholders buy the rights to invest in companies that Safeguard is developing. These rights are relatively cheap, and investors can either exercise them or sell them to someone else. You are allotted rights based on the number of Safeguard shares you own.

Finally, watch out for fraud. Be wary of recommendations from unsolicited e-mail, mail, or cold calls.

RESOURCES

Because researching initial public offers can be so challenging, we provide a list of resources that may be useful.

Alert IPO: E-mail alerts of recent filings. www.ostman.com/alert-ipo

CBS MarketWatch: Commentary and stock picks in its IPO section. www.cbs.marketwatch.com

Edgar Online: Real-time access to company filings with the SEC, e-mail alerts, and advance search capabilities.

Going Public: A newsletter. (212) 432-0045

IPO Central: A joint venture between Hoover's and Edgar Online that offers a list of the latest filings and advanced search techniques. www.ipocentral.com

IPO Data Systems: Another database of IPO filings and a list of upcoming IPOs. www.ipodata.com

IPO Intelligence Online: Research reports, stock picks and commentary from Renaissance Capital. www.ipo-fund.com

IPO Maven: Stories, interviews, alerts, and calendars. www.ipoMaven.com

IPO Monitor: E-mail alerts and Information on the latest offers. www.ipomonitor.com

The IPO Reporter: A newsletter. (212) 765-5311

IPO Spotlight: E-mail or fax alerts of upcoming deals. www.ipospotlight.com

Netroadshow.com: An Internet site where you can watch road shows.

New Issues: A newsletter edited by Norman Fosback. (800) 442-9000

Red Herring: A magazine with an online version at www.herring.com

(continues)

Securities and Exchange Commission Edgar database: Most company filings with a one- or two-day delay; search capabilities.
www.sec.gov

W. R. Hambrecht: An investment bank and brokerage that auctions IPO shares over the Internet. The company was started by William Hambrecht, the founder and former chief executive of the investment bank Hambrecht & Quist.
www.wrhambrecht.com

Yahoo! See the section called US IPOs.

CHAPTER 14

REVERSION TO
THE MEAN

In business school, they teach you that the stock markets are completely efficient. All public information about a company is fully reflected in a stock's price at all times, say the professors.

Many professional money managers know this is a lot of nonsense. They see that stock prices bounce around inexplicably all the time—regardless of whether or not there is news. And when there *is* news, you had better look out. Investors overreact and drive prices to extremes.

A lot of investors make money by taking advantage of these temporary price anomalies. Indeed, entire mutual funds are dedicated to this approach. They are based on the premise that when it comes to the stock markets, the business school professors have it all wrong. A fund that uses this strategy can earn decent returns, despite the trading costs involved.

A good example is the Larger Cap Value Fund, managed by the Numeric Investors, a firm based in Cambridge, Massachusetts, that uses quantitative analysis to pick stocks. Managers at the fund use sophisticated computers to spot undervalued stocks. Then they buy them, or short them, until they are fairly valued again.

Why is it that money managers can make money doing this? "Because the markets are not efficient. They are partially efficient," says Langdon Wheeler. Wheeler founded Numeric Investors in 1989 and helped develop the computer programs behind the Larger Cap fund. "It is not all machines yet. The markets are people and people get carried away. They are out there saying 'I have to buy because he is buying.' Or 'I have to sell because he is selling.'"

And that kind of emotion drives good stocks down to more attractive levels on a regular basis. "Prices slosh around quite a bit," says Wheeler, who studied engineering before starting a career in money management. "Just look at a price chart. You see all kinds of ups and downs when the fundamentals have not changed that much."

Taking advantage of these price anomalies is a bit more complicated than simply "buying the dips," as the strategy is sometimes described in the vernacular. There is more to it–both for you as an individual investor and for money managers. We will explain the best approach for individual investors below. First a look at how the pros do it.

To exploit market inefficiencies, Numeric Investors, which manages the n/i numeric investors family of funds, has developed a complex fair value model that runs on powerful computers. "We try to mathematically model the excesses of human behavior in the market," says Wheeler. The first step is to figure out the "fair value"–how much the market is usually willing to pay–for certain qualities that stocks can have. These qualities include things like book value, expected earnings, the growth rate, the quality or consistency of earnings, and the number of analysts covering a stock.

The market, for example, tends to pay less for volatile earnings that go up in a saw-toothed pattern. Companies that have more predictable earnings get a better financial score from a rating agency like Standard & Poor's, and the market pays up for that. It also puts a higher value on companies that are followed by more analysts. "Every time you double the number of analysts, the equilibrium price of a stock will go up 15%," says Wheeler. More analysts bring in more potential buyers. They also do a better job of getting news about a stock into the market. And these days, having more analysts also means having more "buy" ratings, since analysts are far less apt to issue sell or hold ratings than they once were.

Once the fair value model is up and running, Numeric Investors puts it to work in the following manner. "You figure out how the market prices all these factors each day," says Wheeler. "Then you go back and assign each factor a weight for each stock, and bingo! You have a theoretical price for each stock." The computers X-ray the stock market about once every 90 seconds to see if investors are underpricing any qualities of a company, like its earnings growth or book value. If so, traders at Numeric Investors buy the stock and then reverse the position once the stock is fairly valued again.

"We believe there are two forces in the market: overreaction and underreaction. Investors cause prices to bounce around too much, given the underlying information. And that creates mispricing that will correct over time," says Wheeler. "The market is not efficient, but it is efficient enough. It is seeking equilibrium. If you are good at figuring out what is being mispriced, then you can make a pretty good living out of it."

Usually, the kind of mispricing that the fund exploits is pretty small, but stocks get mispriced by large amounts, too. The fund focuses on the large-cap end of the market because the pricing errors in these kinds of stocks tend to correct more quickly. Despite what you may think, the strategy is not a matter of fast and furious day trading. Managers take positions in stocks expecting to hold them for three to six months.

Wheeler borrowed the idea for the fair value model from a basic concept he picked up as an engineering student: that systems tend to oscillate around central tendencies. Likewise, stocks that wander off the path for no reason usually get back in line. True, stock price movements tend to be more random than other systems in nature. But the "errors" you find in a stock price are more likely to correct than you might think, says Wheeler, who studied engineering at Yale before earning an MBA from Harvard. "Independent of any news announcements, there can be a one-sided market. The price adjustment reflects a momentary imbalance which is excessive, and it will move back." In statistics, the concept is known as *reversion to the mean*. Statisticians have shown that more often than not in nature, traits that depart from their norm tend to come back toward their average, or mean levels.

Sometimes, of course, the fair value model leads fund managers into a trap. Stocks, after all, *do* lose value because of bad news that is not yet circulating widely. "You know you are going to be wrong on some of them," says Wheeler. "But we rely on the law of large numbers." This means that if the odds of doing something are even slightly in your favor, you will come out ahead as long as you do it often enough. "You have to follow the discipline, if you have a discipline that works most of the time. Even a relatively small informational advantage applied over a large number of trials will get you a persistent outcome. Unless you can find what makes the model inapplicable, you have to do what the model says."

One advantage of the system is that it leads Numeric Investors fund managers to value in places where you would not expect them to find it. Says Wheeler: "We have a sharper understanding of the pricing of stocks, and the result is that we can be a value investor in stocks that most value investors would not understand." The system finds bargains not only among the typical down and dirty value stocks, but also among the quality growth stocks.

As an individual investor, you don't need to have complex computers to use a similar strategy. Here are some guidelines on the best way to exploit price anomalies in the market.

HOW TO EXPLOIT PRICE ANOMALIES

Keep in mind that what you are really doing is taking advantage of short-term price reversals in long-term trends. You don't have to sit at a computer screen all day to find momentary blips in a stock price. You can have a broader time horizon. Over the long run, many stocks tend to follow a trend in the same upward direction. The stocks, however, will often go through short-term reversals that can last anywhere from a day or two to a month or so. "The trading strategy is to buy long-term trends that reverse in the short term," says John Bogle, Jr., a money manager who uses quantitative analysis at Bogle Investment Management.

How big a reversal is still safe? Bogle does not feel uncomfortable buying into price declines of as much as 20%, as long as volume is relatively normal and the fundamentals are still the same. "When a stock really breaks down on high volume, you should stay away." If a stock has drifted down by 30% or 40% on no news, then you can be pretty sure there is a problem. And a stock that moves down because there *is* bad news–like a negative earnings surprise or a downward earnings revision–is far less likely to bounce back. Don't buy it. Instead, you want to look for good stocks that have drifted down on normal volume and no news.

When measuring the decline of a stock, stack it up against the appropriate control group. You can compare a stock price to its own chart. But it makes more sense to contrast it with a whole group of stocks that have similar characteristics. The most obvious choice is its own industry group. Why is it better to look for price anomalies against a group of stocks? Because a stock that has deviated from the pack and slipped on its own is much more likely to recover than one that is down with its peer group. "Sectors don't bounce back as much as individual stocks do," explains Bogle. "Don't just buy it because it is down. Buy because it is down relative to similar companies. The price reversal must be residual, and not reflective of a market or sector move."

Aside from picking stocks in the same sector, there are many approaches to building a control group. You can select stocks that are similar in other ways. Bogle suggests using characteristics like market capitalization, valuation measures (price to earnings or price to book ratios), debt levels, and growth rates. The closer your control group is to the stock you are looking at, the better the system will work. "You want to be able to say: 'Gee, I have a company that looks just like this other one. And if this one is down 10% relative to the other one, then it must be a buying opportunity, given that they are so similar.'"

You are going to lose in a lot of cases. Not all of these kinds of purchases will be a success. But you will come out ahead more often than not, says Bogle, and that's all that matters. "I'm not going to say you are not going to get torpedoed. But on average you will win. There are so many investors out there who overreact to news that they create buying opportunities. Statistically, short-term price reversal is an incredibly rewarding strategy. If it is practiced consistently, it will pay off over time. You have to do it over a long period of time to let the law of large numbers work in your favor."

Diversify. Obviously, since you know many of these trades will lose, you don't want to bet your whole portfolio on one price anomaly. Generally, you should never have more than about 2.5% to 5% of your portfolio in any one stock. The idea is that you don't want to give any single stock the power to wipe you out. Avoid big-sector bets as well.

Some kinds of companies bounce back faster than others. Larger companies are more resilient. So are those that have greater financial strength and more consistent earnings. Smaller companies and those that are more leveraged don't recover as quickly.

The best time to look for the short-term deals is in the afternoon. Professional investors tend to be morning oriented. They map out their plans for the day in a meeting before trading starts, based on the news that came out after the previous close. "They are structuring the day's activities prior to market open, and most trades are done early in the day," says Bogle. This means that buyers are usually less attentive in the afternoon because by that time they have probably already finished their mission for the day. Furthermore, since a lot of news is released either after the close or before the open, late afternoon trading tends to be less news driven. For these reasons, you should watch for short-term bargains in the afternoon. "It's better to do this late in the day when fewer people are watching and the news is already out," says Bogle. "There are fewer buyers out there saying, 'This is down 10%, let's buy it.' If you see a stock down in the afternoon, it can be some lazy trader in the market." The best time to spot mispriced stocks is between 2:30 P.M. and 4 P.M.

For these kinds of opportunities, you have to move fast. When a stock drifts down in the afternoon like this, you can't wait a day or two to see what is going on. You have to confirm that there is no news, check that volume is normal, and then move. "By the time you can comfort yourself that there is no news out there, everyone else has done the same thing and the opportunity is gone," says Bogle. "If you see an opportunity at the end of the day, usually it will evaporate at the opening print the next morning."

The longer-term declines that happen over the course of several days or weeks give you more time to do research before buying. But either type of decline is likely to reverse, as long as the fundamentals have not changed. "You just take it as a leap of faith that a company that has underperformed its peer group is likely to bounce back," says Bogle. "Far more often than not, if the fundamentals are fine, it is going to pay to be the contrarian."

Check who owns the stock. When you are thinking about buying a stock that seems to be in a short-term price reversal, look at the Securities and Exchange Commission 13-F or 13-G filings. If the stock is fairly heavily populated with momentum investors, a decline in its price compared to its control group becomes a lot easier to understand (see Chapter 17). Momentum investors often get out of a stock in a sloppy manner, driving down the price, regardless of whether there is something wrong with the stock.

Avoid the temptation to trade. By all means, give it a try if you want. But like most people, you will probably find that trading is a tough way to make any money, especially in a taxable account. As with other techniques in this book, the ones described in this chapter are best used as a way to get a good price on a long-term position in a stock. If you *are* a trader, however, these concepts will be very helpful.

CHAPTER 15

THE BASICS OF
BIOTECH INVESTING

If you put money into biotech companies in the early 1990s, your reaction whenever you hear about the sector now might be: "Never again!" Lots of investors lost a lot of money when the group broke down and these stocks fell out of sight like a rock over the edge of a cliff. Many of the companies simply disappeared. In 1991 and 1992, 101 biotech companies went public, raising $4.4 billion. But by 1998, only 44 of those were still trading, according to Securities Data Company.

Instead of swearing off the sector forever, a better reaction might be to learn from the mistakes of the 1990s biotech mania and find a better approach. The sector is not one to turn your back on. It is where some of the hottest growth occurs. In some ways, the group is only just now hitting its stride. As you read this chapter, scientists around the world are mapping out all human genes in an effort called the Human Genome Project. They should be finished about midway through the first decade of the twenty-first century. The insights gained from this work will lead to the development of drugs for many diseases that are not now curable—unlocking the true power of biotechnology.

For every spectacular success story to come from this and other kinds of research, however, there will be lots of misfires. This chapter tells you how to skew the odds of picking the bottle rockets in your favor, which is what investing is all about.

To be sure, investing in biotech stocks is tricky. The fact that you have to understand complicated medical concepts is only part of the problem. Aside from that, the fortunes of many biotech companies ride on the vagaries of the federal approval process for new drugs and medical devices.

Picking the right biotech stocks gets a lot easier if you follow some of the basic principles outlined by Richard van den Broek, a stock analyst for Hambrecht & Quist. The concepts are easy to grasp, and in some cases surprising, because they go against conventional wisdom. But they are supported by hard data on how biotech stocks perform around each step of the approval process. They make sense if you think them through. Here is the advice offered by van den Broek.

HOW TO PICK BIOTECH STOCKS

Trust your judgment. First, here is a simple point to keep in mind, especially if you aren't trained in the field of medicine. If products or technology do not make sense after several attempts at trying to understand them, it may not be due to your lack of medical experience. It may be that the technology does not make sense. Trust your own judgment and shy away from ideas that don't add up.

Look for companies with "platform technology," or technology capable of launching several products. Single-product ventures can blow up, so the smart biotech investor demands protection against this risk. Look for companies that have technology which can generate several different new products. "You need more than one chance to win," says van den Broek. "The failure rate is too risky for any one product."

In the biotech field, that means finding firms which have what is known as "proprietary platform technology." A company, for example, may have licensed the rights to a unique class of molecules that have the potential to spawn several drugs that can cure many diseases. Or it might be one of several pioneering companies that have each contributed a development that leads to a big breakthrough for a whole field. This is how receptor-based drugs[1] and genomics proceeded.

However it got there, a technology platform is among the most important things to look for—not only because it serves as a hedge against the risk that the development of a product will fail. With it, a

---

[1] Cell receptors receive signals from outside the cell and play a role in modifying cell behavior. Chemical compounds have been developed which limit the sensitivity of cell receptors involved in the development of disease.

biotech company is more likely to get decent financing by trading away some of its potential products. It can also leverage better partnerships with other companies or researchers.

Unfortunately, says van den Broek, just about all biotech companies claim to have a platform technology, even though most of them do not. It is pretty much obligatory for companies to refer to this concept in presentations and reports. But it is actually fairly rare. "The number of companies with a true proprietary platform technology is quite small for the simple reason that it is not easy to discover a technology that is generous enough to generate a flow of product candidates," says van den Broek.

As a basic rule of thumb, remember that the more competition there is in a field, the less likely it is that a company will have proprietary technology. Intense competition, however, is at least a sign that the company is in a potentially profitable area. At the other extreme, a complete lack of competition should raise questions about whether the company's technology has any real value.

In general, you want to look for a history of commitment to specific technologies and expertise protected by patents. Remember that leadership in a branch of technology means a company can stake out a strong proprietary position. Be wary of late entrants to a hot area. It is also good to see investments in a biotech company by several corporate partners. This makes it too expensive or risky for competitors to glom on.

Go for financial strength. Try to find companies with enough cash to cover at least two or three years' worth of expenses. A few biotech stars stand out because they produce exceptional profits, but the vast majority of the 300 or so smaller publicly traded firms in the field are losing money. At the same time, they are burning capital to fund new product development. You have to learn to live with that.

But that does not mean you shouldn't be picky about financial strength. In general, you want to avoid companies that will have to submit to the whims of the financial markets at some point. Firms that are dependent on the financial markets might end up having to give away too much of the company store in exchange for money when a product stumbles or when the business comes upon hard times. They will have to seek additional financing that dilutes future earnings, which means less profits for you, the investor. At worst, it can mean selling half the company for a year or two of cash.

To avoid this risk, van den Broek says you should choose firms that don't need the capital markets at all. Generally, this means looking for companies with at least three years' worth of cash. If not, you have to play it safe and simply assume the company will be making a dilutive offering at some point. Then work that into your earnings and price targets. Even when a company is close to getting final approval from the Food and Drug Administration (FDA), it will probably have to go to the market for financing if it has less than three years' worth of cash. The amount of money needed at that point, however, will probably be less dilutive than financing at an earlier point.

Limiting your investing to companies with at least two or three years' worth of cash does not mean you have to stay with the big, established firms. Many developing companies have enough financial resources, in the form of cash or commitments from partners, to fund development until profits start rolling in.

Remember that a strong balance sheet does not guarantee success with products. It just limits the downside if the company stumbles.

Don't pay too much. Try to pay a price that reflects the "hard assets" of the biotech company. That way you get to speculate on its success for free.

By hard assets, van den Broek means cash, the value of funding from partners, and manufacturing assets. He also includes the present value of any existing royalty streams or product revenues. Unfortunately, biotech companies will trade at their "hard asset value" only when they are out of favor because their prospects look pretty bleak. So it will take strong nerves to buy them at these levels. One approach is to determine the hard asset value in advance and then wait for the price to get near that level.

In general, it makes sense to use the pharmaceutical sector as the valuation benchmark for biotech companies, since that is what a biotech company ends up being when it grows up. Whenever valuations for a biotech company or the sector deviate significantly above or below this benchmark, take positions with the assumption that sooner or later they will come back in line.

Don't gamble on product approval. Why not? The answer is simple. It doesn't pay. During phase I and II of the Food and Drug Administration testing process, products are usually at such an early stage that investing in them is pure speculation. It is phase III testing which removes a lot of the risk and brings a product much closer to reality. Only after this phase is over can realistic financial analysis (discounted cash flow) be performed on a potential drug.

Because this phase is pivotal, it may be tempting to wager in biotech stocks right before results are announced. But this strategy is usually a loser's game, notes van den Broek. If you guess right, of course the pay-off can be huge. But the downside if you are wrong, is even worse.

Studies suggest that investors who owned companies expected to release phase III test data earn about 15% return in the six months before the data came out. That doesn't sound too bad. But those gains would have been more than wiped out by the negative outcomes that occur in over half of phase III trials. In other words, the risk–reward ratio is lousy.

Investors can get better returns at lower risk by waiting for the outcome of the phase III tests and buying the winners. You lose some of the speculative run-up before the phase III results are announced, but you gain more from the increased certainty that the drug will ever get to market. "You can still catch a good part of the upside, but you avoid the potential downside of a product not making it," says van den Broek.

You might think it would be profitable to speculate on biotech stocks only during the run-up period before the release of phase III results. After all, you could simply sell them just before the results come out and then buy back only the winners. In reality, this is difficult because it is nearly impossible to know exactly when the results will be released. True gamblers will be tempted to make educated guesses, however, by the fact that the eventual winners do tend to run up in price before phase III results are released, while the companies that fail the phase III test tend to be weak before the results are released. Evidently, inside information leaks out before the results come out. Or else investors have doubts about the effectiveness of the phase II studies done by the eventual losers, and they unload shares as phase III results seem imminent.

The next steps after phase III are approval from an FDA advisory panel and then by the FDA itself (see below). Once a product has cleared the advisory panel, the chances are a lot better that it will be approved by the FDA, compared to the odds it faced of getting over the phase III hurdle. Indeed, it is almost a certainty. But the penalties for failure are more severe. So investing just after the panel decides—instead of right before—is a more profitable way to buy shares in biotech companies at lower risk, says van den Broek. Once the FDA itself signs off, the product is launched and growing revenue streams start to attract more investors.

Gamblers find it easier to speculate on FDA advisory panel decisions since the dates of all panel meetings are disclosed in the Federal Register. Again, before the release, the companies whose products are eventually approved tend to outperform the losers, just like before phase III decisions. But the difference is not as great.

Look for a good sales franchise. This becomes more crucial as products get closer to the market. Even in the earlier stages, however, a company should have a strategy for dealing with the expensive challenge of marketing its drugs. It might seem like the simplest approach would be to build a sales force once the product is approved. For most biotech companies, however, this is too expensive. Bringing a drug to market can cost over $200 million.

Instead, look for biotech companies that use creative deals to develop a sales franchise. Usually, a biotech company will trade part ownership of a product or technology for financial support.

In a typical approach, a company will give partial product rights—say sales in Europe—to a pharmaceutical company in exchange for support in developing a sales force for the U.S. market. Or a biotech firm might sell worldwide rights to market the drug for one use but keep rights to sell it for another use. Other agreements allow the biotech company to, in essence, rent a pharmaceutical company's sales force for the first few years of the product launch.

However they get a sales and marketing franchise, it is important to look for companies that have this franchise—and not just the technology to come up with products. "The two are distinct assets, and a third-party buyer will find a company more attractive if it already has a presence in the marketplace," says van den Broek.

What is so good about a sales franchise? It has value that can't be beat by even the sweetest royalty deal. Make no mistake, a biotech company with revenue that comes from a royalty deal can be a good investment. But selling a product directly brings in the best profits. A good sales franchise also serves as a magnet for other technology. A young biotech firm or a university department will be much more willing to license its patents to a company with an established record in marketing. A sales franchise allows more mature biotech companies to earn enough money to compete with the big pharmaceutical companies for the best alliances. Having a sales franchise also makes a biotech company more attractive as a buyout target. Direct sales can also provide insight into market demand, which can guide research and development.

Biotech stocks don't normally move as a group. In the technology sector, when Intel announces good results, the computer sellers and other companies that make components for computers will move up. In contrast, when one biotech company does well (or has a setback), it may have an impact on the sector–but it probably won't continue. So don't chase biotech companies when they start to go up on news that seems like it should set off a lasting move in the sector. It probably won't continue because the stocks generally do not move as a group. There are a few exceptions. An external shock from the political world can move the whole group. And the buyout of a biotech leader may spark speculative buying of many other potential candidates. But in general, biotech companies march to their own drummers much more so than companies in the tech sector.

Like tech stocks, however, biotech companies are extremely volatile. So if you invest in them, it is a good idea to be sure you have a stomach for risk. And if you do invest in this group, limit your exposure. Investors fishing in these waters also need to focus on the long term, meaning at least three to five years. Until a biotech company comes up with medication that can do the trick, having a longer time horizon is one of the few things that will limit the queasiness caused by the sector's volatility.

FROM INSPIRATION TO REALITY: A DRUG'S JOURNEY TO MARKET CAN TAKE 10 YEARS OR MORE

STEP ONE: RESEARCH & DEVELOPMENT

A research discovery is followed by preliminary lab and animal testing. Approximate time: one to two years.

STEP TWO: CLINICAL DEVELOPMENT

There are three steps. *Phase I trials* on humans are usually brief tests to evaluate safety and maximum tolerated dosage. At this point, the product is still highly speculative, but approval can cause a brief pop in a stock's price. Approximate time: one year. *Phase II trials* confirm the safety and evaluate the effectiveness of the drug, often using blinded studies. Approval can double or triple the price of small-cap stocks. Approximate time: two years. *Phase III trials* use double-blind tests and placebos, with a larger number of patients. For the drug to move on, there must be statistically significant improvements in patients. Strong evidence that the drug works at this point means it will likely get to market, so investors start factoring potential revenue into the stock price if the drug passes. This phase attracts a lot of speculative interest from investors. But making a bet on approval is risky because only about half of all products clear phase III. Biotech companies have a hard time replicating phase II results in phase III for two reasons. First, to save time and money, they usually run only one phase II trial. Second, the phase III trial is rarely an exact replica of the phase II trial. Approximate time: three years.

STEP THREE: THE REGULATORY
APPROVAL PROCESS

Once out of clinical trials, a drug moves on to an *FDA advisory panel.* This is a group of independent experts, usually from universities. Not surprisingly, the company presents the clinical data in the most favorable light while the FDA challenges the results. The advisory panel discusses the potential risks and rewards of the drug and makes a decision. This phase attracts a lot of speculative investor interest. The panel usually makes a decision on the clinical test results about six to twelve months after the company filed for approval. After that comes the final hurdle: *FDA review.* The FDA nearly always goes along with what the panel decided. The FDA might make up its mind as soon as a day after the panel decides. But it usually takes six to twelve months. During this period, the product label and claims about the drug are negotiated. This determines how the drug can be marketed. Following FDA approval, most products are launched within days. Once a product is launched, speculation turns to whether it will sell as much as the company and industry analysts predict. Typically, it won't.

CHAPTER 16

SHAREHOLDER ACTIVISM

When stocks go down, shareholders often want to sue the company. This usually gets them nowhere. True, even when firms have done nothing wrong, they often settle out of court to make the legal challenge go away. Indeed, many of the lawyers who specialize in these kinds of suits file them precisely because of this "nuisance value." But when the company settles, those lawyers collect big fees, and the shareholders who bothered to get involved receive only cents on the dollar. End of story.

There is a more sensible way to work the legal system to get more out of your investments: participate in shareholder activism. This is when shareholders use the corporate voting machine to bring about changes at a company. It does not cost much, but it can be time consuming and it has its limits. Nevertheless, shareholder activism in the right circumstances can do wonders for the prices of your stocks.

You might think *relationship investing,* as it is also called, is mainly the arena of the big institutional investors and pension funds. You would be wrong. In 1997 and 1998 more than 70% of shareholder proposals came from individual investors or groups of individual investors organized to carry out this kind of activity. The individual investor has used shareholder activism with spectacular results. There is no reason why you can't, too. The key is to raise issues that will get the attention and support of institutional investors.

SOME HISTORY

Shareholder activism dates back to 1934, when Congress approved the Securities Exchange Act. That legislation was an attempt to reverse the abuses of big business at the time, in part by increasing shareholder democracy. As regulators filled in the details, it soon became clear that the law had given shareholders a powerful new voice in corporate policy.

Anyone who owns either 1% or $2,000 worth of shares in a company for at least a year was given an important new right: the power to use the corporate proxy machinery to put issues before all shareholders for a vote. Shareholders can submit proposals that have to be included in the corporation's own annual proxy packages, which get put to vote at shareholder meetings. (Proxy votes exist because investors rarely go to shareholder meetings. Instead, they give someone else the authority to vote shares for them–typically someone at the company.)

The provision of the 1934 Securities Act that allows all this, known as Rule 14a-8 because of its title, was a huge gift to shareholder activists. It spares them the price of independent proxy solicitations, which can cost up to several million dollars. For just $2,000, share-holders not only get the benefit of stock ownership. They can also make other shareholders and the corporation pay for the distribution of proposals and statements. Shareholders can even use this provision to change company by-laws.

In the early days, shareholder activism was carried out by pioneers who shaped the U.S. corporate world for the better in many ways, even though they were branded as oddballs and gadflies at the time. Two of the most famous are John and Lewis Gilbert. They fought battles with companies on governance issues and corporate perks from the Great Depression right through the 1990s. Another outspoken activist was Evelyn Y. Davis, known for her heavily accented tirades against corporate chieftains.

While these early rabble-rousers devoted a lot of time and energy to their causes, many of their colorful tactics made it easy for corporations to discredit them. One of the Gilbert brothers wore a red clown nose at an annual meeting to attract attention. Davis stripped down to a bathing suit before General Motors management for the same reason. To be even more provocative, she once asked Becton Dickinson executives why a rectal thermometer she bought from the company was accurate, but the oral one was way off. (She was told that the oral thermometer does not work properly unless the user knows how to keep her mouth shut.)

SHAREHOLDER ACTIVISM: AT WHAT COST?

No one knows for sure, but shareholder proposals likely cost the corporate world as much as $15 million in a year, according to Alan R. Palmiter, a professor at Wake Forest University School of Law. He bases his estimate on the fact that companies tell the SEC that proposals cost them anywhere between $200 and $900,000 each, with the average cost around $50,000. The SEC puts its regulatory costs at about one staff year.

For all their quirks, the pioneers made significant contributions. Early on, the Gilberts used Rule 14a-8 to urge public companies to adopt consistent financial accounting and more liberal dividend policies. These were visionary ideas at the time, but now they are an accepted part of modern business. Early activists sought the prohibition of inside directors from board committees that deal with compensation and nominations–well before this practice became common. Others demanded better disclosure of executive pay, years before the SEC took up the issue. Activists were also urging AT&T to spin off its operating subsidiaries before the courts ordered the breakup of the company.

It was not until the late 1980s that shareholder activism really started to go mainstream. This was partly because respected members inside of the business community began using Rule 14a-8 to counter some of the more abusive corporate practices of the time. They challenged things like unreasonable poison pill defenses against corporate raiders and overly generous golden parachutes for managers forced out in a takeover.

Much of the credit for bringing shareholder activism into the mainstream goes to Ralph Whitworth. As a young man in Washington, Whitworth dated the daughter of T. Boone Pickens. The relationship did not work out, but Pickens appointed Whitworth chief of operations at a shareholder activist group he founded in 1986 with $26 million. The group was called United Shareholders Association (USA).

Whitworth quickly demonstrated his skill at working all the angles– including the media–when using Rule 14a-8 to make companies more shareholder friendly. He soon developed a reputation as the loudmouth of shareholder activism. But unlike the gadflies, Whitworth knew how to hold back enough to maintain credibility, something even his detractors gave him credit for. Meanwhile, he lobbied in Washington, D.C., for better corporate governance.

For all his success, when it came to shareholder clout Whitworth was never in the same league as the huge institutional investors. But he played an important role. He launched the high-profile public attacks on entrenched management while the multibillion-dollar funds, like the California Public Employees' Retirement System (CalPERS), pressured management behind the scenes.

Together they produced some amazing changes. Probably the biggest was a coup they brought about at IBM in the early 1990s. While IBM's stock sagged, Whitworth and his USA staff lobbed in some tough proxy resolutions to shake things up. They called for things like an independent review of IBM's leadership, the appointment of bankers to consider the sale of assets, an independent nominating committee, and performance-based pay for executives. While Whitworth stoked the publicity machine, the big institutional investors that had coalesced around his proposals put pressure on the board behind the scenes. Before the challenges could come to a head, IBM found a way out by announcing that top managers would leave and that the new management's grip on the company's board would be loosened. Whitworth also provoked some big changes at other large corporations like Westinghouse Electric and Occidental Petroleum, among others.

By the time Whitworth left Washington to start his own career as a money manager employing the same techniques he had honed in Washington, the use of activism by professional money managers to increase shareholder value had become widespread. Major state pension funds like CalPERS were in the forefront. CalPERS took things beyond the simple strategy of scoring victories on narrow issues like antitakeover devices. It began using the broader approach of trying to improve a company's stock price by putting in a better board. With $150 billion in assets under management, CalPERS has a lot of clout. Other major players include TIAA-CREF, which runs pension funds for educators and manages public mutual funds ($250 billion in assets), the State of Wisconsin Investment Board (SWIB) which has $63 billion in assets, and the International Brotherhood of Teamsters.

Studies by Wilshire Associates show that relationship investing has been a big success for shareholders. During the five years before CalPERS started to apply pressure for change at 52 companies looked at in one study, the stocks of those firms lagged the S&P 500 Index by 75%. In the following five years, the stocks outperformed the S&P 500 by 54%.

THE FUTURE

Bolstered by their victories, activists more recently have been pushing the limits of the law—and they may have gone too far. How courts and law-makers resolve the matter will have a big impact on the powers of activists. At the root of the problem is one of the biggest shortcomings of the share-holder votes proposed by activists: They could only *advise* boards on what to do but not order them around. By the late 1990s, activists had found ways around this. "They began wording the proposals in a way that makes them by-law amendments," says Whitworth. "By-law amendments in most states are binding if they are approved by a majority of shareholders."

Stockholders already had the power to adopt by-laws on many sub-jects. They just couldn't do this if it meant they were in effect managing the business. But by the late 1990s shareholders began using by-law amendments to challenge management operational decisions. This was a giant leap. For the first time, shareholders were bossing boards around. Oklahoma courts have upheld this practice. But courts in Delaware, where most big companies are incorporated, may not go along. Ulti-mately, the battle may be resolved by state lawmakers. Meanwhile, many boards have the option of simply repealing by-law amendments adopted by shareholder votes, notes John Coffee, a corporate law professor at Columbia University, even if the public relations costs might be high.

At the heart of the matter is an old debate over who has control of corporations: managers and board members, or shareholders—even though they presumably accepted limited decision-making power along with their limited liability. Traditional business law gives management all the room it needs to succeed or fail—under what is called the *business judgment rule*—and rightly so. If managers are too restricted, they won't be able to carry out their legal duty to act in the interest of sharehold-ers. On the other hand, federal courts have pointed out that the "control of great corporations by a very few persons was the abuse at which Con-gress struck" when it passed the shareholder proposal rules.[1]

PUTTING SHAREHOLDER ACTIVISM TO USE

Enough background and theory. How can you put all this to work for you? Chances are, you won't have the time to become a shareholder

---

[1] *SEC v. Transamerica Corp.*

activist yourself. (If you do, see the tips below.) But that does not mean you cannot benefit. The simplest thing to do is keep an eye on the activities of the major shareholder activists and then invest in the same companies they have set out to improve. Some of the more important groups to watch are CalPERS, TIAA-CREF, the State of Wisconsin Investment Board, Whitworth's Relational Investors, and the Teamsters Union. One of the best ways to follow their activities is to read the financial press. Activist investors love to use the media to make threats against targets and bring pressure on them, garner publicity, and generate support among other investors. So their strategies are no secret. Read over their game plan. If it makes sense, take a position in the company they are targeting, and go along for the ride.

THE GENERAL STRATEGIES USED IN SHAREHOLDER ACTIVISM

Perhaps you want to practice shareholder activism. If so, one of the most important things is to be familiar with the basic tactics that are within the reach of individual investors or small groups, says Whitworth. He uses all of these techniques outlined below, as managing director of Relational Investors LLC, a $750 million investment fund. Some of them may not be as effective if you are acting on your own or with just a small group of other individual investors. That's okay. Remember that a lot of shareholder proposals by individuals succeed anyway because they attract the attention of big institutional investors.

JAWBONING

Simply talking with management and the board or writing letters can help. But only if the company believes you can follow up with more forceful tactics. This is why small investors usually have less success with this technique. Unless individuals have some big institutional investors behind them, they are not as likely to be taken seriously. If you try jawboning anyway, you can help your cause by following the rules of good behavior when addressing companies. Rabble-rousing activists in the past have torpedoed their causes by ignoring this principle. "Because of their style, they gave companies an opportunity to discredit them," says Whitworth. "You will have more credibility at the annual meeting if you conduct yourself professionally."

THE SHAREHOLDER PROPOSAL ALLOWED
UNDER RULE 14A-8

Here is where small investors can make a difference. "Individuals can have an impact with proposals. Very much so," says Whitworth. "I think they can be very effective." The work of activists belonging to groups like Investors Rights Association of America (IRAA) in Massapequa, New York, is a good example. "I give them 90% of the credit for the sea change that we have seen in director compensation, in particular, the virtual elimination of nonemployee director pension plans. There has also been quite a movement away from staggered boards, and many of those proposals have been sponsored by individuals." The IRAA Web site (www.iraa.com) is a good resource for further information about shareholder activism.

When submitting shareholder proposals, you will be much more successful if you strike a chord with some of the big institutional investors, since they can vote a lot of shares. They also tend to be the kinds of investors who actually look at proxy statements and vote. Labor Department rules on pension fund management generally put them under a legal obligation to vote their shares in the best interest of their clients. This can give your shareholder proposal an edge, provided it is written in a way that makes it hard for the big investors not to go along. If the SEC creates the same obligations for mutual funds, there will be an even bigger pool of potential votes to go after.

Whitworth's success in bringing about what he calls "the biggest housecleaning in corporate America" at IBM shows how a relatively small shareholder can have a big impact if he gets the right allies. In that case, the institutional investors let IBM know they intended to vote for Whitworth's proposals as a way of expressing disenchantment with management. In response, the company made enough changes to keep the big shareholders happy and preempt the vote.

SEEK MINORITY BOARD REPRESENTATION

Individual investors typically have a tough time with this one. To succeed, you need to own a big chunk of the shares or have some expertise related to the company's business. Without this, it is hard to get support from other shareholders. With these conditions in place, however, former managers of at least one company have run a proxy contest and gotten on the board, though it is uncommon. Investors who use this approach put their name in place of one person on the management's slate and include the rest of the company candidates.

RUN A PROXY CONTEST FOR CONTROL
OF THE BOARD

Individuals don't have much of a chance here either. For one thing, challengers using this tactic have to pay for the distribution of the proxy statement. This is expensive. Total costs, including legal bills, can run anywhere from $300,000 to $15 million. When institutions use this gambit, they often get the changes they want, even though their slate never goes to vote. That's because the company makes many of the reforms sought by the activists to get them to withdraw their proposal. Or else they make enough of the changes to divide the vote and defeat the proposal.

THE COMMON TARGETS OF
SHAREHOLDER ACTIVISTS

Activists typically try to improve corporate governance by going after companies on the following issues. So if you are looking for an issue that will get broad support from institutional investors, focus on these areas. Even if you don't get involved in shareholder activism, what follows can serve as a checklist of signs that a company gets lousy grades for corporate governance and does not care much about shareholders. This is important to know. It probably makes the company a less attractive investment, since managers put a low priority on shareholder value. What's more, many professional investors stay away from companies that have shareholder unfriendly practices, so these kinds of companies may have a harder time attracting money in the market. On the other hand, lousy corporate governance could make them the targets of powerful "relationship investors" who step in and force them to clean up their act, driving up the stock price in the process.

POISON PILLS

A poison pill sabotages bidders by making unwanted takeovers too expensive. Typically, they work by triggering a massive issuance of shares when an unfriendly suitor buys more than a specific percentage of the company's stock. Under a "dead-hand" plan, directors who would get ousted in a proxy fight are the only ones empowered to rescind the poison pill and sell the company. Activists believe that a lot of poison pills were designed mainly to entrench managers. This prevents shareholders from receiving takeover premiums. Activists usually submit proposals to adopt by-laws that would preclude the board from using poison pills, or put an existing pill to a shareholder vote. Once a poison pill is removed, it gets a lot easier to take over a company.

STAGGERED BOARDS

This means that only a fraction of the board is up for election each year. Staggered boards make it harder for disgruntled investors to oust an entire board and take control. They are often used as a way of blocking takeovers, takeovers that can be good for shareholder value.

OPTIONS REPRICING

When a stock tanks, many companies lower the exercise price of executive stock options. This ends up giving the managers more money at the expense of the shareholder, even though the options were supposed to reward managers for good performance, not bad.

CUMULATIVE VOTING

This allows shareholders to concentrate all their board votes on a single candidate for director. For example, if all 16 directors are being elected, each shareholder will have 16 votes per share to vote for one director. This system can give too much power to a hostile outside group that does not have the interests of all shareholders in mind. On the other hand, cumulative voting gives shareholder activists a voice they would otherwise not have. So it cuts both ways.

GOLDEN PARACHUTES

Not as common as they once were, these guarantee large lump-sum payments to managers when they're fired following a change of control.

INBRED BOARDS

Ideally, a company's board should be made up mainly of independent individuals who neither work for the company nor sell the company goods or services. People who are related by blood or marriage to top-level managers also are not likely to be independent. Activists especially like to see independent directors on the board committees that handle compensation and nominations.

OPEN VOTING

Institutions particularly like to be able to cast votes anonymously, so that they are not bombarded by the company with attempts to sway their decisions. Confidential voting also allows shareholders to vote more freely. This explains why activists like it. But only about 15% of companies have confidential voting.

THE CEO AND CHAIR OF THE BOARD ARE ONE

Activists believe this puts a real limit on board independence.

DIRECTOR PENSIONS, COMPENSATION, AND STOCK OWNERSHIP

How much stock the directors hold can have a big effect on the company's long-term performance. Ideally, directors should own stock worth three to five times the fees they get for being a director. Lavish compensation and pension plans are wasteful. Shareholder activist groups have helped to eliminate such pension plans for outside directors at many companies.

DEBT FINANCING

Is the company taking on too much?

NEW CLASSES OF STOCK

Issuing new classes of stock does more than just dilute earnings. It also diminishes the rights of existing shareholders, when the new classes of shares have superior voting rights compared with existing shares.

WHO ARE THE ACTIVISTS AND WHAT KINDS OF PROPOSALS GET THE MOST SUPPORT?

The overwhelming number of proposals comes from individual shareholders or groups of individual investors. Of the 355 proposals in 1998, 75% came from these types of activists. Institutional investment funds sponsored the remaining 88 proposals. The results were similar for 1977. In that year 72% of the 373 proposals came from individuals or investor associations, and 28% came from funds.

Most votes don't do very well, but that does not mean they failed. They may have motivated managers to make changes. In 1977 and 1998 about 60% of the proposals got less than 20% of shareholder votes, and about 43% got less than 10% of the vote.

The most successful shareholder proposals in 1997 and 1998 were those that tried to accomplish these goals: repeal poison pills, eliminate the staggered election of board members, establish confidential voting, and get permission for shareholders to call for special meetings or "act by written consent," which means to collect votes on an issue without calling a meeting. Each of these kinds of proposals got about 50% of the vote or more.

The next most popular group of proposals sought to do things like restrict pensions for directors who are not employees, block the repricing of underwater stock options, provide for cumulative voting, restrict golden parachutes, get a majority of independent directors on the board, separate the office of CEO and chair, and establish independent compensation and nominating committees. These votes all got between 20% and 34% in 1998 and 1997.

The least successful proposals were those that tried to sell the company, spin off a division, hire an investment banker to look into these options, pay directors in stock, increase board diversity, and restrict or disclose executive compensation. Each got between 10% and 20% of the shareholder vote.

Source: Investor Responsibility Research Center.

THE NUTS AND BOLTS OF SUBMITTING A PROPOSAL

If you plan to practice shareholder activism, the most important thing to know is how to submit a proposal. A proposal must clear several hurdles. First, the subject matter must be *appropriate*. The SEC has created rules stating what kinds of issues shareholders are allowed to raise. The violation of these rules is what most often gets proposals shot down. It is tricky to follow the rules because they create a Catch-22 that would make Joseph Heller proud. On the one hand, proposals cannot be too broad. They have to deal with a "proper subject for action by security holders," according to the definition of what this means in the law where the company is incorporated. State laws are not always clear on this point. However, grand statements about big social issues, for example, are off limits.

On the other hand, proposals are not allowed to address the ordinary business operations of a company. This makes sense because who would want shareholders running the day-to-day affairs of a company? Problem is, if you put the two rules together, you might conclude that most shareholder proposals can be eliminated on the grounds that they are either too general or too specific. Ultimately, the SEC and the courts decide the kinds of issues that can be included. Their interpretations have changed over time. Many matters once excluded as "ordinary business" are now allowed in. These include areas like pay for executives and directors, plant closings, and golden parachutes. Proposals to create advisory committees that report to shareholders were once off limits, but now they, too, are allowed in as well.

Aside from the subject matter, there are many other more straight-forward requirements. First, you may only submit one proposal, and to do so, you have to hold either 1% or $2,000 worth of stock in the company for one year. If you want your proposal to be presented at the annual meeting, the company has to get it 120 days before it sends out its own proxy material.

Proposals cannot contain false or misleading statements, and they must not seek to have the company violate any law. Your proposal cannot be merely an effort to resolve a personal claim or grievance not shared by other stockholders. Proposals are also rejected if they have to do with less than 5% of the company's assets, net earnings, or gross sales for the most recent fiscal year. Proposals cannot address a matter over which the company has no power. They are not allowed to contradict proposals that management plans to submit at the meeting. They will also be rejected if they are similar to other proposals. And they cannot be related to elections for government office.

If your proposal passes through all the hoops, the company is required to circulate it among shareholders with its own proxy material. You are allowed to write a 500-word statement to go along with it. The statement has to be submitted at the same time you send in your proposal. The company can make a statement on your proposal and recommend that shareholders vote in a certain way.

If the company rejects your proposal, it must tell you and the SEC at least 80 days before the annual meeting. It must also say why. You are allowed to appeal the decision with the SEC. If the company plans to include a statement against the proposal, it must share the comment with you 30 days before the company files its proxy statements.

Even if proposals are not approved, they can be carried over to following years if they get enough votes. Resolutions that receive 3% of the vote can be reintroduced the next year. Approval by 6% allows them to be carried over for two years, and the threshold is 10% to make it to the third year. If a proposal gets less than these amounts of the vote, you have to wait five years to submit it again.

Keep in mind that shareholder proposals do not have to win to work. Often they lead to some sort of a settlement or compromise because management wants to avoid embarrassment. Shrewd activists use shareholder proposals as a way to get access to directors and management. And remember that publicity is an important aspect of all this because it gives you more power. Whitworth's USA group often hit home by sending press releases to the local papers in a company's home town. The negative publicity can make managers more cooperative, and it helps get other shareholders behind the cause.

PART FOUR

WHEN
TROUBLE
STRIKES

CHAPTER 17

WHAT TO DO
WHEN YOUR STOCK
BLOWS UP

Sooner or later, one of your stocks will tank. While this is a given, the manner in which you react is not. You have some control over that. What's more, the way you handle yourself in these situations will have a much bigger impact on your long-term performance than the inevitable meltdown of one of your stocks from time to time (assuming you stay well diversified).

If you become too emotional when one of your stocks plummets, you may get shaken out of your position and take an unnecessary loss. On the other hand, if you go into denial and avoid reality, you run the risk of holding onto a losing position for too long, ending up with bigger losses than you needed to take.

Each meltdown is unique in some way. But stocks often get spanked because of the same scenarios that occur over and over again. Below are some of the most common ones, and the thinking that professional investors go through in each set of circumstances.

THE MOST COMMON MELTDOWN SCENARIOS
AND HOW TO DEAL WITH THEM

When bad news strikes. An oil tanker runs aground, a plane crashes, or pieces of glass start turning up in baby food jars. The media latch on to the story. Investors panic, and the price of your stock loses 40% of its value in the blink of an eye. Do you hang on, or bail out before things get worse? This is always a tough call. When crisis strikes, you have to make snap judgments about big questions. Will the company ever recover? Was management really at fault?

Your job will be easier if you ignore all the noise and keep focused on one question: *Does the mishap mean that the fundamentals of the company are different today than they were yesterday?* If not, don't sell. Consider buying more. While public hysteria swirls around you, you need to ignore the confusion and keep your mind on this issue. "Obviously, if the nature of the business has changed and its profit-making capabilities are permanently impaired, it is time to take your losses and move on," says Robert Rodriguez, the chief investment officer of First Pacific Advisors and the manager of the FPA Capital Fund. "But if it is only a temporary impediment to the operations of the business, you can use the price depression to add to your position."

In 1994, for example, Intel seemed to have a disaster on its hands when news broke that its new Pentium chip couldn't handle floating-point division, a complex mathematical function. The company's stock took a hit. It might not have been so easy to tell in the heat of the moment, but the fundamentals of the business were not really that different. Then Intel cleared up doubts about the public relations side of the story by allowing customers to exchange their old chips for debugged ones. The stock rebounded within days. Shrewd investors who figured out that the problem did not really affect Intel's business doubled their money within six months.

When assessing a disaster, you often need to deal with a slightly trickier question. Is the problem a sign that there is something seriously wrong with the company, or was it just plain bad luck? "Very often these little things turn out to be symptoms of bigger problems," says Gary Pilgram, the manager of the PBHG Growth Fund.

Certain difficulties, for example, hint at more trouble below the surface because they cast doubt on the ethics of management. Maybe a government investigation has begun, or there are questions about Medicare billing practices. Or perhaps there is something funny about the financial statements. Things like these can be signs that there are widespread problems that will keep coming out and continue to dog a company.

On the other hand, some events are obviously just plain bad luck. When cyanide turns up in bottles of painkiller, it is pretty clear that this was something management could have little control over. Random events like these don't reflect badly on a company. They have an impact on the stock price, however, creating a selloff that you should either ignore or use as a buying opportunity.

When weighing all the factors in a disaster, consider the size of the company and the nature of its business. In general, you have less reason to get out fast when problems crop up at a large, well-established company with stable earnings. This kind of firm will weather a calamity much better. It also helps a lot if the company has a franchise, meaning it makes products or services that are not interchangeable with those of other companies.

The smaller the company, the worse the damage will be when problems arise because the shares are less liquid. Bigger stocks have many more potential buyers to take up the slack. Growth stocks get hit harder, too. "The growth investors are fast, and they sell and sell, and keep selling for weeks or months," says David Parsons, an equity analyst with USAA Investment Management Company. "I used to think people overreact when a growth stock blows up. But I now think that people underreact."

As a general rule, the smaller the company and the more you can't understand what went wrong, the quicker you should sell. "The difference between a small-growth buyer and a small-value buyer is a long way," says Pilgram. "There is no bank trust department standing in the middle buying shares because it wants to be diversified."

Politicians start to get involved in some way. Companies in the United States have a lot of freedom. But at any point, the government may get involved in day-to-day business operations in some manner. Investors get very nervous in this scenario. "This is uniformly bad. It brings a lot of uncertainty," says Mark Engerman, chief investment officer at Numeric Investors, which runs the n/i numeric investors family of funds. "And investors don't like uncertainty, regulation, and government intervention." So they sell. Often a stock hit by this kind of selling does not recover quickly, especially if the matter gets a lot of attention.

"Once an issue becomes sensationalized in the press and it attracts the interest of regulators and politicians, it almost never turns out well," says Pilgram. "If a company has glass particles in its baby food, it can survive that. It can clean up the problem and move on because the franchise is strong enough to survive. But when you get the federal government involved in holding hearings and regulating, that is different."

Even when there are no hearings, things often turn out poorly when a company becomes a political football. An example is what happened to ValueJet after one of its planes crashed in Florida in 1996. Many investors bought the stock in the selloff that followed. They believed the weakness in the stock was an overreaction to an event that was beyond the control of the company. The accident, they reasoned, could have happened to any airline, and it had nothing to do with the fundamentals of the company. All sound reasoning.

Soon, however, the search for the cause of the accident turned into an investigation of the airline. Then that transformed into a probe of the Federal Aviation Administration (FAA). Suddenly there was intense public scrutiny of the FAA. Then the political heat on the administration caused what many analysts believed was a knee-jerk decision to ground the airline. At that point, the quality of management and business plans was irrelevant.

The threat of government intervention can cause buying opportunities as well, when it is overblown. Health care stocks, for example, got hammered in the early 1990s when it seemed the Clinton administration might introduce a national health care system. Anyone who figured out the reform would not go through made a lot of money buying beaten down health care stocks. "Events like this create opportunity," says Michael J.C. Roth, the chief executive officer of USAA Investment Management Company. "This is where your depth of knowledge, creative thinking, and courage are going to be tested."

Similarly, there is a lot of opportunity when the government deregulates a sector. This hurts the existing players who had enjoyed protection from competition. But it is positive for the new companies that are allowed in. A good example is the deregulation of the utilities in the 1990s. "This really did in the existing utilities because it opened the doors for other companies with lower costs to come in and cherry pick customers," says Alfred Kugel, a former portfolio manager who is the senior investment strategist for Stein Roe & Farnham. "The old utilities were used to being in a protected, monopoly business. Then the regulators changed the rules, after their plants were built and their costs were in place. They did not know how to deal with a competitive market."

Your company misses earnings expectations, or it preannounces that it will. What happens next depends on the size of the miss and the nature of the stock. A shortfall of a few cents by a value stock won't matter that much. A big miss (5% or more) by a momentum stock with a record of beating estimates will cause some serious damage. In this case it's usually best to clear out right away, following the "first out, best out" maxim.

"The stock will go into shock and stay in shock for a long time," says Louis Navellier, a portfolio manager with Navellier & Associates. It depends on what went wrong, of course. But big stocks can take a few quarters to recover, while small- or mid-cap stocks can take a few years. One reason it takes so long is that the first miss after a winning streak usually signals the start of a series of problems. In investing, negative news is very often followed by more negative news. Or as some fund managers like to say: Bad quarters come in fours.

Sometimes you might see a company beat expectations but offer downward guidance for the future. This may not be as negative as it looks. Maybe the company is just being conservative and "managing" expectations. "The company might just be telling everyone not to raise their estimates too much in the future so that they can surprise some more," says Navellier. "That is not a bad thing." If analysts cut estimates shortly afterward, however, you have a problem.

Your stock sells off because a competitor announces bad news about its own business. Obviously, the first thing you have to determine is whether the problem is company specific or something that affects the whole industry. And you have to understand the trends behind the news, which may not be all that bleak for *your* company. After all, bad news for Sears can be good news for Wal-Mart.

One of the most important things to know is whether your company is in a "commodity" business. This is one in which the products of competitors are pretty much interchangeable. If so, bad news from the competition is probably bad news for you, regardless of what anyone says. "Those are the situations you want to be a little more concerned about," says John Bogle, Jr., a money manager who uses quantitative analysis at Bogle Investment Management. Good examples are the steel and semiconductor sectors.

On the other hand, you can feel fairly secure if your company has a "franchise." This has nothing to do with selling hamburgers or other goods in a franchise arrangement with a parent company. It means the company's products or services are special or unique in some way. If your company does have a franchise, it will probably be immune from bad news at firms that work in the same field. "Companies that have the greatest stock-specific component of return are the ones you want to buy in a dip like this, because they are not tied to the industry," says Bogle.

On average, whether or not the companies involved have a franchise, it makes sense to play the contrarian when negative news from one firm affects the whole sector, says Bogle. "People get overly concerned about things like that, so it tends to be an opportunity to buy. But not always."

Announcements of bad news from competitors can be particularly troubling during the so-called preannouncement period. This is the time around the end of each quarter when companies start getting enough results in to know how the quarter is shaping up. The companies that notice trouble with the quarter often preannounce the bad news. It usually happens during the last two weeks of the quarter or the first two weeks of the next one. The problem is that a lot of companies put themselves in a "quiet period" at the same time. This means they bar their employees from talking to analysts while the company is finishing up the books. Companies do this to avoid leaks, not to mention any legal problems that might arise if an investor with better contacts in the firm gets news ahead of other investors.

"When some companies start throwing a shoe and related companies are in a quiet period, it is a very fertile ground for people to create stories and innuendo," says Pilgram. "It is very easy for short sellers to stir up trouble, and they do. This is the time when the goblins come out of the woods and haunt our houses." If you have confidence in the companies you follow, you can take advantage of this situation to pick up stocks at good prices. "The general queasiness rattles stocks that should not be rattled," says Pilgram.

Sometimes a stock you own will sell off because a competitor announces *good* news. To determine whether the selloff is justified, look at why the competitor is doing so well. If that company is hot because the sector is growing, that is fine. If it's because the competitor is increasing market share, you may have a problem.

A decent stock of yours suddenly backs off for a few weeks on no news. A two- or three-week reversal for a strong stock is nothing to worry about as long as there is no news. Stocks in long-term upward trends often experience short-term reversals. Indeed, a successful strategy is to buy the short-term reversals within these long-term trends. Just be careful you are not walking into a trap. When a stock is off 30% to 40% compared to its industry group or it is down on high volume, something is probably wrong. But a stock trading 20% below its peers on normal volume is most likely a bargain, as long as the fundamentals are the same.

Actually making the move and buying that stock will be difficult for you to do. The price weakness will make you feel fear and uncertainty. "This is the time when you are going to find out how courageous you are," says Roth. "But if as far as you can see nothing has changed, then you have to love a stock at $25 if you liked it at $30, regardless of how scared you are. You have to banish fear." It is in times like these that it pays to have a system and stick with it. Allowing your system to decide whether to buy or sell a stock takes a lot of the emotion out of investing.

This makes it easier to take a position in a stock at the right time, even though your stomach tells you to stay away.

The value of your stock erodes over a longer period of time for no apparent reason, in a slow, steady decline. This is one of the trickiest situations to deal with. It can be very troubling to see your stock continue to lose a little value each day for weeks and weeks, on no news. How you react to this puzzle will depend a lot on how smart you think your fellow investors are. Chances are, you fall into one of the two basic camps on this subject. On one side are people who are convinced the market knows more than they do. On the other side are those who believe other investors regularly do foolish things and misprice stocks.

For the second group, a slow, steady decline means you probably have a great buying opportunity on your hands. How can people in this camp be so sure? Well, they reason, if the seller causing the steady decline really had any news, what are the chances that he would be the only one? "Very small," says Engerman. "If anything were really going on, other people would find out and the stock would gap down." The leisurely pace of selling itself says a lot. "The only reason I would sell a stock down slowly is if I knew I had no reason to rush. If I am worried that there is a problem that might make someone come and sell the stock tomorrow, I will sell it down real fast."

Fine. But if there really is no problem, then why is someone selling the stock in the first place? More often than not, the seller causing a slow and steady descent is what is known as a *liquidity trader*. That's a money manager who needs to get rid of some stock to raise money, probably to meet redemptions. When a large institutional client leaves, for example, money managers are given a big lead time to raise the cash. This is the type of trader you want to buy shares from. The kind to avoid, of course, is the *information trader*. This is the person who is selling because he knows bad news you haven't heard about yet.

Of course, it is not always easy to tell the difference between the two. Technical analysts look for signs of urgency in the volume and trading patterns. However you reach your conclusion, if you believe the seller is just a liquidity trader, ignore the decline as long as there is no news. Or buy more. Again, however, this will be difficult because of the uncertainty and fear you feel when a stock moves down. "And inevitably, you will be early," says Engerman.

Why is it so hard to call the bottom of one of these steady declines? Because the price weakness caused by the first liquidity traders often makes other sellers join in. Then a vicious cycle develops, even though nothing has changed at the company. "Eventually, the values get so good that someone starts buying," says Kugel. "You get the short-term people out, and a different group of buyers comes in. This attracts other buyers, and you get a virtuous cycle. Then the stocks take off." Kugel points out that when he says "eventually" he means "some day," not necessarily next week or next month. "It will change, but you can't say when." How long should you wait before you start to get nervous? Many fund managers like to hold on until the next earnings release to see what kind of news comes out and how the market reacts. If the news is good and the price firms up, they hang in there.

So much for the pros who think a slow and steady price decline does not necessarily mean someone knows bad news. In contrast, a lot of professional investors simply don't believe the markets are so inefficient that they would let a stock slip by 20%, even though nothing has changed. For them, a long, steady decline means only one thing. There is news, but you simply have not heard about it yet. The market is usually a lot smarter than you are, notes Lawrence Haverty, an analyst with State Street Research. "There is always a reason, you just don't know what it is," says Hugh Johnson, the chief investment officer at First Albany Corporation. "Never ignore the price of the stock. If it is weak, there is a reason."

"Whenever a stock has reversed a positive trend and established a negative trend, it almost doesn't matter what anyone says. Something is wrong," agrees Pilgram. "The stocks are usually right." Pilgram believes that every stock is surrounded by a few people who know things that the rest of us don't. At some point, their selling sets the tone for the stock, and you have to listen. "Stocks go up and down all the time. The trick is to understand when a downward trend is so strong that it is giving you a message. It is a judgment call. You have to be familiar with how a stock behaves."

People who think a downward trend on no news is a clear sign of trouble are often the kind who believe in technical analysis. This is no surprise because technical analysis is essentially the examination of a stock's trading patterns for clues about what other people know about the stock. Investors in this camp also tend to have strict "sell disciplines." These are trip wires that get them out of a stock as soon as it has declined enough, no matter what. Some managers use strict stop loss limits that they keep in their head. "If it is down 20%, I take mandatory action," says Ben Hock, a portfolio manager at the John Hancock Growth Fund. "I will sell a third or a half of the position. It keeps you from believing your own bull too much. I don't want to be so sure of myself that I ride 'em into the dirt. You have to have some objective disciplines."

Other money managers will sell when the stock price cuts through one of its moving averages. They choose one that has done a good job of catching meaningful moves in the past. Select a moving average that is too short, and it will be so sensitive that it will whipsaw you in and out of a stock at exactly the wrong time.

Your stock tanks because it announces plans to buy another company. Investors frequently sell off the acquirer in a takeover because of a number of negative perceptions they have about mergers. They often think the purchaser is overpaying. Or they believe the merger will not work simply because of the difficulties involved in putting two companies together. Investors also believe mergers increase risk. They think management will be distracted or the business plan is going to change. Very often, investors suspect the transaction will dilute earnings. For any of these reasons, investors regularly conclude a merger is bad, and they sell the acquirer as soon as the news breaks.

Often they are making a mistake. But how do you know during those hours or days after the news comes out and your stock keeps going down and down? The best approach is to look at the deal and figure it out for yourself. But this is not always so easy. Details will be sketchy. The main sources of information—management—will be telling you nothing but how great the merger is. Analysts can help. But if they work for a brokerage whose investment banking arm was involved in the deal, you may not be getting an objective opinion.

If you are not sure about the merger, sometimes the best thing to do is just wait and see. "If the stock of the buyer is consistently underperforming for two to four weeks, then the message is very clear," says Johnson. "This is going to be a very difficult transaction which will hurt earnings for some time to come."

Unless the deal is obviously bad, you should probably at least wait through the initial rush of selling because more often than not, the market is overreacting at this point. "The market tends to view an acquisition as negative because we have all seen acquisitions blow up," says Bogle. "When you are buying a company, you never really know with one hundred percent certainty what you are getting. So the market has a knee-jerk reaction. This tends to mean it is a buying opportunity. More often than not I have been successful playing the contrarian in these situations."

Some money managers like to look at the track record of the buyer's management when it comes to digesting acquisitions. Others wait for a second offer to come through and then hold on tight for a bidding war.

Your company announces plans to issue new stock. The markets don't like this because investors believe the new shares dilute earnings. So they sell the stock down. Depending on the size of the offer, a stock can take a pretty big hit in this scenario. Again, however, this tends to be a knee-jerk reaction, which means you should just ignore the whole thing. If the projects that will be developed with the cash look like they will produce a good enough return, the selloff is obviously in error.

At the very least, when a company issues new stock, you can be pretty sure it won't be coming out with any surprises in the near term. Managers know that if they issue stock just ahead of an accounting problem or an earnings shortfall, they will run into legal problems.

Nevertheless, whenever a company issues new shares, it puts a nagging worry in the back of the mind of the professional investor. Conventional wisdom holds that corporate managers are excellent traders of their own stock—whether it's for their account or on behalf of the company. If so, then it makes sense to think that they are most likely to issue new shares when they believe their stock has peaked for the time being. If managers were really confident that earnings were reliable and growing, they would do shareholders the favor of financing with debt, which does not dilute earnings as much as equity. So an equity financing raises some doubts about the future. "When a company issues new stock, it is a signal that earnings may not be as good down the road," says Bogle. "It should be heeded. But it is more of a long-term concern than a short-term concern."

Don't get overly suspicious, however. Many successful companies do an equity offering shortly after their stock has moved up—and they continue to grow just fine. "A lot of these very profitable, high-growth companies tend to finance when the stock price is very attractive," says Pilgram. "As an investor, I say 'OK, I understand your business is so full of interesting opportunities that you want to raise money at a low cost of capital.' That is not negative. I like it when a company does a financing out of success." Typically, when this happens, the stock will languish for a while as investors wait for the offer to go through. "Then, during the road show the deal tightens up. And people get excited and the whole thing blows over."

Issuing new stock can be downright positive, especially for the smaller companies. Why? Because it widens the circle of interest for the stock. "Mid-cap or large-cap investors start to hear the story," says Pilgram. "And when you get their appetite cranked up, there is another round of enthusiasm for the company."

In some situations it is a real negative to see a company issue new shares. One is when the stock is trading at a low multiple. Why couldn't they wait to get a better deal? It is never a good sign to see a company do a deal under pressure at bad prices. Another case is when a company has to issue stock because it is so leveraged that it cannot issue debt.

Your company announces the sale of stock by venture capital partners or other major insiders. By definition, the venture capital partners who funded the company at the beginning want to cash out at some point. This is how they harvest their reward. So if a stock gets hit on the news that a venture capital partner is selling shares, don't sweat it. Buy more.

The selling may actually be good for the stock because it increases the float. This means more institutional investors will be able to buy it. And don't make the mistake of thinking the sales by the venture capital firms dilute earnings. The stock has already been included when calculating earnings per share.

When the insiders are unloading shares, that is another issue. (See Chapter 3.) Some selling on their part is prudent because they need to diversify. As a general rule of thumb, many fund managers don't start getting worried until they see insiders selling more than 5% or 10% of their holdings. "Insiders sell all the time, and I think it is fine as long as they still own shares," says Navellier. "It is okay to sell a little as long as you own a lot."

One of the accounting newsletters specializing in financial detective work reports that your stock has a problem brewing in the accounts. Ignore the selloff if it occurs, or use it as a buying opportunity. "Most of these things are not so newsworthy," says Engerman. "Good analysts on the buy side or sell side will have already spotted the problem. So to a large extent investors are already aware of it. It is clearly not news by the time the story comes out the fourth or fifth time."

"I would be relatively unmoved by this kind of information," agrees Bill Urban, an investment advisor at Bingham, Osborn & Scarborough in Menlo Park, California. "One newsletter putting any kind of a spin on an accounting number is part of what makes the market efficient, and it is good that they do that. But by itself, this does not have much impact on whether we recommend a stock, any more than one brokerage house recommendation does. The reality is that anyone can look at any accounting statements and come to conclusions that make you wonder about the valuation."

COMING TO THE RESCUE: WHOM
SHOULD YOU BELIEVE?

Whenever a stock is slipping in value, various parties may step in to help out. Here are some of the more common rescue efforts and what you should make of them.

The company says it "knows of no reason" for the stock decline. Given the potential legal problems that it seems a company would face if it were wrong, you might think this kind of comment should instill confidence. Few professional money managers would agree with you. "That is not very reassuring," says Johnson. "Because they may *not* know of a reason. But other people may." For example, notes Johnson, the summer before the Asian economic crisis broke out in the fall of 1997, tech stocks weakened while utility stocks strengthened. This was a sign that someone knew an impending problem in Asia would be bad for the high-flying tech stocks but good for safer stocks like utilities. While the rotation out of tech stocks was going on during the summer, however, managers at many of those companies were saying they "knew of no reason" why their stocks were weak. When the Asian crisis hit, it became pretty clear.

Johnson is not the only one who puts little faith in the "knows of no reason defense". "It is like coming home and telling your wife, 'I don't know how the lipstick got on my collar,'" says Navellier. "It helps a little, but it does not resolve anything."

Roth agrees that the comment is not very reliable evidence that things are okay. "Managers have a legal obligation to tell the truth, but they don't have a legal obligation to spill their guts," he says. Suppose the chairman absconded with all the money. "The company could later say, 'Well, we knew that, but we did not know that this would take the stock down so much.'"

When you call a company to inquire why its stock is weak, it is probably better not to spend too much time on a general question like: "Do you have any idea why your stock is down?" Instead, says Roth, be more specific. "I would rather ask well-thought-out and specific questions, and judge the answers to those."

When you are at the close of a quarter, the "knows of no reason" comment–or pure silence–might just be part of an attempt by the company to buy more time in the hopes that it can turn things around. This is especially true if you are dealing with a high-growth company in the tech or health care field. Many companies like these have "hockey stick" or "back end loaded" quarters. This means a lot of the revenue comes in at the last minute. If that is the case, they really *won't* know until just before they release earnings how the quarter went. As the quarter closes and rumors are driving a stock price down, the company won't feel compelled to respond–if it thinks that not enough information is available to know how the quarter went. A company in this position will wait as long as possible to comment because it thinks it still might be able to turn things around by booking more orders just before the quarter closes.

During a serious selloff, a brokerage house comes out and says the company is still a buy. How reliable is this? "I tend to regard this as an important positive," says Pilgram. "If the analyst has looked into the controversy and can live with it, that is important because those people are paid to be right in those circumstances. Their motives are not sinister. They are stepping into the breach to help. They don't just make a recommendation for the heck of it. They do some research to confirm that the destabilizing element will pass. It does not mean that you always jump on the stock, but it is very helpful."

Pilgram and other money managers note that it is important to check out a few things when weighing the opinion of the sell-side analyst who supports a stock that is melting down. Does the investment banking side of the analyst's brokerage do business with the company? If so, then discount the opinion.

Second, watch what the analyst is doing with earnings estimates. "Maintaining a buy and cutting estimates tends to mean it is time to get out of a stock," says Bogle. "The recommendation alone is far less important than what they are doing with their estimates." It's more reassuring if the analyst is raising estimates and assuring investors that the company will make the quarter, in addition to just reiterating a buy recommendation.

Not all professional investors put so much stock in the reiteration of a rating by analysts during a selloff. "They always say that. You have to make your own judgment," says Arden Armstrong, a portfolio manager at the MAS Mid Cap Growth Fund. "This is not very reliable. I can find you both positive and negative ratings from brokers for all stocks," says Kugel. "I don't use the Street for recommendations," says Haverty. "These guys don't get paid for making me money. It is just noise."

"If they reiterate their rating, you can conclude the firm does believe the stock is a buy," says Roth. "They must have a high degree of confidence that it is true. But whether you can conclude from that that the stock will go up is a whole other matter. Because their judgment might not be any good."

One analyst supports the stock while another is cutting it. Sometimes, when a stock is getting spanked, analysts will come out with opposing opinions. This creates even more confusion. Obviously, it helps to have a sense of who has a better record of making calls for the stock or its sector. But even the best analysts make mistakes. So consider some other factors as well. Did the analyst actually talk with the company? Or is he simply changing an opinion because of trends in the sector, without checking in with management. Believe it or not, this happens, and this kind of rating change is usually less reliable.

Another useful thing to do is look at which analyst is breaking the trend. In general, the analyst who stands out by going against the grain is more likely to be correct. "That's probably the one that bears listening to," says Bogle. "The analyst is taking a risk by being different from the crowd, and they will do so only when they are highly confident that they are right. Staying with the crowd is the low-risk position, so there is not much to be read into that. Go with the trend breaker, not the trend follower. Other analysts are probably going to follow on, and there will be additional sellers."

On the other hand, you have to be cautious about the maverick. "There is tremendous pressure on the analysts to be ahead of everyone else, to be a hero," says Pilgram. "So they reach. Things go on, and analysts extrapolate." The money managers do the same thing, which is what creates buying opportunities in the confusion. "Portfolio managers are the same," says Pilgram. "They hear something, and they say, 'I don't know if it is true or not, but I am going to sell some of the position.' A lot of people are just trading all day based on what they hear, and that has a big influence on an illiquid stock."

Finally, try to understand the opinions of the analysts in conflict and why they are perceiving the same situation differently. When a conflict among the analysts creates turmoil, this is often a good buying opportunity, if you know the sector well enough to make your own call.

Earnings estimates are raised by a brokerage during a sell off. "I like that. That is unusual," says Johnson. "This is a great sign," agrees Navellier.

SOME GENERAL ADVICE

Finally, here are some general tips on what to do when a stock tanks.

The myth of the "dead cat bounce." When a stock is falling fast because of bad news, at some point buyers step in and the stock recoils, moving back up a bit. This is called the dead cat bounce. Because this is so common, it can be tempting to try to predict when it will occur and buy the stock for a quick trade. Bad idea. The chances are you will move at the wrong time and lose money. "This is a suicide game," says Navellier. "It is like catching a knife. There is nothing predictable about the size and duration of a dead cat bounce."

Your stock may be sagging simply because a hedge fund manager or momentum player is getting out in a sloppy manner. Who are the ones to watch out for? They have nicknames like "mad bomber" or "bigfoot" and they share one characteristic. When they leave a stock, they don't care too much about what they do to its price. Even when there is absolutely nothing wrong with a company, momentum players can take it down 20% or 30% in a few days just because they want out. "Some fund managers are klutzes, just like some people are klutzes," says Navellier. The damage they do, and how long it takes them to finish, depend on the size of their position and the liquidity of the stock.

If your stock is tanking on no news, you should check the 13-F and 13-G documents on file with the Securities and Exchange Commission. These list the institutional holders who have had big positions recently. Look for hedge fund managers or momentum investors who have a reputation taking stocks down a lot on their way out. Managers or funds who do this from time to time include Jeffrey Vinik, Ken Heebner at Capital Growth Management, PBHG funds, the AIM funds, Duncan Hearst Capital Management, Nicholas-Applegate Capital Management, and the American Century Ultra fund, among others.

When a stock is tanking, keep your emotions on the sidelines. This is one of those things that is easy to say but hard to do. You can take a few simple precautions that will make this easier to do. First, diversify. When you have many stocks, selling one loser does minimal damage, relatively speaking. Since worries about your financial future are not clouding your judgment, it will be easier to do the right thing and pull the trigger when tragedy strikes.

"It's just common sense," says Charles Dyer, who manages the Hawthorne Sea fund as the chief investment officer of Hawthorne Associates in Boston. "It is an old trick that goes back to the time of the cavemen. You need to have more than one vegetable in your garden." Money management rules depending on your personal situation, but as a rule of thumb many advisors say you should avoid letting any single stock account for more than 5% of your stock portfolio. When this is the case, it is a lot easier to avoid letting emotions interfere with your thinking and analysis, when you need to decide whether to sell.

Another common mistake is getting attached to one of your stocks. Sometimes people become so familiar with a holding that they cannot sell it even though that is the best course. "You can't get married to a stock," says Dyer. "The stock does not know that you own it. If problems arise, you have to just admit that either you were wrong or times have changed, and cut your losses. You can always buy it back. It'll be there."

Next, it is helpful to use this effective test whenever one of your stocks is down. Ask yourself the following question. "If I did not own the stock today, would I still buy it under the current conditions?" This exercise will help you think about the pros and cons in a more objective manner. In fact, at any point, all the stocks in your portfolio should be those that you would still buy if you did not already own them. Always have nothing but the best stocks in your portfolio, according to your system. There is no point in hanging on to a stock if something has changed and it is an obvious dog. When all you have left is hope, it is time to sell and move on. Many people find it difficult to take this step because it is painful to admit they were wrong and take a loss. But you should always have your money where it can be most effective.

"If it really is a busted duck, it will take a while for a company to correct its problem," says Navellier. How long? Maybe a year or more. "Eventually, it will settle into a trading range, if you are lucky. If not, it will decline even more. You have to be careful about being too patient." Sometimes, having too much patience can make you lose everything. "The thing about these situations is that the lower a stock goes, the more bad things you find out," says Pilgram. "The next thing you know the company can't pay its bills, and it is about to be liquidated. The business world does not guarantee survival."

CHAPTER 18

WHEN GOOD
STOCKS GO BAD

The market for certain stocks has come to be dominated by momentum investors. These are the fund managers who invest by searching for a checklist of growth characteristics they believe will propel shares higher and higher. They go after companies whose earnings and margins, for example, are rising rapidly. Some even chase a stock simply because it is going up fast. In what is almost a self-fulfilling prophecy, they reason that momentum begets momentum.

Often they are right. Momentum funds are frequently the ones you see posting those 50% gains for the year. They control the money behind many of the high-flying stocks in the market. The problem is, when the momentum factors that were driving the enthusiasm peter out, these stocks crash fast.

Two things are most likely to trigger this kind of reversal. One is a negative earnings surprise. When the managers behind high-flying momentum stocks fess up to having a bad quarter, the shares in their companies can lose as much as half their value in the blink of an eye. The same thing happens when earnings estimates get sliced by a large enough amount. A negative earnings surprise or a cut in estimates are two of the surest signs that whatever momentum factors were revving up a stock are going away. So when these things happen, the momentum managers beat it, and these stocks drop out of the sky.

After observing enough of these spectacular flameouts, other investors in the market often come up with a bright idea. Surely the panic selling that happens as the momentum investors flee must create a good buying opportunity. After all, if these momentum players drive a stock up too high when they pile in, doesn't it make sense that they drive it down too low as they leave? Besides, the same management that turned in the great performance is still in place after the stock crashes.

For all these reasons, the shares that get crushed by the momentum investors must be a good value. So why not troll the momentum trash for bargains? All you have to do is stick out a rough quarter or two at most, and these stocks will be back on their feet and up near their old highs in no time, right? Probably not.

The chances are good that momentum stocks that tank because of a bad earnings surprise or a cut in estimates will underperform for as long as a year or more. Trolling the momentum trash, in other words, simply does not work that well. Stocks on the momentum garbage heap are more likely than not to stay there, according to research by Claudia Mott of Prudential Securities.

"Some investors think, 'We missed the stock the first time around, so this is a great buying opportunity,'" says Mott. "Well, our research provides proof that this is not the case. When it comes to the momentum names, these blowups do not turn out to be buying opportunities."

Portfolio managers who use momentum strategies agree with Mott's findings. "Once these stocks get hit, they bounce along the bottom for some time," agrees Louis Navellier, of Navellier & Associates. "The big-cap stocks can bounce back a lot quicker. But the small ones can take as much as two years to recover."

In her study, Mott screened for momentum stocks that had moved up quickly and then got hammered—either because of downward revisions to earnings estimates of 10% or more or because of negative earnings surprises. Then she looked at how long it took them to recover. Her study covers the time between early 1994 and early 1998, when momentum investing really got popular. The results: Overall, fewer than half of the fallen angels outperformed their benchmark indexes after a year. This means the odds of picking the successful rebound candidate are against you.

The least likely to bounce back were mid-cap stocks that got hit because of downward earnings revisions (see Table 18.1). A year later, only about a fifth of these stocks outperformed their benchmark, the S&P MidCap Index. As a group, these stocks trailed their benchmark by 14% after a year. But mid-cap stocks suffering from negative earnings surprises did not fare well either. About 40% of them recovered enough to be ahead of their benchmark after a year. As a group, however, they lagged by about 7%.

Table 18.1

Momentum Trash Results[a]

	Percentage of Companies Outperforming			Average Excess Return		
	3 mon.	6 mon.	12 mon.	3 mon.	6 mon.	12 mon.
Small-cap stocks						
Negative earnings surprise	43.4%	46.9	40	–.82%	9.58	–.54
Downward earnings revision[b]	44.3	35.7	32	–1.75	–1.11	–12.47
Mid-cap stocks						
Negative earnings surprise	39.7	40.7	39.6	–3.62	–7.85	–6.96
Downward earnings revision	33.9	22.4	21.3	–5.45	–10.97	–14.33

[a] From January 31, 1994 through April 30, 1998. Small-cap performance is relative to the Russell 2000; mid-cap is relative to the S&P MidCap Index.
[b] Negative revision of 10% or greater.
Source: Prudential Securities

The most likely to recover were small-cap stocks that tanked because they missed earnings estimates. About 40% of them outperformed their benchmark, the Russell 2000, after one year. And the group overall had more or less caught up to their peers after a year. Small-cap stocks getting hit by downward revisions, however, did not do well. About 70% of them lagged after a year, at which point the whole group trailed its benchmark by about 12%.

"Some people think that because more money is being invested these days using momentum strategies, stocks deserve a rebound if they get extremely beaten up when they are sold haphazardly by momentum players," says Mott. "But just because more money moves out when momentum players pull the trigger, it doesn't mean the performance after a negative surprise is any better."

Not all momentum stocks that get hammered by bad earnings news are destined to stay in the dumps, however. Whenever a stock tanks on this kind of news, you need to look things over carefully before making a move. Above all, you have to consider company-specific matters. Beyond that, here are some general tips on how to handle bad earnings news.

WHAT TO DO WHEN BAD EARNINGS NEWS STRIKES

Look at the volume. Usually it is better to take a hit and get out as soon as bad earnings news strikes and the momentum investors start to flee. The price is likely to continue to erode after the first move downward. "And then the stock will probably be in shock for several quarters," says Navellier. One thing to check before deciding what to do, however, is the volume. "If a stock sags on light volume, I might wait till the next quarter. If it goes down on big volume, I take the money and run."

How much were estimates cut? If the stock is selling off because of downward revisions, look at how much the estimates were cut. Trimming estimates by 2% or 3% might not matter that much. But a cut of 10% or more in the consensus earnings can be devastating. "If it is more than 3%, I think you are in trouble," says Navellier. "As a rule of thumb it is better to sell, unless it is a nonrecurring factor that does not affect operating earnings."

Size matters. Big-cap stocks will bounce back the fastest. Navellier estimates that mid-cap stocks (with a market cap of between $1 billion and $5 billion) will be weak for two to six quarters after an earnings shock. Small-cap stocks (below $1 billion in market cap) can take as much as three quarters to two years. "Once small-cap stocks get hit, they stay down for some time," says Navellier. "Small-cap stocks can take as much as two years to come back. Big-cap stocks rebound a lot quicker."

Wait and see. If you are tempted to bottom fish, you may want to wait until the next earnings report to see if the trouble behind the negative earnings surprise or downward earnings revision was an aberration or a real change on the company's business, notes Mott. Companies that beat expectations the quarter after turning in disappointing news are more likely to outperform.

Talk to me. How a stock behaves after bad earnings news comes out depends a lot on how well the company communicates with Wall Street analysts. If a company fails to soften the blow of an earnings disappointment by warning analysts and investors ahead of time, it will probably stay in the penalty box for a long time. Companies that make this mistake can come out with positive earnings surprises for two or three quarters afterward, but investors will still not trust them. Intel is an example of a company that does not suffer as much from bad news because it does such a good job of keeping Wall Street informed. "It all boils down to how well management communicates and whether they come across as being credible," says Navellier. "The ones that come out and fess up tend to do better. If a stock has been hyped a lot and then its estimates get cut, that is devastating."

What about the market makers? Also important are how much the market makers support a stock and how widely it is covered. Stocks followed by big houses like Merrill Lynch and Salomon Smith Barney will probably bounce back sooner, after damaging earnings news. "At the minimum you want good regional coverage from a firm like A. G. Edwards or Piper Jaffray," says Navellier. "On the other hand, if they are all firms you have never heard of, you are probably in trouble."

CHAPTER 19

AFTER-HOURS
MARKETS

It's a familiar scenario to anyone who owns stocks. Normal trading has closed, and news comes across the wire that one of your holdings is going to miss earnings estimates for the quarter. Or maybe some other disaster strikes.

You want to get out of the stock right away, but the only place to do so is in the "after-hours" markets. Thanks to recent changes in the securities markets, you can get access fairly easily. Your broker might even be part of one of the new after-hours trading systems. Or else it offers access to an electronic trading network (ECN) like Instinet, which is run by Reuters, POSIT, or AutEx. These systems match buy-and-sell orders that are entered electronically by investors, until the network shuts down or there are no more matches.

Some day you might even be able to trade with "itinerant agents," a form of software that can be sent out on the Internet to check all exchanges and private networks everywhere in the world, find the best price, and execute a transaction.

Even without this technology, trading in the after-hours market has some clear advantages. The biggest one is that you can act quickly on news released after the close of the normal trading day. Now that ECNs are available, the ability to do this is no longer the privilege of big institutional investors. Because companies like to wait until after normal hours to release big news, having access to the aftermarkets can be handy, even if there are risks because the volume is lower.

"You are more vulnerable to misinformation in a period of greatly diminished liquidity," says Gary Pilgram, the manager of the PBHG

Growth Fund. "But if you really know something and you can benefit from what you know by getting out, I don't see anything wrong with that." It works the other way, too. There are many success stories of traders who have picked up stocks at bargain prices in the aftermarkets right after good news was released and then sold for much more the next day when regular trading began.

Despite the potential advantages, the after-hours market may not necessarily be the best place to do your investing. There are several good reasons why you might want to think twice about rushing in or out of a stock in the relatively murky world of night trading.

THE DISADVANTAGES OF AFTER HOURS MARKETS

There's not much liquidity and too much volatility. You can find good depth to the markets for some stocks in the after-hours forums. But in many cases there is a shortage of buyers and sellers, which dramatically reduces liquidity. In these conditions, prices can swing around wildly. Even Securities and Exchange Chairman Arthur Levitt, a champion of small investors, thinks this lack of liquidity creates "a number of practical difficulties and a great deal of risk for any individual investor."

Many professional traders agree. "You can really get hurt because of the volatility and lack of liquidity," says Tom Menzies, an equity trader for USAA. Part of the problem is that there are no market makers in the after-hours forums. During normal trading, these market makers stabilize prices to some degree by buying and reselling shares. They make money on the spread between the bid and the ask price, but their inventory serves as a cushion in the market. Without the market makers, after-hours forums are more like an electronic swap meet among the investors who have access. "We like to have more of a transparent market and see what the market makers are doing," states Menzies.

True, liquidity in the regular market has gotten worse. That's because spread trading became a lot less lucrative for the market makers, with the implementation of the Limit Order Handling Rule in 1997. The rules were designed to give investors a better deal by limiting the spread market makers could charge. It worked. In 1997 alone, spreads fell by over 40%. That's another way of saying the prices that market makers charge fell by 40%. No wonder they don't play as active a role anymore in buying and selling stocks during regular trading.

Despite these changes in the regular markets, liquidity and volatility are much worse in after-hours trading. Some market analysts argue that for every person who bought too high in the aftermarket, there is someone else who feels that she got out at a great price. By this logic, volatile night trading is good for someone half of the time. True, but when prices are swinging around so much, you never really have a clear understanding of whether you will be the winner or the loser. If you do venture into these volatile markets, trade with limit orders, which lock in the price at which you will buy or sell. Market orders are too risky in a fast-moving market; for this reason many of the after-hours trading systems only allow limit orders.

The prices are not "real." In a market that has little depth, you don't get "accurate" pricing. The true prices for a security are established in a broad market. An after-hours price is less likely to represent the natural supply and demand present during normal market hours. "The risk in after-hours trading is that there isn't enough activity to determine the real price of the stock in an open market," says Michael Murphy, editor of the *California Technology Stock Letter* based in Half Moon Bay, California. "Once regular trading begins, the market may not react to the news the same way the after-hours traders did. You could find out in a hurry that you paid too much or sold for too little. The stock could open three or four points away from where the after-market traders thought it would be."

Lack of information. Trading in a stock in the after-hours market probably won't be very active unless there is some sort of news. And when there is news that sparks trading, that news is likely to be a pretty big breaking story. In this situation, the individual investor is unlikely to have as good a grip on the meaning of the news as the well-connected money manager. "If there is an informational asymmetry, it will most likely work to the individual's disadvantage," says Mark Engerman, the chief investment officer at Numeric Investors. "The individual investor won't know what the Merrill Lynch analyst just said." John Markese, president of the Chicago-based American Association of Individual Investors, has the same concern. "Who gets the information first after hours? My guess is it's still the institutions." If you listen to an after-hours conference call, be sure you understand what is really going on (see Chapter 2).

Someone may be manipulating the market. Thin markets are easier to manipulate. A crafty investor with sufficient capital will do enough trades to make a stock look strong and then dump a big position. "There are a lot of games that get played," says Murphy. "And the spreads are wide. You are sort of walking into the lion pit with the current systems, but it is clearly going to evolve."

Give us a break! Stock market regulators like to halt trading in a stock when there is breaking news. In some circumstances, they even shut down the entire market. They do this to let investors absorb the news and get some perspective. With all the various types of after-hours markets opening up, the trend is in the other direction—more and more trading regardless of whether there is market-moving news. Is this a good thing?

"Personally, I always found it to be a relief when markets closed at the end of the day," says David Meese, an investment counselor with T. Row Price. "People could collect themselves after a particularly disturbing session. And if someone needed to break a big story, it was very convenient to wait for the market to close and release the news. It takes time for things to percolate, for people to look at the numbers and figure them out. It is very useful to have the market closed for a period of time when company officials can come out and tell their story."

Investing is better than trading. Picking good stocks is what counts. For someone who has held an excellent stock like Microsoft from its early years, it doesn't really matter to them now whether they bought it in the morning or the afternoon.

The real money is made outside of the markets. "You don't get wealthy from investing," says Michael J.C. Roth, the chief executive officer of USAA Investment Management Company. "You get wealthy from being entrepreneurial. And things like the after-hours markets perpetuate the idea that you can get wealthy from investing." In addition, the after-hours market encourages people to trade instead of invest for the long term, which is a better strategy. "People who do the best are the ones who buy good companies and hold them. When you trade, you latch on to some pattern and all of a sudden the pattern breaks with a vengeance and you get hammered. You win a nickel, win a nickel, win a nickel. And then you lose five dollars. That's why investing beats trading."

CHAPTER 20

AVOIDING THE CON ARTISTS

You might believe you are too experienced to get suckered into an investment scam. Try telling that to Emile Murnan.

"I'll be 79 years old later this year, and you would think I wouldn't be dumb enough to do what I did," lamented Murnan, at a press conference in an attorney general's office in Manhattan. Prosecutors were announcing the results of a 1997 nationwide crackdown on crooked brokers, and Murnan was one of the victims. The Midwesterner said he let a cold caller convince him to open an investment account for about $6,000. Then the broker wiped it out by overtrading.

As Murnan knows, scammers are good, and they have a lot of tricks up their sleeves. Indeed, one of the most common laments from those who have been had is: "If only someone had warned me!" Consider this chapter your warning. One of the best ways to avoid crooks is to know the nature of their game. This makes them easier to spot. Here is a roundup of the most common scams you are likely to come across.

FRAUD ON THE INTERNET

The Internet is a dream come true for swindlers. It gives them an efficient and inexpensive way to reach you and millions of other people. What used to take weeks can now be done in minutes. No more sacks of junk mail or hours on the phone to nail one victim. And, of course, the anonymity of the Internet allows crooks to close up shop and start again elsewhere at the first hint of trouble.

What's more, the Internet is so huge our regulators have a hard time rooting out all the crooks, says the Government Accounting Office (GAO), a research branch of Congress. In short, it is up to you to know how to stay away from them. Above all, you should beware of the false sense of security that may come over you when you see something written on the Internet. Next, be familiar with the typical kinds of fraud that occur there. The thieves use all the techniques from the old, unwired days, outlined below. But the Net provides new opportunities for the imaginative scammer.

Take bogus copies of the websites of legitimate brokerage firms, for example. It's hard to believe, but a fake version of the Web site of an online brokerage in California was up and running for 10 months, says the SEC. It was used to dupe foreign investors into sending money to the crooks. They did. The same thing happened to a broker dealer based in Washington State.

Regulators have also gotten a fraud conviction against someone who posted a fake *Bloomberg News* page announcing that a small technology company called Pairgain Technologies was being taken over at a nice premium. The report spread to the Internet investing chat rooms and other sites frequented by stock traders, who quickly bid the stock up by more than 30%. Speaking of chat rooms, you have to be careful with them, too. Investors use these Web-based bulletin boards or newsgroups to share information by posting messages to "threads." Many of the messages are legitimate, but a lot of them are simply attempts to tout a stock. Furthermore, the boards are a good place for anonymous scammers to use the old trick of talking up a microcap stock and then selling into the rally.

In one such ploy investigated by the SEC, con men lied about a company's technology and purchase orders and then dumped $3 million worth of its shares. Once these scammers get done selling their shares and stop hyping the stock, the price falls and investors lose their money. Conversely, short sellers will spread false bad news so that they can gain when the price goes down. These scams are most commonly used with small, thinly traded companies about which there is little public information, because their stocks are easier to manipulate. If you come across one of these being talked up in a chat area, be careful. You might have met a swindler.

There are other problems with the chat areas. For one thing, you never really know who you're dealing with or whether they're credible. Most of the sites hosting chat areas allow participants to hide behind aliases. People claiming to be unbiased observers might really be insiders, large shareholders, or paid promoters.

And if a scammer knows how to work the Net well, it may be hard to track him down, once you have been ripped off. "In general, it's tough," says Andrew Lih, the director of technology at the Center for New Media at Columbia University's Graduate School of Journalism. "If the people are smart, they will make sure that they have left at least three layers of uncertainty between their final words on the screen and the place where they entered. If they use three layers, it's pretty tough to find them. But it's not impossible."

One common ploy is to steal someone else's Internet account. Other scammers use the initial free hours offered by online providers without registering, or they open accounts under a false identity. They may use computers at a public library or cybercafe, or an open terminal at a col-

REALLY DUMB

Even if the crooks don't catch up with them, some investors have no trouble scamming themselves–by being just plain silly. Take the case of Appian Technology, a dormant circuit manufacturer, for example.

Shares in the penny-stock soared over 37,500 % one trading session in early 1999, before finishing the day up over 18,500 %. Why all the action? Because traders thought it was a different stock. They confused it with a potentially hot Internet company that had filed for an initial public offering the day before, hoping to trade under Appian's ticker symbol.

Without bothering to check things out first, traders rushed into shares of Appian, which was listed on Nasdaq's OTC Bulletin Board under the ticker APPN. This just happened to be the same symbol that the Internet IPO, called AppNet Systems, said it wanted to use when it started trading on the Nasdaq Stock Market.

Even though that IPO was still several weeks away, traders confused the two stocks, debating "APPN" in chat rooms–apparently thinking they were talking about the e-commerce company, App-Net. Because of this case of mistaken identity, the wrong stock traded over 3.6 million shares for two days in a row, rising from a low of from about 0.007 cents to a high of 20 cents. It eventually fell back down to the price it had before traders confused it with the Internet IPO.

lege campus. Scammers also hide by running their messages through anonymous "e-mail reflectors." It's up to the people behind the reflector to identify the sender, and usually they don't, says Lih. Law enforcement subpoena powers can help. But this gets tricky when the reflector services are located in other countries.

Even if you are not being scammed outright, the chat areas can be hazardous to your wealth in another way. One of the big problems with them is the group think that tends to predominate. In the stock chat areas, bulls often gang up on bears and berate them until they go away. This leaves the thread dominated by bulls, who put an overly positive spin on every little bit of news that comes out and on a lot of news that doesn't come out.

The bulls may be satisfied by the false sense of security and comfort this provides. In reality, however, group think and crowd psychology are among the investor's worst enemies. Once you have lost your independence, you are only free to make the same mistake as the crowd. And in investing, the crowd often makes some very big blunders. As for the bears who get run out of the threads, keep in mind that many professional investors say it is as important to know the bear case for your stock as the bull case. Smart investors welcome both sides. When there is group think, you only get one.

Going back to the outright scammers, another common tool they use online is the Web site that looks like a legitimate investment newsletter. These are set up by stock promoters who are paid to talk up low-priced shares in tiny companies. Not only do they lie about the firm's prospects, but they also fail to let you know they are being paid to promote the stock. Once they work their magic and move the stock up, they sell their own shares for a fast profit. Some of these Web sites may try to stay within the law by telling you that they are getting paid to promote a stock—in a lengthy, densely written document tucked away in some hard-to-find corner of the site. Lots of these sites are out there. In a successful year, the SEC will bring charges against several dozen promoters who get paid millions of dollars in cash and shares to tout hundreds of stocks.

Another favorite Internet tool of the scammers is e-mail. In one case investigated by the SEC, paid stock promoters sent out more than 6 million e-mails used together with bogus Web sites to tout two small, thinly traded microcap companies. Their massive spam campaign triggered the largest number of complaints the SEC had ever seen. Your best bet is to just ignore those messages promising "Exciting, Low-Risk Investment Opportunities" and huge overnight gains.

It's amazing how silly some of the Internet-based scams are. Investors have bought stock in companies developing time travel technology. One crook offered stakes in an eel farm predicted to net a "whopping 20% return." Another scammer carried out a direct public offering over the Internet for a fake company, raising $190,000 from 150 investors. He used the money for stereo equipment, groceries, and other personal purchases. Many of the scams, however, do have an air of legitimacy. Investors, for example, have lost hundreds of millions putting money into bogus Hollywood movie theme restaurants and offshore gambling enterprises.

Securities regulators say investors can avoid online scams by following some simple advice. Treat any offer with a healthy dose of skepticism. Don't rely solely on what you read online to make an investment, especially in small, thinly traded companies. Resist being pressured into making a decision quickly. All of this sounds obvious. But people have made these mistakes hundreds of times, and they will next week, too.

COLD CALLERS

Aside from the Internet, crooks often weasel their way into your life through what is known as the *cold call*. Using a charm offensive, they might start off with chit chat about your town or the local ball team. Other cold callers will employ a more sophisticated, three-part approach. Their first call is a warm-up designed to build your trust. They ask permission to call again if an "exciting" deal comes along. Naturally, one does. You are told about it in the "set-up" call. The broker "thinks" he might just be able to get you in on the deal. In the third, or "close" call, you are urged to buy into the deal now or miss out.

Many of these pitches are made from boiler rooms in or near New York City "in the shadow of Wall Street which lends an air of legitimacy to their operations," says Mark Griffin, president of North America Securities Administrators Association (NASAA). South Florida, Colorado, and Utah are also common home bases. Reading from scripts, forked-tongue cold callers use banks of telephones to pressure victims into buying stocks. They lie about their experience and performance. They lie about the investment. They typically push "house stocks" from their own inventory, stocks that the firm buys and sells as a market maker.

Again, their goal in many cases is to talk a stock up so they can sell their own holding into the rally in what is known as a "pump and dump" scheme. Once you have opened an account, they might conduct unauthorized trades that run it down to zero. Or they might fail to complete trades that you asked them to make, putting you instead into some other stock that promptly tanks. "The pattern is always the same," says Griffin. "First they tell you what they need to tell you to get your money. Then, they execute trades without your permission. Then when you complain, they route you around the firm and give you the royal runaround, and you can't get your money back."

To keep the scammers at bay, regulators advise you to remember the following points when a cold caller is on the line. If you feel pressure to place an order, hang up. And don't fall for leading questions. "You do want the best for your family, don't you?" An appeal to your sense of greed or guilt over a missed opportunity is a clear sign of trouble. Does the caller guarantee results? This type of selling is against the law. Be suspicious of callers who rush you into making a decision without giving answers to your questions. "If you wait for the annual report to arrive, these shares will go to other investors who are smart enough to act quickly." These are all bad signs.

You should also be on guard if the caller seems to care little about whether the investment suits your financial means. "Don't worry about investing the money. You'll have it back and more within three months." Watch out if the caller hedges when asked about his brokerage house. "If you have not heard of my firm, you have not been investing for long. We are one of the biggest names in the business." Is the caller looking for an investment that is way beyond your budget? Any of these things are signs the broker is not on the up and up.

Not all brokers who call are scam artists, of course. But since some are, be sure to take notes of the conversation if one calls, in case you need them later to help prove what was said. If you are considering doing business with a broker, check out his disciplinary and arbitration records at the National Association of Securities Dealers website (www.nasdr.com).

MICROCAP FRAUD

Accurate information about microcap companies can be tough to find because many of them do not file financial reports with the SEC. This is another dream come true for the fraudsters. They love to take advantage of the shortage of information to spread rumors and manipulate a stock.

One of the most common ways is to pay promoters who tout the stocks through talk shows, Internet chat boards, newsletters, or phony press releases without letting on that they are being paid. Sometimes, payment is in the form of the very stock they are touting, which gives them an extra incentive to tell tall tales. All of this is illegal. Securities laws require promoters to disclose who paid them, the amount, and the type of payment. If you are thinking about buying a microcap stock, above all take your time and do the research, and don't let yourself get pressured into a deal. You should never feel the need to rush into a stock because, as they say on Wall Street, there is always another train leaving the station.

When doing your research on a microcap company, be on guard for the following red flags. First, look for peculiar items in the footnotes of the financials. A lot of microcap fraud involves strange transactions by people connected to the firm, like unusual loans or the exchange of dubious assets for stock. You should also be concerned if there has been a change in accountants or if a company's auditors have refused to certify the books. Next, if assets are huge compared to revenue, this is a warning sign. Microcap companies sometimes assign high values to assets that are worthless or have nothing to do with their business.

If insiders own large amounts of the stock, be careful. In many microcap fraud cases company officers and promoters own big blocks of the shares. This makes it easier to manipulate the stock. Next, has trading in the stock ever been suspended? This is a bad sign. The SEC has the power to halt trading for up to 10 days if it thinks information about the company seems suspicious. Is this what happened? Finally, beware of brokers pushing microcaps if they tell you the investment is a "once-in-a-lifetime" opportunity or one that's based on "confidential" information. These are the hallmarks of fraud.

If you try to find the SEC filings and they are not available because the company is too small, ask your broker for what's called the Rule 15c2-11 file. This will have useful information. Or else check with a research service like Dun & Bradstreet, Hoover's, or Standard & Poor's. And ask your state regulators. Companies that don't have to register with the SEC might have papers on file in your state. When it comes to researching banks, keep in mind that they file reports with their own regulators. These regulators all have Web sites where you can find the documents you need. Check the Federal Reserve System's National Information Center of Banking Information (www.ffiec.gov/NIC), the

Office of the Comptroller of the Currency (www.occ.treas.gov), or the Federal Deposit Insurance Corporation (www.fdic.gov).

THE MOB AND STOCK FRAUD

More often than you would like to know, law enforcement officials are arresting members of organized crime families–with nicknames like "Butch" and "Boobie"–for running classic "pump and dump" stock market scams. In some cases, mob members use threats of violence to get the cooperation of senior managers at brokerage companies. In other instances, these crooks have found ways to get really cheap stock from insiders or offshore accounts. They do this by getting access to restricted Regulation S stock issued overseas. Since the stock is not allowed on the market, they can buy it cheap. Then they sell it to the public at huge markups. These scams take place in what are known as chop shops. Chop is slang for the spread, or the difference between the price paid for the stock and the price at which it is sold to the public.

CURRENCY TRADING SCAMS

One of the more unusual corners in the world of investment fraud is the currency trading shakedown. In this ruse, crooks first entice victims by advertising openings for highly paid "account executives" trading foreign currency for customers. And guess what! There is no experience needed and little risk involved! Another approach might be to invite you to a free seminar.

Once you have accepted your "job," however, you find you have to pony up your own money to invest. Not only that. You may also be pressured to get friends and relatives to invest through the firm, too. Meanwhile, none of the "trades" you make in your new "job" is really taking place. To the victims, things seem above board because bogus account statements are produced to "show" that the trades occurred. In reality, the new "account execs" are being had.

The currency confidence game might seem like a rarity. But it was so common during the late 1990s that the U.S. Commodity Futures Trading Commission (CFTC) issued public warnings. "The companies will give the impression that they are taking orders for forex and matching these orders on an exchange," says Daniel Nathan, the deputy director of the CFTC enforcement division. "Often they will say there is an office

GENERAL TIPS ON HOW TO AVOID SCAMS

One of the best ways to protect yourself against fraud in the small-cap market, say stock market watchdogs at the SEC, is to use some good old common-sense precautions. They offer the following tips.

- Be on the lookout for classic warning signs that you are getting a bogus pitch. You might be encouraged to send money "right away" so you don't "miss out." This tactic, however, is really meant to give you little time to think. You should also be on guard when the salesperson claims to have inside information. Another common ploy: The company you are asked to invest in has a name that, just coincidentally, sounds a lot like the name of a large reputable firm. Promises that you "just can't miss" or that there will be quick, astronomical profits are another red flag.

- Beware of anyone who insists on handing over documents in person. They may be trying to avoid using the mail, so they can sidestep prosecution under much more stringent federal mail fraud charges.

- Since fraud often starts on the phone with a "cold call," or on the Internet, be suspicious of anyone who approaches you through either of these means. Many fraudsters prey on the elderly. If you belong to this group, be especially careful. The SEC offers a brochure called Cold Calling Alert, available at (800) SEC 0330.

- Your best defense is knowledge. Ask a lot of questions about the stock, and review a prospectus before investing. Check to see if the broker or brokerage firm you are dealing with is registered with the SEC or National Association of Securities Dealers.

- Fraudsters take advantage of the errors in judgment caused by raw human emotions like greed. So when you hear about an amazing investment, keep in mind the age-old advice: If it sounds too good to be true, it probably is. "When they call you, they talk to you like they are your brother," says Billy Hellums of New Mexico, who says he lost money after getting duped by a cold caller promising big profits in small-cap stocks. "But the quick money these people convince you that you can make is just not there. You are better off going to Las Vegas."

overseas that is taking the orders. They create the illusion of a back-office trading operation."

But what happens if you are actually *good* at currency trading and you want to cash out? At this point, the victims are usually encouraged to invest more with the extra "value" in the account. On the other hand, if positions "lose" money, the victims will be asked for more margin. "At the end of the day, the money will all go, one way or another," says Nathan. "If it is not obtained by these fictitious means, the shops close their doors, and there is no forwarding address."

Unfortunately, many of these scams are carried out against those who can least afford it: retired people or recent immigrants who may not have enough of a financial foothold to be able to afford losses. Russian, Chinese, and Indian immigrants have been targeted. What's worse, the victims who bring in new "clients" from their community are unwittingly scamming their own friends because no one has caught on. All told, during the 1990s over 3,600 people lost over $250 million in this kind of ripoff.

Currency trading operations can be legitimate. To avoid the bogus ones, the CFTC offers the following tips. Be wary of "job opportunities" as a currency trader. Many ads draw victims in by offering openings as "account executives." And be suspicious of firms that tell you there is little or no risk. Trading *is* risky. Anyone who tells you otherwise has something up his sleeve. Be careful about sending cash via the Internet or the mail. Phony currency trading firms use the Internet as a cheap way of reaching a large pool of potential customers. And once you have transferred money to a foreign firm, it may be impossible to recover.

If you do trade currencies or futures, don't risk more than you can afford to lose. Don't trade on margin unless you really know what it means. The bottom line: Margin trading can make you responsible for losses much greater than the amount you initially deposit. Before signing up, ask about the company's track record, and if it is not forthcoming, be on guard. If you are suspicious, contact law enforcement officials before trading. You can also check with your state's attorney general's office, consumer protection agency, or Better Business Bureau.

FINANCIAL STATEMENT FRAUD

By law, the reports that companies file with the SEC must tell the truth. They are also supposed to present all the facts that people might need to make an investment decision. Sometimes they do neither. Stock regulators try to catch the funny business, but some of it slips through.

Part of the blame lies with regulators themselves because they don't do a good enough job of checking for problems. This was the conclusion of the GAO in a harsh report on one of the biggest penny-stock fiascoes of the 1990s. The case involved a fingerprint-identification company called Comparator, whose stock rocketed from a few cents a share to $2 before plunging again back in 1996. The incident raised "serious questions" about how well market watchdogs are keeping an eye on the penny-stock arena, said the GAO in a report to Congress. The company was eventually delisted because of questions about its accounting. Meanwhile, asked the GAO, how was it possible that a firm whose assets had no real value could have met the Nasdaq Small-Cap Market listing requirements? Regulators defended themselves by saying that more than half of Comparator's assets were patents and licenses in obscure technology, which made it easy to inflate their value.

Whoever was right, the lesson to learn from this story is that you can't assume financials are accurate just because they have been approved by regulators. Companies are not supposed to lie. But regulators aren't guaranteeing that the financials are accurate either. Every year, enforcement actions are brought against companies who've "cooked their books," or left out important information.

THE PYRAMID SCHEME

One classic ripoff that lends itself to the Internet is the pyramid scheme. A typical headline introducing one of these scams might read: "How to Make Big Money from Your Home Computer!!!" Or "Turn $5 into $60,000 in Just Six Weeks." In the pyramid scheme, organizers count on the continuous recruitment of fresh members to kick in money that flows back to those at the top. The promise of "big money" for those who recruit new members keeps a fresh supply of participants on hand.

In theory, the descending layers of suckers in the pyramid will continue to generate income for everyone involved. But at some point, of course, it becomes hard to find new members and the whole system breaks down. This leaves most of the participants at the bottom in the lurch. Sometimes pyramid schemes occur on a massive scale with serious consequences. When a huge pyramid scheme in Albania collapsed in 1997, it got the whole country so angry that the government collapsed.

Political risks aside, the real problem with pyramid schemes is that they can masquerade as legitimate multilayer marketing plans. In these schemes, participants are asked to send money in exchange for the "right" to distribute products. Often, these products have little, if any, real value, and existing members are leaned on heavily to recruit new participants and keep the cash flowing in. This makes the whole thing look a lot like a pyramid scheme, which would be illegal, since pyramids are really nothing more than a form of deceit. They promise participants that they will make money, when in reality most of the people involved will inevitably lose.

To identify a pyramid scheme, look at the source of your potential income. "If the money is coming in as a result of recruiting new people, as opposed to selling a product, then it is a pyramid," notes Claudia Bourne Farrell of the Federal Trade Commission. Regulators try to keep on top of these scams on the Internet by deploying search engines to patrol for suspicious phrases like "guaranteed moneymakers." But they can't find all of them, so it is up to you to be on your guard.

THE S-8 SCAMMERS

The SEC originally created "S-8" forms to give companies a quick way to register shares used to compensate employees. No messy prospectus is needed because the SEC figures employees already know about their company. So far, so good. But then in 1990, the SEC decided to let companies use the form to register shares meant to be used to pay consultants as well. Voila! A loophole is born.

Scammers quickly figured out that companies could use this route to register shares for "consultants" whose only real "service" was to turn around and sell those shares to the public. In other words, they found a way to get new shares in the market and pay touts to sell them, without even having to file a new prospectus. The SEC has tried to take steps to shut down the use of this form to register shares that go to "consultants" who are really brokers in disguise. To keep track of things, it also wants a list of the names of any "consultants" who get shares through the use of this EZ registration form.

THE REGULATION S SCAM

"Reg. S" lets companies avoid registering shares with the SEC, as long as those shares are to be sold offshore. After all, reasons the SEC, if the stock is going to another country, let them worry about it. Some brokers, however, abuse this rule by bringing these shares back into the U.S. markets. In the typical offshore scam, an unscrupulous microcap company sells unregistered Reg. S stock at a deep discount to partners posing as foreign investors. These scammers then sell the stock to U.S. investors at inflated prices. Of course, they pocket huge profits, which they share with the microcap company insiders. The flood of unregistered stock into the United States can tank the stock, leaving unsuspecting U.S. investors with big losses. The SEC has strengthened Regulation S to make these frauds harder to conduct. In general, be extra careful when considering any investment opportunity that originates in another country because it's difficult for U.S. law enforcement agencies to investigate and prosecute foreign frauds.

GAMBLING ADDICTION: ARE YOU SCAMMING YOURSELF?

Many people, it turns out, are their own worst enemies. This is the case with those who are so compulsive about playing the market that they are really nothing more than problem gamblers. The Internet, offering cheap and easy trading, has been good for investors but bad for gamblers. How do you tell the difference? If you find yourself spending lots of time trading online and your losses are starting to pile up, you may be wondering about this very question. After all, what is the distinction between an addict and someone who just really enjoys doing something?

Experts say it's important not to jump to conclusions. The reason is that channeling healthy enthusiasm into an activity can be quite productive and rewarding, says Judith Klavans, a Columbia University professor who has studied Internet addiction. "It is like being addicted to reading. What you can do with it is tremendously powerful if you have it under control."

And that's what the question comes down to. Does your interest in online trading control you, or do you control it? Jon Horvitz, an assistant professor of psychology at Columbia and an expert in compulsive gambling, says there are a handful of basic warning signs that distinguish healthy pleasure in a pastime from an addiction.

- First, he says, compulsive gamblers keep on gambling in spite of the downside—like damage to relationships with family or friends, lost time from work or school, or financial loss. "The fact that a person continues gambling despite the negative consequences is what gives it the label 'compulsive,'" says Horvitz. "That is the key to distinguishing between addiction and just doing the things that we like to do."

- Compulsive gamblers use their addiction to escape worries and problems. Are you trading because you think, if only you make enough money, everything will change in your life? Not only is this a sign of addiction, but it will inevitably lead to bad trading decisions. Sooner or later, when you trade using your emotions in place of a rational system, the market will get you. As Martin Pring points out in *Investor Psychology Explained* (John Wiley & Sons, 1993) the market is constantly probing you for character flaws to exploit. Greed is high on the list.

- The range of pleasure-seeking behavior addicted gamblers engage in will narrow down to the addiction. "If you used to spend a lot of time going to movies or dinner, these activities are cut back and replaced by the behavior you are preoccupied with," says Horvitz.

- Investors figure out their goals and how long it will reasonably take to get there. Then they take appropriate risks as part of their plan. Gamblers risk large sums to make fast money and experience the excitement of the action. They "play" the market.

- Addicts experience withdrawal symptoms, unlike people who simply enjoy an activity and know when to stop. Watch for negative emotions like restlessness, anxiety, or depression when you are not able to trade.

- Like other addicts, compulsive gamblers experience "tolerance." In other words, the amount of financial risk needed to give them a thrill grows and grows.

If many of these traits apply to you, you may have a gambling problem. You should probably seek help before you do too much damage.

What causes the risk-seeking and self-destructive behavior that lies behind gambling and other addictions? Some theorize that risk, like cocaine or other drugs, may be just another way of increasing the amount of dopamine that gets to the brain and causes pleasure. The original link between dopamine and the pleasure sensation, experts say, was meant to reward constructive experiences like eating the right kinds of foods. "Sweets allow you to stock up on calories, so they taste good. This is how the brain evolved," says Horvits. "Usually things that are pleasurable are good for us."

For some reason, though, addicts are compelled to overstimulate the pleasure centers of the brain. "And it is possible that the thrill of gambling is activating this reward system in a big way," says Horvitz. Experts don't know what creates the need for this overstimulation, but they doubt that a single cause lies behind addiction in each individual. The source of gambling urge may be similar to the sources of other risk-seeking behavior or self-destruction. Alcoholism, for example, can be inherited. "This has not been shown with gambling, although that is not to say it is impossible," says Horvitz.

The experts are pretty certain about a few things. Gambling addiction is often associated with another addiction like alcoholism. Gambling addicts have often suffered the loss of a parent during childhood. Compulsive gamblers may also have a father who either had a gambling problem or was alcoholic. Compulsive gambling is more often seen in men than women.

One problem for stock market gamblers is that there is something about playing the market that makes it more compelling than other kinds of wagering. With a casino or the lottery, winning is a random event. But performance in the stock market is not totally up to chance. You do have some control over the outcome. This could make wagers in the market more appealing, especially to educated gamblers. Remember, it is possible to have a gambling problem in the stock market even if you have never gambled anywhere else before in your life.

For a quiz that will help you determine if you have a gambling problem with the markets, visit the Web site of the Connecticut Council on Problem Gambling at www.ncpgambling.org or contact them at (203) 453-9142.

PART FIVE

EPILOGUE

CHAPTER 21

TRICKS OF THE PROS

Professional money managers typically have a number of analysts who carry out a thorough examination of a company before the fund takes a position. And each money manager, of course, does extensive homework as well. At the end of the day, however, fund managers tend to zero in on just a handful of factors over all others. They weigh all the variables, but they have a short list of characteristics they really like to see.

You can learn a lot about investing by studying what the pros have on their list of "acid test" features. With that in mind, money managers in this chapter explain the three most important qualities they look for in a stock. The managers represent a range of styles, from growth, momentum, and value to short sellers, technicians, and specialized sector investors.

SCOTT SCHOELZEL, MANAGER OF THE JANUS TWENTY FUND

One: *A common-sense business model.* Instead of doing a lot of "inane calculations," Scott Schoelzel likes to fall back on common sense. "The lay investor thinks that there is some sort of secret code that Wall Street knows. But it really boils down to common sense. Is the business getting better? Or are they going through a lot of financial gymnastics to get their results?"

To know the difference, it is important to avoid sectors that are too complicated for you to fully comprehend. "I look for a simple business that I can understand or identify with. I have never owned big positions in the semiconductor capital equipment manufacturing sector because, quite frankly, I don't understand it. The Gap, Microsoft, America Online, companies like that I can understand."

Along the same lines, Schoelzel says it is best to try to keep it simple when doing investment analysis. But don't expect this to be easy. "It is very difficult to focus on the two or three trigger points because you get all this input. Sometimes when I meet with the analysts I say to myself, 'Whoa, I am getting a headache just listening to this!' If I can't express why I own a stock in a sentence or two, and if I can't explain the whole investment on one sheet of paper, then I am reaching." To help narrow his focus, Schoelzel likes to limit his portfolio to around 20 holdings, compared to the 60 or more stocks that the typical mutual fund has at any one time. He says as few as 11 stocks can keep an individual investor well diversified, if you are in seven different industries.

Two: *Improving margins.* "There are complex returns on invested capital calculations, but really it boils down to this: As sales increase, is the business becoming more profitable? Are the returns on the incremental money spent to build the business improving, staying the same, or getting worse?" To find out, check to see that both gross margins and operating margins are expanding. "It is very straightforward," says Schoelzel. "I want to see that the company is getting more leverage from its sales force." Schoelzel also likes to stick to sectors with above-average growth, like telecom, technology, health care, pharmaceuticals, biotechnology, media, retailing, and financial services.

Three: *Quality management.* "We have all met people in our lives who are extraordinary. It could be a college professor, a writer, a physician, or the guy who paints your house. You can't necessarily identify one characteristic that makes that person stand out, but you know it when you see it. I want to come away from a number of meetings with management feeling that the people I am investing with are extraordinary. You don't need to spend more than about 10 minutes with John Chambers at Cisco to realize that this guy is someone special. I don't care if he is selling routers or if he is in the retail business, he would be a success. It is the same with Tom Meredith, the chief financial officer at Dell, Bob Pittman at AOL, and Scott Cook at Intuit. Their stocks may not go up all the time, but it is not because they are not giving 100%." The qualities that make managers stand out are hard to define, says Schoelzel, but it is usually some combination of "vision," integrity, leadership, and a strong work ethic.

CHARLES FREEMAN, MANAGER OF THE
VANGUARD WINDSOR FUND, A VALUE FUND

One: *Depressed valuations caused by indiscriminate selling, also known as the baby thrown out with the bath water.* "The number one best thing is flat out anomalies, where the market's taking a whole group down," says Freeman. "The market tends to be indiscriminate on the downside."

Two: *Solid management and a strong balance sheet.* Freeman looks for a debt to equity ratio of no more than 25% to 30%. And he wants companies to have enough free cash flow to give them flexibility. "I also like to see an intelligent approach to the deployment of free cash flow. We like to hear management say that it has an acquisition strategy or an investment plan and that if it can't find opportunities that are better than buying back stock, it will buy back stock."

Three: *Oversold stocks anywhere, any time.* "We try to know a little bit about everything at any point in time so we can act quickly when there are price opportunities," says Freeman. "We are opportunistic. We are looking for the same things other people are looking for, we just don't like to pay a lot." Freeman, in other words, tries to buy into weakness and then sell into strength.

AL KUGEL, SENIOR INVESTMENT STRATEGIST,
STEIN ROE & FARNHAM

One: *Strong market for the company's product.* "You have to analyze the growth potential for the company's products and services. If you are looking at small companies, you want to make sure they are dealing with things that have a large potential market, so they can grow for a long time," says Kugel, who managed the Stein Roe Capital Opportunities fund from 1975 to 1989. "And you want to think the company's product is as good as, or better than, any competing product."

Two: *Steady growth.* "Second, I look at how consistent the growth was over the past three to five years. The market will pay a very big premium for consistent growth. If growth wiggles around a lot, the market does not like that."

Three: *Financial strength.* "Do they have the resources to carry out their plan? Look at the financial statement to see if they have a lot of debt, and whether they can raise capital."

Stock selection is one thing, but it is important to use prudent investment tactics as well, says Kugel. When building a portfolio, for example, avoid buying so many stocks that you lose your focus. "You don't want to overdiversify. You can't follow that many stocks. You dilute your effort." When he managed the mutual fund, Kugel used what he calls the rule of the thirty-sixth stock. "We held 35 stocks, and to put a new one in, we had to take one out. It is like weeding your garden." Individual investors should stop at 12 stocks, unless they have a multimillion dollar portfolio. Just be sure to be diversified across several sectors.

It is also important to let your winners ride and avoid the temptation to trade in and out of stocks. "If you sell a good stock and take a profit, you will pay about 25% in taxes. So when you sell, you have to invest your after-tax money in a stock that is not only going to do well. It must do 25% better than the one you had. That ain't easy."

LOUIS NAVELLIER, NAVELLIER & ASSOCIATES

One: *What everyone else likes.* Navellier uses computers to test the market on a regular basis to see which qualities in stocks are being rewarded the most. Then he buys stocks that have those attributes. His system examines 36 characteristics, including factors like operating margins, return on equity, earnings revisions, earnings surprises, and sales and earnings momentum.

Two: *Strong product cycle.* While Navellier selects stocks based on these models, there are a few things he always likes to see. One is a solid product cycle that seems to have staying power. He also likes management that knows enough to stagger product launches so that they constantly follow one another. "Good companies rotate their products. Microsoft, for example, releases them one at a time, so they each get a big Woop Dee Doo." Lotus, on the other hand, is an example of a company that hurt itself by bunching up product releases too much, says Navellier. "Lotus had a lot of good products. But overnight they came out and said, 'Look we have these 30 products' and nobody paid attention. Lotus issued too many at once, and they did not give each one the right recognition. Companies have to manage their product cycle to keep their margins fat and happy. A good company wants to have a regular flow of wire stories on it."

Three: *Solid operating margin growth.* "Get a company when it is growing and when margins are expanding. As long as margins are expanding, earnings are going to grow faster than sales. If operating margins are under compression, avoid the stock."

HUGH JOHNSON, MARKET STRATEGIST AND MONEY MANAGER AT FIRST ALBANY

One: *Relative price strength.* "I am a closet technician. I like to see consistent, positive relative stock price performance over a long time. This is the acid test for me. If a stock underperforms the S&P 500, the odds are it underperforms for a reason."

Two: *Relative earnings strength.* And usually you don't have to go far to find the reason, says Johnson. "Generally it is because earnings growth is inconsistent, or it is too low. So the second thing I look for is consistent relative earnings growth." For both price and earnings, Johnson compares stocks to the S&P 500. "I like to see a company whose stock price and earnings growth has beaten the S&P in eight of the last ten years. If a stock has not outperformed the S&P in the past, then my conclusion is that the odds are it won't in the future, unless my analysts build an extraordinary case that the Zebra is about to change its stripes. But that almost never occurs."

Three: *Relative value.* First, Johnson takes the average price earnings multiple for the stock for the past five years and divides that by the average p/e for the S&P 500 over the same time period. This gives him a relative value measure. "Then I look at what it is now, whether it is trading above, below, or equal to what it normally trades at relative to the S&P 500. You want to see it cheaper than its average."

ROBERT RODRIGUEZ, MANAGER OF THE FIRST PACIFIC ADVISORS CAPITAL FUND, A SMALL AND MEDIUM-CAP VALUE FUND

One: *Market leaders.* How can you tell who they are? "We go to distributors and ask how the companies compare to each other. We ask customers in the same sector who they purchase from most of the time, and why. And we ask the company." But doesn't every company say it is the market leader? "No. They don't all say 'We are number one.' Most companies are fairly straightforward about that. Sometimes they say 'We are number two or three.' Of course, if you define the industry narrowly enough so you are the only one in it, then you are number one. We do have to look out for that. We also go to the trade journals where there are third-party rankings of companies."

Rodriguez does not turn to the sell-side analysts much when trying to figure out whether a company is the market leader. Instead, he uses them more as consultants. "The main reason is that most analyst recommendations come out because they are timely. That is, people will buy the stocks because the trends are obvious and it is easier to make the sale. We say to the analysts, 'In your area, what are you *not* recommending, and why?' Or maybe we phrase it differently like, 'If you had a longer time frame of three years instead of six months, would you still have this as a hold?' They might say, 'No this is a great stock and we would recommend it. It is just that it won't go anywhere in the next six months.'"

Two: *Depressed profit margins that seem likely to bounce back.* "We look at where the profitability levels are today compared to where they have been in the past, and secondly, whether they are likely to recover. And if so, whether they will return to prior levels or go higher." Rodriguez looks mainly at operating profits, return on equity, and return on assets. "Our analysis focuses on whether there has been a permanent erosion in the underlying profitability, or whether it is a transitory issue."

Three: *Strong balance sheets.* "If we are going to invest in a company that is out of favor or unloved, in an industry that is having difficulty, we like the potential leverage." Rodriguez looks at the ratio of total debt to total capital. This means short- and long-term debt divided by the value of total debt and shareholder's equity combined. "Our typical company has around a 20% total debt to total cap ratio. The Russell 2000 has 38% total debt to total capital, while the S&P 500 is at 48%."

In addition, Rodriguez likes to see free cash flow or a trend that means the company may soon have some. "This typically happens after a major capital expansion has been completed or is nearly completed. A company might have just finished building a new plant or expanding its distribution system. This means it does not have to use large amounts of cash to fund that anymore, and now it is going to start entering the process of throwing off cash." If you can't talk with managers, you can learn about where the company is in the capital spending cycle by looking at the financials and comparing current capital spending to the historic levels. "If capital spending is high now, it will most likely trend down." Another way is to compare capital spending to the company's depreciation rate. Again, if the former is much higher, there is probably a capital spending program going on that will soon come to a close, freeing up cash.

One of the toughest things about buying stocks that are cheap because the company has some problem is that you can never really be sure how much worse things will get. "You always have doubts. The idea is to try and increase the odds, and that comes from information and study. You really have to get inside and understand the business. As Ben Graham said, that is the difference between investing and speculating. That is why value investing is very lonely. It is part of human nature to want to have a lot of third-party verification. It's the idea that if everyone is doing it, it must be right. But rarely do you buy an asset at a cheap price if everyone is doing it. That is why people sell things through auctions, to get everyone together in one room and get the frenzy going so everyone will bid everyone else up. We prefer to go to an auction where we are the only one there."

In other words, to be a value investor, you have to be psychologically strong enough to buck the trend. "Momentum investors are betting that positive trends will continue. When we purchase at very depressed levels, we are betting against the continuation of a negative trend. Usually, the expectations are far worse than the reality, and once that is recognized, the stock goes up."

NEIL HOKANSON, PRESIDENT OF HOKANSON CAPITAL MANAGEMENT

One: *Strong sectors.* "A great deal of investing has to do with industry conditions," says Hokanson. "If oil prices are going up, you don't need to be a rocket scientist to make money in energy stocks. But if times are tough for the sector, even good companies will have trouble." Hokanson doesn't favor strong sectors so much because he is trying to position himself ahead of other investors he thinks will rush in and drive up stocks. "It's more because companies in a strong sector have the wind at their backs. This allows them to get away with the types of mistakes that companies make when they are growing."

Two: *An excellent management team.* "Companies succeed and fail because of the people running them and the people working for them. Even if everything does not fit perfectly, if you really believe in the management team, if they are focused and intelligent and they really want to succeed, that is a big plus." The reverse is also true. "If a company is in a good industry and has poor management, it will fail."

Three: *Repeat business.* "I have a bias for recurring revenue streams. I like companies that get paid on an ongoing basis, companies that don't have to go out and sell. When there is a steady demand, it is easier to get a handle on the numbers, and our confidence in the numbers goes up." An example would be a firm that carries out credit card or payroll processing. At the other end of the spectrum is a company like Cray Computer. "They don't sell a lot of supercomputers, and if they miss one or two big-ticket sales, they have a bad quarter."

Along the same lines, Hokanson likes to see some kind of franchise or barriers to entry as well. "We look for high retention among clients and companies that can sell one product on top of another. We like situations where it is difficult for a client to go elsewhere." This means the company has pricing power. The epitome of the kind of business that lacks this asset are those in fashion-related sectors. "Companies like Tommy Hilfiger or the Gap can be hot. But when they get the wrong line of clothing, you are stuck with an earnings estimate that does not mean anything. In a business like this, you have to constantly recreate yourself and stay just ahead of people's tastes. That is an incredible business challenge. The hat has to be off to managers who have to come in every week and start over."

GARY PILGRAM, MANAGER OF
THE PBHG GROWTH FUND

One: *High-growth companies that are beating expectations.* "We are driven towards stocks based on whether they are meeting or beating expectations for sales and earnings," says Pilgram. "As long as a company stays on track and has high growth, we are content to hang on and see where it takes us."

Two: *Momentum, regardless of valuations.* Pilgram says it is important to let your winners run. "Don't let anyone spook you out of your good stocks. Don't let anyone tell you they think they know when stocks are overpriced. Leave good stocks alone, and don't worry about valuation. Don't try to use valuation tools with growth companies." Likewise, when the fundamentals change and a stock runs into trouble, don't let anyone talk you into holding on to it, says Pilgram.

Three: *Spotless performance.* "If a company grows at an exceptionally high rate for a long enough time, it will invariably produce returns that beat the market. But this is a very risky part of the world, these shooting star investments, and you have to wire yourself to be risk adverse. You will have 10 huge winners, and you don't want 20 losses to wipe it all out."

This means you have to be alert for trouble and get out quick if it looks like things are starting to go wrong. "Our buy and sell decisions at the margin are based on the perception of whether things are getting better or starting to falter, and whether there are a lot of excuses from management about why the income statement or balance sheet are not where they are supposed to be."

A big warning sign is when companies miss sales or earnings expectations. "Companies guide analysts on what to expect, and we get concerned when that guidance breaks down. Variance from guidance makes you uncomfortable because it is often the first step toward things falling apart."

Pilgram also watches inventories, accounts receivable, and deferred revenue for signs that the company might be taking advantage of the flexibility in accounting rules to paint a false picture of growth and prosperity. "Be careful when there is an abrupt change. It does not always mean there is a problem, but when there is some smoke you have to look into it. If you see accounts receivables shoot up, for example, this should make you suspicious that the company struggled to make sales estimates for the quarter. Since receivables went up, they must have closed sales late in the quarter. So what did they do to get those sales? Some last-minute discounting? When something dramatic changes on the balance sheet, you want to know how much it helped the company meet expectations and whether it is sustainable."

GARRETT VAN WAGONER, MANAGER OF THE VAN WAGONER EMERGING GROWTH FUND

One: *Market growth.* "The overall market for the company's product or service must be growing, whatever they are doing."

Two: *Barriers to entry.* "The company must have some barrier to entry, superior products, a better distribution system, some unique aspect of the business that allows it to bar competitors from entering."

Three: *Good management.* "We have to have the sense through our interview process that the management knows how to grow the company."

WILLIAM FLECKENSTEIN,
FLECKENSTEIN CAPITAL,
SHORT SELLER

One: *"Crummy" businesses.* William Fleckenstein thinks investors pushed the markets into precarious territory by the end of the 1990s. They did this by flocking to fund managers who were pure momentum players and neglecting those who used tried and true investment analysis. "All the money is flowing to the crazy momentum guys. Bad money is driving out the good. We need to have that totally shattered and to have people realize how delusional they have been, to get back to investing. Business analysis won't come back and matter until we have a market crash." Until that happens, Fleckenstein likes to play the short side. (Shorting means you borrow a stock and sell it, hoping that you can buy it back cheaper and return it for a profit at some point.) Fleckenstein starts by looking for "crummy" businesses that are priced too high.

What is a crummy business? "It is one where you can't erect barriers to entry." Internet stocks fit the bill perfectly, he says. But Fleckenstein is reluctant to short them because there are no meaningful fundamentals like earnings or sales to grasp. The personal computer business is another area where firms are vulnerable because there are no barriers to entry. At the other extreme are companies that manage billboards. "This is a nice business, because you can't build more billboards. It has barriers to entry."

Other factors can make for a "crummy business." Fleckenstein, for example, likes to target companies in sectors that are at the end of their natural business cycle. An example might be auto companies in the final stages of an economic expansion. When the economy falters, people lighten up on big-ticket purchases because of the uncertainty. Fleckenstein also finds bad companies among firms that are short on free cash flow because they constantly have to plow money back into the business.

Two: *Insider selling.* "You have to have the insiders telling you that you are right," says Fleckenstein. "Insiders never miss the chance to get out of their own stock before it gets crushed."

Three: *A catalyst.* "This is more of a tactical thing," explains Fleckenstein. "You want to see some reason that will make people reevaluate their position. It could be anything from an earnings report or price cutting in the sector to a huge inventory stockpiled somewhere."

MARC KLEE, CO-MANAGER OF
JOHN HANCOCK'S GLOBAL
TECHNOLOGY FUND

One: *Good management.* "The most important thing, no matter what, is management. Because good management can take even a fair company up to the next level." The individual investor who is unable to meet with managers, unfortunately, will have some trouble sizing them up. One thing to do is look for relevant experience. "If you have a bunch of engineers running a company and no one has any marketing experience, that should be a red flag." Another good way to judge managers is to watch whether they do the right thing when a problem arises.

Two: *Financial wherewithal.* "If you have a strong balance sheet, you can afford to take different kinds of risks than if you are financially weak." A strong company can afford to invest in things like acquisitions, marketing programs, and research and development. "If you are financially strapped, you have to go out there and accept what the market has to offer." A weak company will also be forced to concentrate mainly on improving cash flow. This means it will focus on short-term decisions, at the expense of strategic matters. When assessing financial strength, look first at the "change in cash position" statement in the financial. Be sure to read the footnotes and develop a sense of how conservative managers are with accounting practices as well.

Three: *Good value.* "You can have a great situation, but if the valuation is already accounting for that, it does not do you much good as an investor."

By valuation, Klee means the price of the stock compared to earnings over the course of the economic cycle. This is different from the standard price to earnings ratio, which compares a stock price to recent or expected earnings. Instead, Klee likes to use "normal" earnings, which he calculates by smoothing out the ups and downs over the whole economic cycle. Then he weighs that against today's stock price. "We ask what you would get if you had normal profit margins, not the margins you get when everything is going right. We make assumptions about what would be happening in a normal economy growing at 2.5%, instead of one that is growing at 4%."

Another way to do the same thing is to compare current margins to their historic range. "If a company has been earning between 5% and 10% pretax margins, and today it is earning 10%, the odds are there is not a lot of upside there." This kind of analysis is more important for cyclical companies—the ones that are more sensitive to the economic cycle. Technology companies are an example, because spending on their products declines a lot when economic growth slows. At the other end of the spectrum are companies that have more stable earnings—either because their products are necessities or because their products are trivial in terms of cost. Utilities companies and soft drink producers are examples of these.

TIM GHRISKEY, MANAGER OF THE DREYFUS FUND (BLEND OF GROWTH AND VALUE), AND THE DREYFUS GROWTH OPPORTUNITY FUND

One: *Price momentum.* "I like it when the market is confirming that there is interest in a stock. There are some times when the market flips back and forth on a stock, but most of the time it is in a trend. I like to see the price indicating interest in the stock." To measure price momentum, Ghriskey compares stocks to the S&P 500 index.

Two: *Earnings momentum.* To confirm that this exists, Ghriskey looks for positive earnings revisions and positive earnings surprises.

Three: *Decent potential revenue growth.* This is where fundamental analysis of the company and the sector comes in. "There are no hard and fast rules. You have to think through the company and its situation." Also consider the historic growth rate. A company with a hot growth record is bound to cool off. But normally the markets overestimate the extent to which it will slow down.

JACK RYAN, MANAGER OF THE VANGUARD WELLESLEY INCOME FUND

One: *Dividend yield.* As an income-oriented investor, Ryan first looks for nonutility stocks that have a dividend yield about twice that of the S&P 500. (A bit less when the S&P 500 is paying more than the 1.2% dividend of the late 1990s.) Then he blends in some utilities to increase the dividend payout of his portfolio.

Two: *Growth.* Ryan goes for decent total return in addition to income, so he looks for growth in earnings and revenues as well as dividends. "If you have a very high dividend yield and no growth, you are probably better off buying a bond in the same company." To boost total return,

Ryan will give up a little dividend yield to get more growth, assuming the two companies are in the same industry and have a similar valuation and level of risk.

Three: *A decent price.* Ryan first calculates expected earnings and cash flow for a company. Then he adjusts down the price investors should pay for that level of earnings and cash flow in order to account for risk factors. Risk factors include things like uneven historic earnings, leverage, and weak cash flow. He also considers the quality of management and looks at the extent to which they are being compensated with stock, which is a positive. Once he has done the calculations, he compares the risk-adjusted price earnings ratio to the valuations of similar companies. If a company is trading cheap, he buys. "Since just about all companies that pay high dividends are mature and growing in line with the economy, you can use the price earnings ratio to differentiate among them, as long as you are adjusting for risk factors."

Ryan says it is very important to consider capital flows in an industry. If too much investment money is building out too much capacity, he shies away. This is often the case with a hot sector, like the telecom sector in the late 1990s. "Investors tend to be too focused on the demand side, and hardly focused on the supply side at all. I focus on the supply side. If you have excessive rates of capital investment, that increases the risk that you are not going to achieve the expected returns. The revenue may go up substantially, but it may not be enough to compensate the capital that is arriving. So despite the fact that revenue is increasing a lot, return on capital might decline. I look for opportunities where the demand growth is higher than capacity growth."

MARIO GABELLI, MANAGER OF THE INTERACTIVE COUCH POTATO FUND, INTERNATIONAL GROWTH FUND, AND GLOBAL OPPORTUNITIES FUND

One: *A good business.* Gabelli looks for things like a brand name, a franchise, barriers to entry, good margins, and the generation of cash. He also likes predictable growth, which means he wants to see a product that gets consumed often and on a regular basis. He doesn't like it when a company is forced to reinvent its product every so often. "To me, that is not as simple as trying to figure out whether people will continue to shave or drink Coke every day."

Two: *Shareholder-friendly management.* Gabelli looks closely at how the company approaches corporate governance. "How well do they communicate with shareholders? We don't want to see Berlin Walls put around our shares." Gabelli looks for the usual negatives, including poison pills which prevent takeover premiums or the failure to use cash to buy back stock when managers have no better ideas. He also watches for signs of extravagance, like golf club memberships, secretaries in miniskirts, and directors who have too many other board memberships. Gabelli says you don't have to meet with the company to figure out how friendly managers are to shareholders. "The essence of the culture comes through in the reports. If you read enough annual reports, you start to get a feel for the culture of the company." One turnoff: when the company does a poor job of explaining the dynamics of the business, or buries it in the footnotes.

Three: *Value and a catalyst that will unlock it.* Gabelli uses the standard value investor's techniques to figure out what the business would be worth to a buyer. He gets interested if it is selling for 50% below this "intrinsic value." But he also wants to see a catalyst that will bring the stock price up to this level. That could be anything from an accounting rules change that speeds up mergers to regulatory reform or the arrival of an aggressive, new chief executive officer.

RON MUHLENKAMP, MANAGER OF THE MUHLENKAMP FUND, A VALUE FUND

One: *Decent return on shareholder equity.* To get return on shareholder equity, divide earnings by equity capital. Equity capital is all assets minus all debt. What is decent return? "The corporate average since World War II has been about 14%, so our rule of thumb is we want something over 15%." But if interest rates are high, the cutoff rate gets higher as well.

Two: *A bonus plan that makes managers sweat.* "As investors, we look at ourselves as partners in the business with management. We just want to make sure they view themselves as partners with us. If their bonuses kick in at 8% return on equity, that is not good enough. If they kick in at 13% and get real nice at 15%, we know they have high standards, and we like that. So we go along for the ride. If they set their standards too low, they will go off and spend their money on dumb stuff." Companies also have to use the right benchmarks for their bonus programs. Return on capital or cash flow benchmarks are fine, but sales growth is not. "We are not interested in a company that is out only for sales growth."

Three: *Bargain prices.* In a low-inflation environment, Muhlenkamp likes a company when its price to earnings ratio is below the return on equity. But when inflation is higher, he looks for better value. "When inflation was 7%, I wanted a p/e less than half of the return on equity." Put another way, the cutoff depends on the rate of return on the alternative investment used as a benchmark in business analysis, the long bond. Suppose the bond yield moves from 6% to 12%. "If the alternative investment gets twice as attractive, I will pay half as much for the income stream that comes from a company."

HEIKO THIEME, MANAGER OF THE AMERICAN HERITAGE FUND

One: *A good concept.* "It has to be unique. A company must distinguish itself in its sector." If it does, a company has pricing power, which allows it to keep expanding margins.

Two: *Good management.* "I look for management vision, experience, and realism." Because this is so important, Thieme gets to know the top executives at many of the companies he is thinking of buying. "We won't invest in a small company unless we know the management personally, or someone we trust has a good grasp on who they are."

Third: *A good price.* Thieme waits for the right one to come along. "Ultimately, you really buy a price."

JOHN LAPORTE, MANAGER OF THE T. ROWE PRICE NEW HORIZON FUND, SMALL-CAP GROWTH

One: *Good management.* This is by far the most important aspect of a company for Laporte. "What I have learned is that when you are buying small companies you are really buying management. You have to make sure they have their heads screwed on right, that they have a viable business strategy, and that the proper incentives are in place. You want to see a management that can successfully execute a difficult strategy and take a company from the embryonic stage to full development." To find out, Laporte or his analysts meet with management face to face. "I really believe you have to look 'em right in the eye." Once his fund has a position, analysts meet the managers about four times a year and talk with them once a month. "We have constant contact."

Two: *Fertile fields.* "I am looking for small companies with huge market opportunities."

Three: *Growth.* Laporte has a minimum hurdle of 20% earnings growth. He also likes to see top-line growth around the same level, and he wants the company to be able to finance that growth by itself, out of cash flow.

DAVID TICE, MANAGER OF THE PRUDENT BEAR FUND, A SHORT SELLER

One: *Bad businesses.* "I like to be short businesses that generate low returns on capital, which to me is the definition of a bad business." To calculate return on capital, he divides operating income by the amount of capital employed, which is debt plus equity. Any return on capital below 20% starts to look attractive. Tice says targets often turn up among retailers, restaurants, and distributors. These are some of his favorite sectors to short anyway because companies in these areas have few barriers to entry to shield them against competitors.

He also likes situations in which investors complacently accept the excuse that return on capital is low because a company is just starting out. Sometimes this is a legitimate explanation. But in many cases it is not. He says there are a lot of examples among the Internet stocks. True, many managers in this space have developed business plans that stand a good chance of producing gains in the return on capital. "But other managers think, 'If we are making money on the stock options, what difference does return on capital make? As long as we can sell the story, everything will be all right.'" Investors accept the sales pitch, buy the stock, and drive up its price, giving Tice what he thinks is an excellent shorting opportunity.

Two: *Mistaken consensus.* "We want to find a company where our position about the future is significantly different from the consensus." He does this by analyzing the company's business model and its sector, and then comparing his conclusions to what Wall Street thinks. "A lot of times this can be fairly simple."

Three: *Hype.* Tice likes to see so much hype surrounding a stock that the consensus expectations are unreachable. "I like ultra-confidence on the part of the bulls that the stock is the greatest thing since sliced bread, so that there is almost a cult following. I look for situations where people don't care about the analysis when they buy a stock. They just buy it because it is going up. I like to see a frenzy." This means that Tice finds himself searching among stocks that have outperformed the market by a wide margin. Stocks often start looking like excellent candidates to Tice once they are more than 100% off their lows for the year or when the price to sales ratio is greater than 5.

When Tice finds good candidates, he doesn't just rush in. "It can be very dangerous to short a rocket ship that is going straight up," says Tice. So he uses a few tactics to take away some of the risk. For one thing, he likes to take a short position after a stock has already started to underperform the market for about four weeks. "A lot of times when you have a high-priced stock that has disappointed its supporters, the supporters do not race back in too fast. So this is a good time to short. We still might short a stock that is 30% off its high, and it will still make a good short position."

Tice also likes to stay away from stocks that are already being heavily shorted. True, academic studies show that stocks with large short positions tend to underperform. "It gives you some confidence." Nevertheless, Tice shies away from these stocks. Why? "Some short sellers have more staying power than others. If the stock goes up three points, one of your compadres may rush to cover." This means they close out their short position by buying the stock back and returning it to the lender. Their purchase normally moves the stock up. "And that causes another short to do the same thing. Before you know it, all the shorts rushing to cover drive the stock up, and you have to cover as well."

MICHAEL MURPHY, MONEY MANAGER AND EDITOR OF THE CALIFORNIA TECHNOLOGY STOCK LETTER

One: *Good revenue growth.* "It has to be strong enough to prove that that the company is creating its own future," says Murphy. How strong is that? Generally, revenue growth must be at least 15%.

Two: *Good profit growth.* Again, Murphy looks for at least 15% growth as a sign that "there is something special going on."

Three: *Strong "price to growth flow."* Murphy prefers this measure over the traditional price to earnings ratio. To figure out price to growth flow, take the stock price and divide it by the total of earnings plus research and development costs. Murphy likes this measure because he says it does a better job of capturing a tech company's potential. "With earnings you have to wait for R&D to turn into new products, and then into sales, and then into earnings. That is when Wall Street will get excited. But we want something that will get us into stocks earlier. Stocks look cheap on price to growth flow before they look cheap on earnings." Murphy says a company is attractively priced when its price to growth flow is less than half its growth rate. "So if it is growing 30% a year, we would pay up to 15 times growth flow."

The price to growth flow measure is also useful for valuing tech stocks that have been hit because earnings fell sharply, says Murphy. If a stock's price and earnings go down in tandem, it may still have a fairly high price to earnings ratio. "But it will look cheap on price to growth flow, because the R&D did not go down."

An attractive price to growth flow by itself does not mean a stock is a buy. You still need to have some certainty that the R&D will actually pay off. "You always have to do the research to figure that out. But this measure lets you work in a universe of stocks that have the potential to do extremely well, if they execute and bring out the products."

Price to growth flow in tech companies, by the way, is similar to price to cash flow measures for industrial companies. That's because R&D costs at a tech company are more or less the same thing as depreciation expenses in an industrial firm. To derive cash flow at an industrial firm, you add depreciation, amortization, and taxes back in to net income.

BEN HOCK, MANAGER OF THE JOHN HANCOCK GROWTH FUND

One: *Favorable big picture trends.* "First, I look at the economy to see which sectors are making a contribution," says Hock. "I pay a lot of attention to macro trends and GDP numbers. This points me in the right direction. It helps me choose a group, so I can use my time efficiently. We kick an incredible amount of tires."

Two: *Good fundamentals.* Next Hock looks for positive signs in the standard financial statement measures like return on equity and operating margins. He prefers companies that are self-financing. "I also want a long-lived product. Not three years."

Three: *Decent potential reward.* "If I don't see 25% upside, I don't buy it. I am not going to get distracted by trading opportunities, a pop from 45 to 48. I don't think that is a good use of time."

MARTIN WHITMAN, MANAGER OF THE THIRD AVENUE VALUE FUND

One: *Quality of resources.* "The first thing we want to see is the absence of liabilities, whether on the balance sheet, in the footnotes, or in the real world. For instance, we would not invest in tobacco companies because the potential liabilities worldwide cannot be counted." When it comes to debt, Whitman will accept a large amount only if it is "nonrecourse" debt. This means that in the case of default, the lender can take the property purchased with the debt but not the other assets of the company. Next, Whitman wants to see a lot of high-quality assets. "We are in very few companies where cash alone does not exceed total book liabilities." Another thing Whitman likes to see is a decent amount of free cash flow. "We don't want to look at companies that have to dedicate all their cash flow to capital expenditures or inventory." Cash on the balance sheet is reassuring, as is a franchise that protects sales.

Two: *Price.* Whitman ignores the price to earnings ratio. Instead, he looks at the price of the stock relative to the "quantity of resources," or an assessment of the company's net asset value. The manner in which he calculates this varies, depending on the nature of the business. But once he has a number, the next step is always the same. "We don't want to pay more than 50% of what a business is worth as a private company or as a takeover candidate."

Three: *A catalyst.* "There has to be something that might come along that could make the stock go higher." This could be anything from a merger to a share repurchase plan. Other possibilities include a hostile takeover, a restructuring, the liquidation of some assets, the spinoff of a division, or a refinancing that frees up cash.

Overlaying all three qualities, Whitman wants to see high-quality management. "Determining the ability of the company to translate the first two factors into long-term worth is more than anything else an appraisal of management, which is the toughest thing to do. We meet with management, but we are much more document intensive."

ARNOLD L. LANGSEN, FORMER FINANCE PROFESSOR AT THE UNIVERSITY OF CALIFORNIA AT BERKELEY

One: *The Growth Opportunity (GO) ratio.* Langsen believes that the price earnings ratio is a poor way to value a stock. Instead, he says, the amount you should be willing to pay depends on several other factors. The first is the GO ratio. This measures the portion of the stock price that investors are paying for future growth. As long as it is not too high, the stock price is probably okay.

To determine the GO ratio, first divide the trailing four quarters' worth of earnings by the 30-year bond yield. This tells you how much investors are paying for the current earnings. If a company earns $2 a share and the bond yield is 10% then investors are paying $20 for current earnings, or $2 divided by .1. "And if the stock is trading at $30, then $10 of the stock price is a bet on the future growth of the company." Put another way, $10 is the present value of future growth.

In this example, it works out to be one-third of the stock price, which isn't bad, according to Langsen. He reckons anywhere between 20% and 40% is acceptable. Values between 50% and 80% mean the stock is a hold. "If the growth factor is 80% or more of the current price, I have to look very closely at that company to see if the return on investment or some other factor like reinvestment rate justifies this." According to his research, the chances are good that they won't. Stocks with a GO ratio above 90% should generally be avoided. If the ratio is below 20%, the company is either undervalued, or it has some problem that means earnings growth is about to slow down.

Two: *Adequate reinvestment.* One way to judge whether a company's GO ratio is reasonable is to look at the company's reinvestment rate. Is it big enough to support the expected growth rate implied in the stock price? The first step is to figure out the reinvestment rate. To do so, multiply return on equity by one minus the payout ratio. For example, if ROE is 20% and the company pays half its earnings in dividends, then the reinvestment rate is 10%.

Next, compare that to the GO ratio. "If the GO ratio is big, which means that a very large amount of a stock's current valuation is a bet on the future, but the company only has a 10% reinvestment rate, then the chance of it reaching its goal is not as great as it should be." Generally, if the GO ratio is less than 40% and the reinvestment rate is greater than 12%, then the growth expectations priced into the stock are reasonable.

Another way to check whether the reinvestment rate is adequate is to compare it to the rate at a group of similar companies or to an appropriate benchmark like the S&P 500 Index, the NASDAQ 100, or one of the Russell indexes.

Three: *The Momentum ratio.* Finally, Langsen considers a measure of recent momentum designed to weed out stocks that have recently been either too strong or too weak. To get this ratio, he divides the rate of return for the past 13 weeks by the rate of return for the past 10 trading days. A ratio of anywhere between 2 and 12 is acceptable. Above 12 means that the shorter-term performance has petered out too much and momentum is slowing, a sign of possible trouble. Below 2 means the stock has come up too much during the past 10 days, implying that it will probably pull back in the near term because it has been running at a pace that cannot continue. A value between 2 and 12 indicates the recent momentum is likely to continue.

CHAPTER 22

SOME BASIC POINTERS

Here are some basic pointers that you should keep in mind at all times because they can save you a lot of money and peace of mind if you invest in the stock market.

- Never invest money you can't afford to have tied up. You don't want to be forced to liquidate a good position that is temporarily under water, just to manage your personal cash flow.

- Follow sound money management principles. Never put all your money in just a few stocks. Never have more than about 5% of your portfolio in any single holding. Many advisors point out that you need at least 10 stocks to be well diversified. Be careful with margin. It can make you lose more than you originally invested and wind up in debt to your broker.

- Have a system and stick with it. It does not matter much what system you use, as long as it works more often than it does not *and you stick with it.* Many investors make the mistake of temporarily adopting a system they do not understand well. When the going gets rough because the stock sinks, they don't understand the reasons for being in the position, so they get too nervous, or worse, they get shaken out too easily.

- The single biggest mistake many investors make is to hold on to losing positions for too long. When your original reasons for being in a stock change and you are left with only hope, sell and take your losses. You should always put your money to the best possible use in the best stocks. Besides, there is something liberating about confession.

- Don't try too hard to make fast money. If you are in this mode, there will be a lot of emotion behind your stock selection and investment decisions. That emotion will interfere with your thinking, and your poor judgment will make you lose money.
- Don't give or accept stock tips, especially among friends. If the advice turns sour, there will be at least some resentment in the relationship. And if you do not do your own research and fully understand an investment, you won't have the courage to stick with a position that goes against you. You might not be able to discern when the original reasoning no longer applies, a change that would mean it is time to take a loss and move on.

INDEX

Accounting, 72, 218
  aggressive, 75-79
  change of accounting firm, 54, 65, 66
  differing approaches used by companies, 17, 70, 79
  fraud, 66, 67, 71, 75-79, 221, 222, 237
  tricks, 70, 71, 75-79
Accounts payable, 88
Accounts receivable, 60-64, 67, 78, 79, 88, 237
Accruals, 66, 67
Accustaff, 137
Acorn funds, 81
Acquisitions. *See* Mergers and acquisitions
Addiction, gambling, 224-226
A. G. Edwards, 8, 207
AIM Aggressive Growth Fund, 9
AIM funds, 201
Aircraft companies, 82
Albania, 223
Alcoholism, 226
Alert IPO, 123, 155
Alliance Capital Management, 4
America Online, 230
American Association of Individual Investors, 210
American Century Ultra fund, 201
American Heritage Fund, 29, 243
Analysts, 3-27, 206, 230, 234, 237
  the axe, 9
  bullying by companies, 9
  buy-side, 4, 23, 31, 33
  conference calls, 31-33
  conflict of interest 3-8, 18, 19, 21, 23, 65-67, 141, 142, 199
  interpreting their reports 3-26
  price targets, 15, 16
  ratings and recommendations, 3, 5, 11, 13-15, 21, 22, 31, 199, 200
  sell-side, 3-26, 31-33
Analysts' Accounting Observer, 69
Annual reports, see Securities and Exchange Commission, 10-K

Appian Technology, 214
Applied Materials, 29
AppNet Systems, 214
Argus Research, 23, 44, 46, 83
Armstrong, Arden, 199
Assets, 24, 25, 60, 67, 72, 166, 247
  current, 88
  held for disposal, 78
  useful lives of, 77
AT&T, 173
Auditors, 65, 66, 218
AutEx, 208
Auto stocks, 72, 91, 238
Auto and truck sales, 98, 99
Average workweek, 94, 100

Baker, Tom, 5
Balance sheet, 60, 61, 67, 80-89
Baltic Freight Index, 103
Banc of America Securities, 149
BankBoston Robertson Stephens, 137
Bankers Trust, 82
Banking sector, 18, 75, 91, 94. *See also* brokerage stocks
Barriers to entry, 74, 236-238, 241, 244
Basic industry stocks, 62, 63
Bear Stearns, 149, 150
Becton Dickinson, 172
Beim, David, 87
Bench marking, 140
Beneficial owners. *See* insider buying and selling
Best offer, 153
Bettis, Carr, 40
Big foot, 201
Billboard companies, 238
Bingham Osborn & Scarborough, 5, 197
Biotechnology sector, 81, 163-170, 230
Bizjak, John, 40
Bloomberg News, 213
Body language, 30
Boeing, 82

Bogle Investment Management, 160, 191
Bogle, John Jr., 160-162, 191, 195, 196, 199, 200
Bonds, 90, 91, 94, 97, 104, 144, 240, 243
Book value, 75
Boroian, Patrick, 141
Bourne Farrell, Claudia, 223
Bousa, Edward, 72
Bradshaw, Mark, 65
Breimeyer, Frederick, 99, 104
Broek, Richard van den, 164-170
Brokerage houses, 31
  analysts' reports, 3-26, *See also* Analysts
  Chinese walls, 4, 13
  commissions 4, 5, 8, 146
  investment banking, 4, 5, 7-10, 18, 19, 23, 65,
    117, 118 122, 141-156,199
  online, 146, 151
  regional 20, 21
Brokerage stocks, how to analyze, 23-26
Brooks, Russell, 45
Brown Brothers Harriman, 24
Browne, Will, 82, 83, 86
BT Alex. Brown, 149, 150
Building permits, 101
Bulletin Board, 154, 214
Bureau of Labor, 97
  statistics, 103
Business cycle, 91, 98, 99, 101, 238-240
Business inventories, 99-100
Business judgement rule, 175
Business services stocks, 62, 63
Butman, Robert, 110, 111
Buying opportunities, 11, 58, 64, 72, 75, 92, 109-
    134, 157-162, 191, 193, 194, 195, 197, 199,
    204

Cahn, Rosanne, 96
California Public Employees' Retirement System,
    174, 176
California Technology Stock Letter, 210, 245
CalPERS. *See* California Public Employees'
    Retirement System
Capacity utilization, 92, 98, 101, 102
Capital Growth Management, 201
Capital investment, 102
Capital spending, 12, 81, 82, 234, 235
Capital spending stocks, 62, 63
Cash flow, 67, 68, 77, 86, 231, 234, 235, 238,
    239, 241, 242, 244, 246, 247
Cash from operations, 67, 68
Cash, 80-89, 118, 247
  definition of, 88, 89
  net, 88
  ready, 88
Catalyst, 238, 242, 247
CBS MarketWatch, 155
Center for Financial Research & Analysis, 69
Center for New Media at Columbia University's
    Graduate School of Journalism, 214
Certificates of deposit, 88
Chambers, John, 230
Charles Freeman, 231

Charles Schwab, 146
Chat rooms, Internet, 27, 213, 215, 218
Chefitz, Robert, 137
Cheung, Eddie, 61
Chicago Purchasing Managers Index, 100
Chief executive officer (CEO), 28, 30, 38, 41,
    181, 242
Chief financial officer (CFO), 30, 32, 34, 35, 42
Chop shops, 219
Church, John, 82, 87
Ciesielski, Jack, 69
Cisco, 230
Clinton administration, 190
CMG Information, 154
Coca Cola, 9, 74, 82
Cockroach theory, 115, 116
Coffee, John, 175
Cold callers, 216, 217, 220
Coleman, David, 37, 39, 40, 44, 48
Colorado, 216
Columbia Business School, 87
Columbia Law School, 51
Columbia University, 175, 224
Commerce Department, 98, 102
Commodity Futures Trading Commission, 219,
    221
Commodity Research Bureau's Futures Price
    Index, 97
Commodity-type business, 191. *See also* Franchise
Compaq, 42, 82
Comptroller of the Currency, 219
Computer software sector, 81
Conference calls, 9, 27-36
  code words, 35
  interpreting, 27-36
  structure of, 30, 31
Confessions season. *See* earnings
Conglomerates, 87
Connecticut Council on Problem Gambling, 226
Consumer confidence, 98
Consumer cyclical stocks, 62, 63
Consumer Price Index, 96, 97, 103
Consumer services stocks, 62, 63
Consumer spending, 94, 97, 98, 101
Consumer staples stocks, 62, 63
Contrarian, 191
Cook, Scott, 230
Cookie jar reserves, 77
Corestaff, 137, 138
Cornerstone Growth Fund, 75
Corporate filings. *See* Securities and Exchange
    Commission
Corporate governance. *See* shareholder activism
Cost cutting, 12, 13
Cost of goods sold, 68, 76, 79
Cost savings, 140
Costs, immaterial, 78
CPI. *See* Consumer Price Index
Crane, Ryan, 9, 13, 15, 19, 20
Cray Computer, 236
CRB Index. *See* Commodity Research Bureau's
    Futures Price Index

Credit Suisse First Boston, 96, 149, 150
Cumulative voting, 179, 181
Cuneo, Richard, 44, 47
Currency trading scams, 219, 221
Cushing, David, 126
Cyclical stocks and companies, 26, 71, 72, 82, 84, 91, 139, 239, 240

David L. Babson & Co., 145
Davis, Evelyn Y., 172
Day traders, 110, 159
Days sales outstanding, 31
Dead cat bounce, 200, 201
Debevois & Plimpton, 122
Debt to equity ratio, 231
Debt, 17, 77, 80-83, 161, 180, 231, 234, 241, 244, 247
  nonrecourse, 247
December effect, 130
Deferred revenue, 237
Delaware, 175
Dell, 12, 13, 39, 82, 230
Dell, Michael, 39
Depreciation and amortization, 17, 76-79, 246
Direct public offers, 153, 154
Dirks vs. SEC, 34
Disclosure, 53
Discount rate, 94, 105
Discount retailers, 75
Diversification, 154, 161, 201, 202, 232, 250
DLJ Direct, 146
Dog and pony show. See road show
Dollar cost averaging, 115
Donaldson, Lufkin & Jenrette, 126, 141, 149, 150
Dopamine, 225
Dow Jones Industrial Average, 124
Dowd, Richard, 136
Drexel Burnham Lambert, 110
Dreyfus Fund, 240
Dreyfus Growth Opportunity Fund, 240
Dun & Bradstreet, 218
Duncan Hearst Capital Management, 201
DuPasquier & Co., 8
Dyer, Charles, 201, 202

E*Trade, 146
Eade, John, 23
Earnings before interest and taxes, 79
Earnings before interest, taxes, depreciation, and amortization, 77
Earnings from continuing operations, 17, 18
Earnings, 13, 27, 28, 34, 66-68, 71-77, 82, 85, 86, 90, 91, 94, 118, 136, 158, 196, 197, 203-207, 233, 239-241, 244, 248
  confessions. See Earnings preannouncements
  estimates, revisions, and surprises, 9-13, 17, 19, 60, 65, 110, 111, 141, 160, 190, 191, 199, 200, 232, 233, 236-238, 240
  manipulation, 70, 71, 75
  preannouncements, 65 109-116, 191-192
  release, 122
eBay, 143

EBIT. See Earnings before interest and taxes
EBITDA. See Earnings before interest, taxes, depreciation and amortization
ECI. See Employment Cost Index
ECN. See Electronic trading network
Economists, 90-106
Economy, 72, 90-106
  forecasting, 38
Edgar Online, 48, 49, 53, 56, 118-120, 123, 155
Edgar. See Securities and Exchange Commission
EdgarScan, 53
Electronic trading network, 208
E-mail scams, 215
Employment Cost Index, 92, 100
Employment, 90-93, 96
Energy stocks, 62, 63
Engerman, Mark, 189, 193, 197, 210
Entertainment and media sector, 81, 82, 230
Efron, Eric, 31, 35
Extraordinary costs, 17
Extraordinary Poplar Delusion & the Madness of Crowds (Mackay), 113

FAA. See Federal Aviation Administration
Fair value, 158
FDA. See Food and Drug Administration
Fed. See Federal Reserve Board
Federal Aviation Administration, 190
Federal Deposit Insurance Corporation, 219
Federal funds rate, 104
Federal Open Market Committee Meeting, 104, 105
Federal Reserve Board, 90-106
Federal Trade Commission, 223
Fedspeak, 105
Fidelity, 4, 146
Fiduciary duty, 34
Financial services stocks, 62, 63, 230
Firm commitment, 153
First Albany, 111, 194, 233
First Call, 8, 11, 14, 16, 20, 29, 47, 111, 112, 115
First Pacific Advisors, 188, 233
Fisher Investments, 70
Fisher, Ken, 70, 71, 74
Fleckenstein Capital, 6, 32, 238
Fleckenstein, William, 6, 32, 238
Flipping, 145-147 151
Florida, 216
FMOC Meeting. See Federal Open Market Committee Meeting
Follow-on offer, 117, 118, 197, 198
Food and Drug Administration,
  advisory panel, 170
  approval process, 164, 166-170
Fosback, Norman, 155
FPA Capital Fund, 188
Franchise, 74, 191, 236, 241, 247
Frank Russell Company, 124-131
Freidman, Billings, Ramsey, 150
Froehlich, Robert, 110

Gabele, Bob, 38, 39, 44, 47

Gabelli, Mario, 241, 242
Gamblers, 167
GAO. *See* Government Accounting Office
Gap, The, 230, 236
Gasparac, Michael, 25
Gates, Bill, 39
GDP. *See* Gross Domestic Product
General and administrative costs, 68, 76, 79
General Motors, 82, 172
Generally accepted accounting principles, 66
Ghriskey, Tim, 240
Giblin, James, 82
Gilbert, John, 172, 173
Gilbert, Lewis, 172, 173
Gillette, 74
Glenmede Equity, 82
Glickenhaus & Co., 81
Glickenhaus, Seth, 81
Global Opportunities Fund, 241
Going Public, 155
Goizueta, Roberto, 9
Golden parachutes, 173, 179, 181, 182
Goldman Sachs, 14, 15, 20, 22 149 150
Goldschmid, Harvey, 51
Good will, 77
Government Accounting Office, 213, 222
Graham, Ben, 88, 235
Green shoe, 58, 153
Griffin, Mark, 216, 217
Griggs and Santow, 93
Gross Domestic Product, 101, 246
Gross profit margins, 68, 73-75, 230
Growth investors, 4, 86-89, 203-205
Growth opportunity ratio, 247, 248
Growth stocks, 61-63, 74, 75 159, 189, 190, 203-207
GTCR Golder Rauner LLC, 118, 136, 139

Hambrecht & Quist, 28, 156, 164
Hambrecht, William, 156
Harvard, 158
Haverty, Lawrence, 194, 199
Hawthorne Associates, 201
Hawthorne Sea fund, 201
Health care stocks, 62, 63, 114, 190, 230
Heebner, Ken, 201
Heller, Joseph, 182
Hill, Chuck, 8, 14, 20, 29
Hock, Ben, 194, 246, 247
Hokanson Capital Management, 6, 11, 22, 29, 86, 235, 236
Hokanson, Neil, 86, 87, 235, 236
Home building stocks. *See* Housing sector
Hong, Harrison, 19
Hoover's, 218
Horvitz, Jon, 224-226
Hourly earnings, 94, 100
Housing sector, 72, 95, 99, 101
Housing starts, 101
Human Genome Product, 163, 164
Humphrey Hawkins hearings, 92, 105, 106
Hype, 244, 245

IBES International, 6, 11, 16, 110, 115
IBM, 44, 174, 177
Income investing, 240
Indicators, economic, 90-106
Inflation, 90-106
   small-cap stocks and 126-127
Information trader, 193
Initial jobless claims, 102
Initial public offering, 25, 28, 57, 117-119, 127, 143-156, 215
   quiet period, 7
Insider Bulletin, 48
Insider buying and selling
   beneficial owners, 42, 56
   interest rate forecasting and, 38
   interpreting 37-49, 197, 238
   key SEC forms for, 42-43, 55
   loan programs, 41
   microcap stocks, 218
   options and, 43, 44
   researching, 48-49
   zero-cost collar, 40
Insider trading. *See also* Insider buying and selling
   illegal, 34, 37, 38
Insiders' Chronicle, 38, 47
Instinet, 208
Institutional Investor, 8, 9
Insurance industry, 18
Intel, 29, 82, 115, 168, 188, 206
Intellectual property, 82
Interactive Couch Potato Fund, 241
Interest rates, 26, 90-106
forecasting, 38
International Brotherhood of Teamsters, 174, 176
Internet stocks, 71, 143, 215, 238, 244
Internet, fraud on, 212-216, 220
Intuit, 230
Inventory, 13, 31, 60-64, 66, 67, 82, 88, 99-100, 237, 238
Investment banking. *See* brokerage houses
Investment Psychology Explained (Pring), 113, 225
Investor relations, 17, 27, 206, 242
Investors Rights Association of America, 177
IPO Central, 123, 155
IPO Data Systems, 155
IPO Intelligence Online, 123
IPO Interactive, 123
IPO Maven, 123, 155
IPO Monitor, 155
IPO News, 123
IPO Reporter, 155
IPO Spotlight, 155
ITG Research, 126-128, 131
Itinerant agents, 208

January effect, 130
Janus Twenty Fund, 229, 230
Japan, 85
Jawboning, 105, 176
John Cabell, 33
John Hancock Financial Industries Fund, 24

John Hancock Funds, 7, 22, 30, 239
John Hancock Global Technology Fund, 7, 29, 239
John Hancock Growth Fund, 194, 246
Johnson, Hugh, 111, 112, 194, 195, 198, 200, 233
Jordan, Michael, 28
Journal of Commerce, 97
Journal of Finance, 19, 151
Journalists, financial, 93, 105, 106, 176

Kahn, Alan, 82, 83
Kemper Funds Group, 110
Keynes, John Maynard, 35
Kim, Steve, 128, 129, 131
King World Productions, 84
Klavans, Judith, 224
Klee, Marc, 7, 21, 29, 239, 240
Krigman, Laurie, 151
Kugel, Al, 110, 111, 190, 193, 194, 199, 231, 232
Kurlak, Tom, 9

Labor costs, 100, 103
Labor Department, 95, 103, 177
Langsen, Arnold, 247, 248
LaPorte, John, 243
Larger Cap Value Fund, 157
Las Vegas, 220
Lason, 137
Legg Mason, 72
Lehman Brothers, 149
Lemmon, Michael
Leverage. See debt
Levitt, Arthur, 34, 209
Lexis Nexis, 49, 53, 148
Liabilities, 72, 84, 88, 247
Lih, Andrew, 214
Lim, Terence, 19
Limit order handling rule, 209
Limit orders, 152 153, 210
Lipton Financial Services, 8
Liquidity, 125, 128, 130, 154, 189, 208-210
Liquidity trader, 193
Livedgar, 53
Lockup release, 52, 55, 57, 58, 117-123, 153
Long, Perrin, 24, 25
Lotus, 232

Mad bomber, 201
Male, Robert, 24, 25
Manhattan Bagel, 152
Manley, John, 116
Manufacturing sector, 82, 96, 98, 99, 101
Margin, 221
Markese, John, 210
Market makers, 206, 207
Market orders, 152 153, 210
Market Profile Theorems, 45, 48
Markets, after hours, 208-211
MarketWatch.com, 143
Marquardt, Sil, 7, 9, 13, 22, 30
MAS Mid Cap Growth fund, 199
Massachusetts Institute of Technology, 19

Material event, 52, 55
Material information, 35, 57, 78, 114, 147, 198
Medical device companies, 74
Meese, David, 151, 211
Mellon Private Asset Management, 112
Menzies, Tom, 209
Meredith, Tom, 230
Mergers and acquisitions, 4, 5, 13, 25, 34, 57, 58, 65, 77, 78, 86, 87, 135-142, 195-196, 239, 242, 247
Merrill Lynch, 9, 14, 19, 20, 93, 125, 128, 131, 149, 150, 207
Microcap fraud, 217, 218, 224
Microsoft, 12, 18, 19, 29, 39, 44, 73, 74, 81, 115, 125, 154, 211, 230, 232
Mid-cap stocks, 52, 61-63
Momentum investors, 51, 162, 201, 203-205, 232, 235-238, 240
Momentum ratio, 248, 249
Money managers, 4, 56, 70, 73, 84-88, 109, 110, 131, 157 158, 174, 178, 181, 197, 229-249
Money market instruments, 88
Morgan Stanley Dean Witter, 149, 150
Mott, Claudia, 61, 130, 204-206
Moving average, 195
Muhlenkamp Fund, 23, 73, 82, 242
Muhlenkamp, Ron, 23-25, 73, 82, 83, 242, 243
Multilayer marketing plans, 223
Munder Microcap Equity, 154
Murphy, Michael, 210, 211, 245, 246

n/i numeric investors family of funds, 158, 189
NAPM. See National Association of Purchasing Managers Index
NASDAQ 100 Index, 248
Nasdaq small cap market, 222
NASDAQ, 154, 214
Nathan, Daniel, 219, 221
National Association of Manufacturers, 102
National Association of Purchasing Managers Index, 95, 100
National Association of Securities Dealers, 217, 220
National Information Center of Banking Information, Federal Reserve System's, 218, 219
Natural resource companies, 139
Navellier & Associates, 30, 114, 190, 204, 232
Navellier, Louis, 30, 31, 114, 190, 191, 197, 198, 201, 202, 204-207, 232
Nelson, David, 72-74
Net income, 17, 67, 68, 76, 79
Net profit margins, 68, 73-75, 230, 232-234, 239-241, 245, 246
Net working capital, 88
Netroadshow.com, 155
Network Appliance, 39
New Issues, 155
New Mexico, 220
New York Stock Exchange, 154
New York University, 144
Newsletters, accounting, 197

Nicholas-Applegate Capital Management, 201
Noel, Joe, 28, 30
Nonfarm payrolls, 94, 100
Nonrecurring costs, 17
North American Securities Administrators
 Association, 216
November effect, 130
Nuisance value, 171
Numbers bump, 12
Numeric Investors, 111, 157-159, 189, 210

O'Shaughnessy Capital Management, 70
O'Shaughnessy, James, 70, 73-75
Occidental Petroleum, 174
Oklahoma, 175
Olstein Financial Alert Fund, 69
Olstein, Robert, 69
Operating income, 17, 76, 79, 244
Operating leverage, 72
Oprah Winfrey Show, 84
Options, employee, 32, 39, 43, 44, 50, 52, 57,
 58, 100, 180
 repricing, 179, 181, 241, 244
Options, put and call, 40
Options repricing. See Options, employee
Orders, 92
 domestic, 96
 durable goods, 98, 99
 export, 96
Organized crime, 219

Painchaud, Michael, 45
Pairgain Technologies, 213
Paley, Alan, 122
Palmiter, Alan R., 173
Paper stocks, 72
Parsons, David, 189
Patricof & Co. Ventures, 137
Paulsen, James, 100
Payout rate, 248
PBHG Growth fund, 188, 201, 208, 236
Peg ratio, 25
Personal computer companies, 238
Personal income, 95
 spending and savings, 102
Peter Schliemann, 145
Pharmaceutical companies, 74, 163-170
Pickens, T. Boone, 173
Pilgram, Gary, 188, 189, 192, 194, 196, 199, 200,
 208, 236, 237
Piper Jaffray, 207
Pittman, Bob, 230
Planet Hollywood, 152
Platform technology, 164, 165
Poison pill, 173, 178, 179, 181, 242
Poof companies, 136
Pornography, investment, 8
Portfolio managers. See money managers
POSIT, 208
PPI. See Producer Price Index
Pradhuman, Satya, 125
Pre-tax income, 79

Price book ratio, 16, 25, 70, 72, 76, 161
Price earnings ratio, 16, 25, 70-72, 76, 85, 86 161,
 241, 243, 245, 246
Price to cash flow, 246
Price to growth flow, 245, 246
Price to sales ratio, 70-79
Prices paid, 96
Pring, Martin, 113
Producer Price Index, 103, 104
Product cycle, 35, 232, 246
Production, industrial, 92, 95, 96, 101, 102
Productivity, 92, 103, 104
Profit margins, pre-tax, 24, 239, 240
Prospectus, 52, 57, 120, 121, 147, 148
Proxy contest, 177-179
Proxy statements, 182, 183. See also Form 14a
 under Securities and Exchange Commission
Proxy votes. See shareholder activism
Prudent Bear Fund, 244
Prudential Securities, 61-63, 130, 204
Psychology, investor, 14, 31, 113, 114, 187, 192,
 201, 202, 215, 224-226, 235, 244, 245, 250,
 251
Pucci, Richard, 6
Pump and dump, 217
Putnam Equity Income Fund, 72
Pyramid scheme, 222, 223

Qualified opinion, 65
Quality of earnings ratio, 66-68
Quality of Earnings Report, 69
Quarter, back end loaded, 35, 198, 199, 237
Quarterly reports, see Securities and Exchange
 Commission, 10-Q
Quiet period, 192
Quote.com, 48

R&D. See Research & development
Rauner, Bruce, 118, 136-138, 140
Receptor-based drugs, 164
Recession, 72, 101
Red Herring, 155
Red herring, 57, 147 148
Registration statements, 56-58
Reinvestment rate, 248
Relational Investors, 176
Relationship investing. See shareholder activism
Renaissance Capital, 155
 IPO Plus Aftermarket Fund, 154
Research & development (R&D), 77, 239, 245,
 246
Reserve accounts, 77
Restaurant stocks, 244, 152
Restructuring charges, 17, 18
Retail sales, 90, 97, 98
Retail sector, 82, 244
Return on assets, 234
Return on capital, 242, 244
Return on equity, 25, 80, 83, 86, 234, 243, 246,
 248
Return on shareholder equity, 242
Reuters, 208

Revenue. *See* sales
Revenue recognition, 17, 66, 67
Reversion to the mean, 157-162
Richards, Gordon, 102
Richardson, Scott, 65
Ricker, Jeff, 3, 18
Ritter, Jay, 145
Road show, 148, 149, 151, 196
RS Microcap Growth fund, 154
Rodriguez, Robert, 188, 233-235
ROE. *See* return on equity
Roll-ups, 135-142
Roth, Michael J.C., 190, 192, 198, 199, 211
Rule 15c2-11 file, 218
Russell 1000, 124, 125, 130, 248
Russell 2000, 124-126, 130, 205, 248
Russell 3000, 125, 145, 248
Russell reshuffle, 124-131
Ryan, Jack, 240

S&P 500 Index, 74, 124, 174, 233, 240, 248
S&P MidCap Index, 204
Safeguard Scientifics, 154, 155
Sales and revenue, 12, 16, 24, 25, 60, 62, 64, 68,
    70-79, 84, 87, 100, 136, 230, 240, 243-245
    recurring, 12, 236, 241
Salomon Smith Barney, 116, 149, 150, 207
Sanford Bernstein, 8
Santow, Leonard, 93, 105
Savings, personal, 25
Schachter Capital Management, 10, 29
Schachter, Howard, 10, 29
Scott Schoelzel, 229, 230
Scudder Kemper Investments, 96
Sears, 191
SEC vs. Transamerica Corp., 175
Secondary issue. *See* Secondary offering
Secondary offering, 13, 57, 65, 117-120, 197
Securities and Exchange Commission (SEC), 24,
    34, 35, 37, 114, 148
  8-K, 52, 54
  10-K, 29, 35, 52, 54, 57, 64
  10-Q, 29, 35, 52, 54, 57, 64
  13-D, 42, 43, 51, 56
  13-F, 53, 56, 201, 162
  13-G, 42, 43, 51, 56, 162, 201
  14-D, 56
  424B, 51, 57, 58, 120, 121
  accounting, 76, 78, 79
  corporate filings, 50-59
  Edgar 48, 49, 52-56, 64, 118-120, 156
  Form D, 54
  Form 3, 52, 53, 55
  Form 4, 42, 43, 47, 53, 55
  Form 5, 52, 53, 55
  Form 14a, 43, 44, 52
  Form 144, 43, 46, 47, 52, 53, 55
  insider buying and selling, 45, 46, 48, 49
  insider trading, 41, 42,
  investor fraud, 215, 218, 220-222, 224
  Offering circular, 54
  Regulation A, 54

S-1, 52, 57, 120, 121
S-2, 52, 57, 120
S-3, 52, 57, 120
S-4, 57
S-8, 57
sanctions for manipulating earnings, 66
SB-1, 57
SB-2, 57 Form 10, 57
S-8 scams, 223
Securities Data Company, 163
Selective disclosure, 34, 114
Services, 98, 99
Shareholder activism, 52, 56, 171-183, 242
  history 172-174
  rule 14a-8, 172 173, 177
  Securities Exchange Commission, 172 173, 177,
    182, 183
  submitting a proposal, 181-183
Shareholder proposals. *See* shareholder activism
Shareholders' meeting, 58. *See also* Shareholder
  activism
Shaw, Wayne, 151
Shipley, Stan, 93, 97
Short sellers, 31-33, 192, 213, 238, 244, 245
Silvia, John, 96, 101
Skolnick, Sheryl R., 137-139, 141
Sloan, Richard, 65, 67, 68
Small-cap stocks, 5, 52-54, 57, 119, 124-128, 130,
    131 143-156 161, 169, 189, 191, 204-206, 231,
    243, 244
  analyst coverage of 18-21
  effect of new analyst coverage on, 20, 158
  fraud, 217-220
  inflation and, 126, 127
  rollups 135-142
  Russell reshuffle, 124-131
Small companies. *See* small-cap stocks
Soft drink companies, 240
Solloway, James, 83
Specialty retailers, 114
Spread, bid-ask, 5, 8 129, 209, 210, 211
Sprout Group, 141
Staggered boards, 179, 181
Standard & Poor's, 8, 24, 158, 218
Standard & Poor's 500 Index. *See* S&P 500 Index
Stanford University, 19
State of Wisconsin Investment Board, 174, 176
State Street Bank, 99
State Street Research, 194
Steel sector, 81
Stein Roe & Farnham, 110, 190, 231
Stein Roe Capital Opportunities fund, 231
Stein, Jeremy, 19
Stern School of Business, 144
Stocks:
  interest rate sensitive, 94
  marriage or attachment to, 15, 202
  ratings. *See* Analysts
  Regulation S, 219, 224
  restricted or unregistered, 55
  share buybacks, 12, 87, 247
Strausberg, Marc, 118

Stuffing the channel, 78, 79
Supermarkets, 74, 75
Supplier delivery, 96
Sylla, Richard, 144
Synergies, 87

T. Row Price New Horizon Fund, 234
T. Row Price, 151, 211
Takeover premium, 179
Tax loss selling, 130
Technical analysis, 47 193, 194, 233
Technology stocks, 62, 63, 82, 114, 198, 230, 240, 246
Telecom sector, 230, 241
Tender offer, 56
Testing, Phase I, II and III, 166-170
theglobe.com, 152
Thieme, Hieko, 29, 30, 243
Third Avenue Value fund, 32, 84, 247
TIAA-CREF, 174, 176
Tice, David, 244, 245
Time value of money, 85, 94
Tips, stock, 251
Tobacco companies, 247
Tom Finucane, 24
Tommy Hilfiger, 236
Torpedo ratios, 60-68
    calculation of, 64
Total debt to total capital ratio, 234
TQA Investors LLC, 110
Traders, 91, 92, 99, 110, 117, 193, 194, 209
Trading, 5, 8, 25, 110, 115, 122, 128, 160-162, 200, 208-211, 221
Treasury bills, 73
Tweedy Browne, 82

Underwriters and underwriting, 5, 23, 25, 58, 117, 121, 122, 144-156
Unemployment rate, 94, 100
United Shareholders Association, 173, 183
University of California at Berkeley, 247
University of Florida, 145
University of Michigan School of Business Administration, 65
Urban, Bill, 197
USAA Aggressive Growth Fund, 31, 33
USAA Investment Management Company, 24, 189, 190, 209, 211
USA Today, 123
Utah, 216
Utility stocks, 62, 63, 81-83, 91, 94, 101, 190, 198, 240

Value investors, 42, 56, 71-74, 84-88, 231, 233-235, 242, 243, 247
Value Line, 8, 24
Value, relative 233
Value stocks, 61-63, 74, 75, 88, 89 159, 190, 239, 241
ValueJet, 189, 190
Van Wagoner Emerging Growth Fund, 237
Van Wagoner, Garrett, 237, 238
Vanguard Wellesley Income Fund, 240
Vanguard Windsor Fund, 231
Venture capital 42, 52, 57, 121, 136 , 148, 154, 197
Vickers Weekly Insider Report, 44, 46, 47
Vinik, Jeffrey, 201
Volatility, 209
Volcker, Paul, 144
Volume, 205, 206

Wachovia Securities, 136
Wake Forest University School of Law, 172
Wal-Mart, 12, 13, 191
Wanger Asset Management, 81
Wanger, Ralph, 81, 85
Ward's Automotive Reports, 99
Watershed Asset Management, 37
Weaver, Daniel, 14, 23
Wells Capital Management, 100
Westinghouse Electric, 174
What Works on Wall Street (O'Shaughnessy), 70, 73
Wheeler, Langdon, 111, 157-159
Whitman, Martin, 32, 84, 86, 247
Whitworth, Ralph, 173, 174, 176, 177, 183
Wiese, Carl, 6, 11, 22, 29, 33
Wilshire Associates, 174
Winans International, 7
Winans, Ken, 7, 17
Winters, Vernon, 112, 113
Wit Capital, 146
Womack, Kent, 151 152
Working capital, net, net, 88
W.R. Hambrecht, 156

Yahoo!, 123, 156
Yale, 158

Zacks Investment Research, 11, 16, 110, 115
Zacks, Ben, 11, 21
Zickland School of Business at Baruch College, 14
Zurich Kemper Investments, 25